Challenges to the United Nations

Building a safer world

edited by
Erskine Childers

CIIR
Catholic Institute for International Relations

St. Martin's Press

First published 1994
Catholic Institute for International Relations (CIIR)
Unit 3, Canonbury Yard, 190a New North Road, London N1 7BJ, UK

First published in the United States of America 1995
St. Martin's Press, Scholarly and Reference Division
175 Fifth Avenue, New York, NY 10010, USA

British Library Cataloguing in Publication Data
A catalogue record for this book is available from the British Library

Library of Congress Cataloging in Publication Data applied for

paperback **ISBN 1 85287 128 8** (CIIR)

hardcover **ISBN 0-312-12566-6** (St. Martin's Press)
paperback **ISBN 0-312-12575-5** (St. Martin's Press)

Cover photos: © Crispin Hughes

Top: Mogadishu, Somalia. Pakistani checkpoint on October 21st Road, site of the ambush which killed 24 Pakistanis.
Bottom: Belet Huen, Somalia. German military doctor, part of the German UN peacekeeping force in Somalia, treating a Somali baby.

Design: Jan Brown Designs
Printed by the Russell Press, Nottingham, UK

Contents

THE UNITED NATIONS SYSTEM:

International Court of Justice	General Assembly	Economic and Social Council

- Main and other sessional committees
- Standing committees and *ad hoc* bodies
- Other subsidiary organs and related bodies

▶ UNRWA

■ IAEA

▶ INSTRAW

▶ UNCHS

▶ UNCTAD   ▶ WFP

▶ UNDP   ▶ ITC

▶ UNEP

▶ UNFPA   ● Functional commissions
        Commission for Social Development

▶ UNHCR   Commission on Human Rights
        Commission on Narcotic Drugs

▶ UNICEF   Commission on the Status of Women
        Population Commission

▶ UNIFEM   Statistical Commission

▶ UNITAR   ● Regional commissions
        Economic Commission for Africa (ECA)

▶ UNU   Economic Commission for Europe (ECE)
        Economic Commission for Latin America

▶ WFC   and the Caribbean (ECLAC)
        Economic and Social Commission for Asia

▶ UNDCP   and the Pacific (ESCAP)
        Economic and Social Commission for
        Western Asia (ESCWA)

- Sessional and standing committees

- Expert, *ad hoc,* and related bodies

■ ILO
■ FAO
■ UNESCO
■ WHO

World Bank Group
■ IBRD
■ IDA
■ IFC

■ IMF
■ ICAO
■ UPU
■ ITU
■ WMO
■ IMO
■ WIPO
■ IFAD
■ UNIDO
■ GATT

Principal Organs of the United Nations

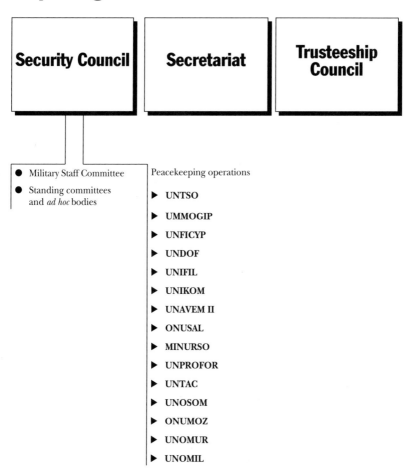

Security Council

Secretariat

Trusteeship Council

- Military Staff Committee
- Standing committees and *ad hoc* bodies

Peacekeeping operations

▶ **UNTSO**

▶ **UMMOGIP**

▶ **UNFICYP**

▶ **UNDOF**

▶ **UNIFIL**

▶ **UNIKOM**

▶ **UNAVEM II**

▶ **ONUSAL**

▶ **MINURSO**

▶ **UNPROFOR**

▶ **UNTAC**

▶ **UNOSOM**

▶ **ONUMOZ**

▶ **UNOMUR**

▶ **UNOMIL**

Key
- ▶ United Nations programmes and organs (representative list only)
- ■ Specialised agencies and other autonomous organisations within the system
- ● Other commissions, committees and *ad hoc* and related bodies

Glossary

ACC	Administrative Coordinating Committee
ECOSOC	UN Economic and Social Council
ESC	Economic and Social Council
FAO	Food and Agriculture Organisation of the UN
G-7	Group of Seven most industrialised nations (Canada, France, Germany, Italy, Japan, United Kingdom and United States)
GA	General Assembly
GATT	General Agreement on Tariffs and Trade
IAEA	International Atomic Energy Agency
IBRD	International Bank for Reconstruction and Development
ICAO	International Civil Aviation Organisation
IDA	International Development Association
IFAD	International Fund for Agricultural Development
IFC	International Finance Corporation
ILO	International Labour Office
IMF	International Monetary Fund
IMO	International Maritime Organisation
INSTRAW	International Research and Training Institute for the Advancement of Women
ITC	International Trade Centre (UNCTAD/GATT)
ITO	International Trade Organisation
ITU	International Telecommunication Union
MINURSO	UN Mission for the Referendum in Western Sahara
OECD	Organisation for Economic Cooperation and Development
ONUMOZ	UN Operation in Mozambique
ONUSAL	UN Observer Mission in El Salvador
SC	Security Council
UN	United Nations
UNAVEM II	UN Angola Verification Mission II
UNCHS	UN Centre for Human Settlements (Habitat)
UNCTAD	UN Conference on Trade and Development
UNDCP	UN International Drug Control Programme
UNDOF	UN Disengagement Observer Force
UNDP	UN Development Programme
UNEP	UN Environment Programme
UNESCO	UN Educational, Scientific and Cultural Organisation
UNFICYP	UN Peace-Keeping Force in Cyprus

UNFPA	UN Population Fund
UNHCR	Office of the UN High Commissioner for Refugees
UNICEF	UN Children's Fund
UNIDO	UN Industrial Development Organisation
UNIFEM	UN Development Fund for Women
UNIFIL	UN Interim Force in Lebanon
UNIKOM	UN Iraq-Kuwait Observation Mission
UNITAR	UN Institute for Training and Research
UNMOGIP	UN Military Observer Group in India and Pakistan
UNOMIL	UN Observer Mission in Liberia
UNOMUR	UN Observer Mission in Uganda-Rwanda
UNOSOM	UN Operation in Somalia
UNPROFOR	UN Protection Force
UNRWA	UN Relief and Works Agency for Palestine Refugees in the Near East
UNTAC	UN Transnational Authority in Cambodia
UNTSO	UN Truce Supervision Organisation
UNU	UN University
UPU	Universal Postal Union
WFC	World Food Council
WFP	World Food Programme
WHO	World Health Organisation
WIPO	World Intellectual Property Organisation
WMO	World Meteorological Organisation

Acknowledgements

This book has been prepared with all the care which I have come to observe the CIIR gives to all its publications, with many contributions that deserve grateful recognition.

First, to authors Barbara Adams, Nassau Adams, Phyllis Bennis, Amir Jamal, Maximo Kalaw, Angela Penrose, Paul Rogers, Myriam Vander Stichele, and Katarina Tomaševski. We thank them for their penetrating analyses, and for cheerfully responding to an exacting editorial process.

Key in that process have been highly qualified readers, whose thoughtful suggestions on drafts I am sure all authors including myself have greatly appreciated: Sam Daws, John Gittings, Iqbal Haji, Tony Hill, Edward Mortimer, and Colm Regan.

We must also express our gratitude to the innumerable sources of data and analysis upon which we have drawn. Needless to say we are solely responsible for our ultimate use of such assistance.

I have been told that CIIR staff are never acknowledged in the institute's books, one saying to me, 'It's our job, after all!'. I beg to break this rule to thank a friendly and immensely hard-working publications team whose dedication to the goals of the United Nations has been a continuous inspiration.

Finally, it is with much gratitude that we acknowledge the financial support of Cafod, Christian Aid, Save the Children and Trócaire.

Erskine Childers

Introduction

ERSKINE CHILDERS

When the Cold War seemed to end, there was a burst of euphoria across the Northern part of the world, that now, at last, there would be 'an era of peace'. Some said the world would at last be policed by the major powers together, and that the United Nations (UN) – apparently 're-discovered' during the Gulf Crisis – would come into its own. In the event, instead of the era of peace, we are in an era of constantly expanding eruptions of civil collapse, violence, and mass human misery to which no culture or region is immune. In this extremely dangerous world 'the UN' has seemed even more perplexing to many in Northern countries, while hopes placed in the world institution by the vast majority of humankind in the South have diminished, but for very different reasons.

There never were any grounds for the Northern euphoria. It only served to demonstrate how distracting the Cold War was from the real world's long-accumulating real problems – and from the ravages that the East-West contest wrought across the South even as its peoples struggled out of colonialism. The ability of the United Nations to cope with the consequences is in balance. This book lays out the key elements in this fragile equation.

To an extent which few Northern citizens could know because they were kept so ill-informed about it, the UN has always been a remarkably well-attuned echo chamber of the human condition, including the most dangerous division in the history of our species – that between the North and the South. But this is nothing like enough. Citizens of the planet are entitled to insist on much more, and to remind their governments that they are legally committed to use the UN System to the utmost to make the world a more friendly, just and secure place for all our children. And the time we have to get moving on our global problems is inexorably reducing, as the years of neglected causes accelerate their transformation into violent and inhumane effects.

A section immediately following this introduction will describe the machinery of the System and its present resources. But we must also place the UN and its System in the tumultuous history of the last 50 years in order to understand how it has suddenly been confronted by so many gigantic problems, and seems so weak in the face of them.

The founding of the UN System

In 1945 much of the world lay in the ruins of the deadliest war in history, and in a poverty that was not new but newly perceived as no longer tolerable, or safe. The UN was born on a great tide of yearning among ordinary people for democratic multilateral institutions – institutions that would harness humanity's best intellectual and scientific resources to tackle problems which must never again result in such hideous conflict.

The founders did not, however, envisage decolonisation even within this century. Winston Churchill had declaimed that he had 'not become His Majesty's First Minister in order to preside over the dissolution of the British Empire'. The Soviet Union, one in every eight of whose citizens had been killed in yet another war from the West, was not going to dismantle its imperial ramparts either. The architects of UN headquarters were told to make allowance for only some 70 ultimate members – mostly more European countries – where today 184 delegations fill its halls from every corner of the globe. Yet, almost as if some unseen but more far-seeing hand was guiding the drafters, the purposes and work-programme in the Charter provided a remarkably sound framework to tackle the whole world's problems when liberation did suddenly sweep like grass-fire across the South and make the UN universal.

Read today, the Charter proclaimed from San Francisco on 26 June 1945 seems to respond marvellously to these needs, because the smaller countries of the North and Latin America, and the few from the colonial South able to be there (like India and the Philippines), insisted on creating more than a great-power policing organisation. Wise and progressive statesmen even from the great powers – people like Philip Noel-Baker and John Maynard Keynes – vitally helped to give the UN at least the mandates for balanced action, not only to halt armed conflict but to tackle its economic and social causes.

The words of the resultant Charter reached out all over the globe, lifting people in the hope of saving 'succeeding generations from the scourge of war' … of employing 'international machinery for the promotion of the economic and social advancement of all peoples', and of 'international peace and security with the least diversion for armaments of the world's human and economic resources'. The Charter made the vital connections between political and military, and socio-economic security, stating that 'conditions of stability and well-being (are) necessary for peaceful and friendly relations among nations based on respect (for) equal rights and self-determination …'.

Taken together, the constitutions of the System gave humanity a comprehensive international social contract for the first time. The constitution of the new Food and Agriculture Organisation of the United Nations (FAO) committed governments 'to contribute to the expansion of the world economy and to liberate humanity from hunger'. That of the World Health Organisation (WHO) declared that 'the health of all peoples is fundamental to the attainment of peace and security'. Approaching the same web of problems with another causal insight, the constitution of the UN Educational, Scientific and Cultural Organisation (UNESCO) avowed that 'since wars begin in the minds of men it is in the minds of men that the defences of peace must be constructed' (one occasion in a UN document when the word *men* is entirely apposite).

Unacknowledged achievements

In the ensuing decades the UN System has accomplished vastly more than most of its citizens have ever been told about, because the world's dominant media, oriented to great powers and bad news, paid it so little attention until only yesterday. For example, the development of human rights related by Katarina Tomaševski will be described by future historians as a remarkable testament to the UN's ability to get governments to acknowledge common problems and work together on them. Indeed, every page of this book could be filled with details of little-known concrete achievements and innovations by the UN and its agencies.

How many citizens know of the World Meteorological Organisation's 24-hour World Weather Watch? Of FAO's Early-Warning machinery for famine and drought (so often and so criminally unheeded by governments)? Of the one million-plus teachers trained through UNESCO and UNDP in only 20 years, over half in Africa? How many know that in scarcely 30 years the entire body of law governing human use of the oceans and seas and their very beds was transformed at the UN for the first time in 300 years? Or that the ages-old scourge of smallpox was eliminated from the face of Earth by the WHO in tandem with the rest of the UN System, from 15 million afflicted in 1967 to only one ten years later, and then none?

Deeper even than this lack of information has been confusion, especially in the affluent, educated, and media-drenched North, about what makes up the United Nations. For example, only during 1993 and 1994 did Northern media begin to qualify their use of the very words 'the UN', and explain that 'it' consists at any one moment of either the Secretary-General and the civil services, or of governments and their policies – more often the latter, more often policies of the major powers.

Even these elementary clarifications only arose when media found themselves baffled by weak interventions of 'the UN' in crises where it then turned out that the powers were refusing to give the Secretary-General needed resources and authority, or were continuing to interfere bilaterally and then blaming 'the UN' for resultant chaos. But behind the long years of indifference to the UN (except for periodic bashing by right-wing ideologues in some governments and media) there is a more fundamental problem.

The legacies of empire

From 1945 until the 1960s the West held a US-led majority in the UN. A young Burmese delegate, the future Secretary-General U Thant, observed in 1952 that it was 'like a one-party system functioning in the General Assembly'. The arrival in the early 1960s of the new majority from the South was an epochal development in world history. Yet the profound implications for the position of the Northern minority in the new at least legally liberated world and in the now universal United Nations were not debated. The Charter itself, with a one-nation one-vote principle that had been inscribed only for what had originally been perceived as its limited membership, ironically made the UN's transformation too easy. Many decent, world-minded Northern citizens would remain unaware that their leaders would go right on trying to run it: a minority of governments (and population) determined to retain control while preaching democracy to the majority.

The Cold War further deflected attention from the UN. It was a monstrously expensive and menacing period of suspended animation amid ever-increasing urgency to build a just and peaceable world community. In a very real sense it froze all the dangerous, long-accumulating cultural, ethnic, political and economic problems the world had inherited from the age of the Northern empires – both Western and Russian-Soviet. The UN itself was bound to reflect the premises inherited from those centuries in some degree, but the Cold War also froze its evolution away from them.

Legally, the United Nations was constructed on the thesis of sovereign nation-states, and of the sanctity of the frontiers of each under the Charter. This presupposed that such frontiers corresponded at least tolerably well to the cultures and other attributes of social identity of each community of citizens within them. The harsh fact was, however, that almost every kilometre of the frontiers of the colonial South had been drawn by officials of empires without any consultation with the peoples on either side of them – usually ripping apart ancient societies and vital kinships.

These colonial frontiers (or even more provocative partitions) had to be accepted by liberation movements as a price of independence. In an irony that will tax the UN for years to come, these harsh sunderings of real societies were then made sacrosanct in UN membership. So, too, were other dismemberments, like the separation of the 10 million Quechuans of the Andes within the frontiers of four already independent members of the UN. The same supposition was involved in the membership of the USSR and of Yugoslavia. How many ancient but riven identities, and how many animosities, were thus concealed and suppressed inside sanctified UN member-state boundaries, and not allowed to evolve in healthy relationships? Untold trouble was being stored up for the future, all across the world.

Politically, the foundations of the UN presupposed that one, centrist nation-state model of governance, developed in Europe and imposed everywhere else in the age of empires, would prove acceptable and viable for as long ahead as anyone could predict. It requires but a moment's reflection to realise that this was an enormous assumption for the great majority of human beings in societies totally outside Judeo-Christian culture, possessing their own ancient heritages of governance and representation. But no one anywhere has thought of any alternative beyond the post-Westphalian nation-state for over 200 years.

If the peoples of the South had been genuinely free at last to resume their own, indigenous evolution of political systems, pluralism and democratic accountability could have been advanced in far more societies, with gradual adjustment of the inherited European nation-state model. Instead the Cold War brought, to peoples who had nothing to do with its origins, dictatorships installed or fostered by intelligence agencies. Lavishly financed and armed, these regimes were also often used as bases to destabilise neighbouring countries. In all of this 'the UN' was virtually powerless. Today it is supposed to cope with what are suddenly called 'civil wars' in countries like Angola and Mozambique or 'tribalism' in Rwanda, with precious little help from the powers directly responsible for these ravages and the divide-and-rule legacies of internal dissension.

It could have been predicted, but it was not, that as soon as centrist authoritarian rulers fostered, financed and armed by intelligence agencies of the great powers lost their Cold War-driven support, these exogenously constructed states might crumble. When Somalia did, the powers, with the same astonishing capacity for forgetting responsibility, promptly turned to the UN to pick up the tragic pieces. Yet they neither resourced it adequately nor left it alone to try. Phyllis Bennis analyses these syndromes in the unfolding history of UN peacekeeping. Angela Penrose analyses the challenge to the UN System of the constantly growing scale of man-made humanitarian crisis, and discusses the weaknesses in its machinery and in the behaviour of its member-governments that must now be redressed.

Economic and social regression

Economically, the UN System at its creation obviously presupposed the continuation of the economies of the empires. Yet here again the smaller founders had miraculously seen to it that the roles it was *mandated* to perform fully matched the needs of the peoples of developing countries when

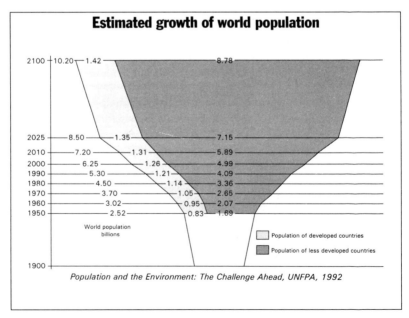

Estimated growth of world population

2100	10.20	1.42	8.78
2025	8.50	1.35	7.15
2010	7.20	1.31	5.89
2000	6.25	1.26	4.99
1990	5.30	1.21	4.09
1980	4.50	1.14	3.36
1970	3.70	1.05	2.65
1960	3.02	0.95	2.07
1950	2.52	0.83	1.69
1900			

World population
billions

Population of developed countries

Population of less developed countries

Population and the Environment: The Challenge Ahead, UNFPA, 1992

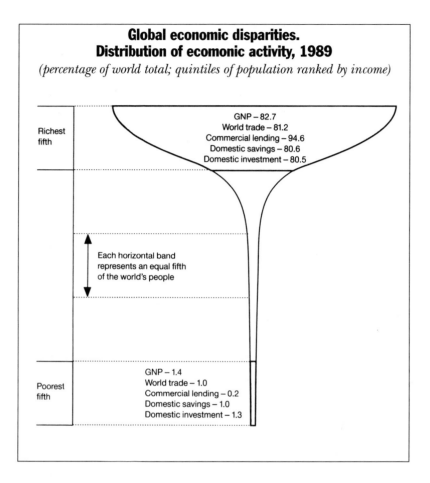

Global economic disparities.
Distribution of ecomonic activity, 1989
(percentage of world total; quintiles of population ranked by income)

Richest fifth

GNP – 82.7
World trade – 81.2
Commercial lending – 94.6
Domestic savings – 80.6
Domestic investment – 80.5

Each horizontal band
represents an equal fifth
of the world's people

Poorest fifth

GNP – 1.4
World trade – 1.0
Commercial lending – 0.2
Domestic savings – 1.0
Domestic investment – 1.3

these were revealed. The Charter's commitment of all members to employ the UN System for the economic and social advancement of 'all peoples' was there when 'all peoples' could at last be reached. The Economic and Social Council (ECOSOC) was supposed to have high-calibre commissions which would, among other things, tackle 'methods of increasing productivity and levels of consumption in the less-developed regions [and] the effects of industrialisation and technological change on world economic conditions'.

The UN's mandates thus provided all the bases for a new multilateral and equitable management of the commanding heights of the full world's economy, for everyone's benefit. Nassau Adams, Amir Jamal, and Myriam Vander Stichele discuss in more detail what has happened to the machinery that was supposed to be put to work for these ends. The story of how, instead, the UN System's economic and social capacities have been steadily weakened by industrial powers raises in question whether their elites ever intended to honour their commitments in this vital cause-addressing part of the original design. Today there is increasing impoverishment, more – not less – inequitable world trade, and an end to all semblance of multilateral management of world money and exchange. Combined, these factors not only keep hundreds of millions of our sisters and brothers in abject misery, but now powerfully exacerbate cultural, political and ethnic tensions throughout the world.

All of the forces sketched above were at work throughout the Cold War and, as noted, were even intensified by it. But in place of the euphoria that swept across the North, the deferred reckonings with history became very quickly evident, like old minefields buried under ice and suddenly re-exposed across the world in a sudden thaw ... all the more deadly for their long neglect.

Gulf crisis: sign of the times

The 1990-91 Iraq-Kuwait Gulf crisis was much more than one episode in 'the volatile Middle East', as Western commentators like to call it. History seemed, indeed, to be insisting in those months that the world wake up to all that it had neglected, everywhere. The Gulf crisis mirrored virtually every one of the delayed reckonings – artificially imposed but UN-sanctified frontiers, poverty adjacent to unbridled affluence, failure to come anywhere near to international management of global commons. It also demonstrated the ability of a handful of states to assemble and unleash all the devastation of their high-technology 'conventional' weaponry: five times the combined explosive power of the Hiroshima and Nagasaki bombs was dropped on Iraqis, one-third the total tonnage dropped by the Allies on Europe between 1943 and 1945. In Chapter 6 Paul Rogers provides a thorough overview of weaponries and disarmament syndromes in our world today.

In the Gulf War the world divided over not only the origins, not only the blocking of all efforts to negotiate a settlement, but over what the crisis signified for the United Nations. The factor of imbalance in power available to the Security Council on the one hand, and the General Assembly on the other, is also discussed by Phyllis Bennis. One element within this imbalance, which even the highly alert smaller countries could not predict in 1945 and therefore guard against in the Charter, shows how the increasing impoverishment of developing countries can pervade every aspect of the UN. Citizens in the North were told that the Gulf War was prosecuted 'under the UN Charter and UN resolutions'. This briefly contributed to the 'rediscovery' of the UN. Northerners were not, of course, informed of the use of huge bribes, or brutal economic menaces (loss of 'aid' or debt relief or IMF credit), to secure votes or silence delegations so that the war would seem to have been prosecuted – as Washington and London repeatedly claimed – 'with the support of the whole international community'.

How fragile the UN's world bases of support can be while it is thus abused on one hand, and under-used on the other, can be seen from the view of it from the South during and after the Gulf crisis and war. It was theoretically the same one 'UN'. But where many Northern journals were hailing its 're-birth', their Southern counterparts were forecasting its death. The political cartoonist of *The Times of India*, Laxman, depicted diplomats standing around a grave below the UN headquarters building as headstone, with the epitaph, 'Here Lies the UN, Victim of the Super-Powers'.

Causes for hope

As this book is published, however, the United Nations that belongs to all of us is still very much alive. We can be immensely thankful that the majority of humankind have not given it up, even though the industrial powers continue in every sphere to exert 'carrot and stick diplomacy' to keep it under their control. We could, indeed, be on the eve of genuine new advances for the world organisation and thus for all of humankind, if a number of healthy trends are strengthened.

The first of these is that a major and increasingly transparent debate on the entire future of the UN's roles in the maintenance of international peace and security has been launched. The most healthy aspect of this debate is that it is not confined to and circumscribed by the powers in the Security Council. The General Assembly has insisted on treating the *Agenda for Peace* report by the Secretary-General as *its* business, in a special open-ended working group that is being taken seriously, not least by the 'Permanent Members' of the Council.

Every member state has been asked to submit its views, in writing, for publication, on the future composition of the Security Council and its roles in relation to the General Assembly; the issue of permanent Members and whether there should be any more, or none; and the question of the veto. This is one UN reform area where the last thing we need is haste, lest it result in the worst of compromises: a 'trade-off' admitting Germany and

Japan to the archaic club of the 'Permanents', but seducing some large Southern countries to join as well.

In a parallel development the majority in the General Assembly have insisted that, if there is to be an *Agenda for Peace* then there will also be an *Agenda for Development*. In the summer of 1994 the President of the Assembly took the unprecedented step of convening 'Public Hearings' on this second agenda, where eminent and more popularly rooted unofficial views were invited, and were debated with the governmental delegates. In their rejection of a draft paper from the Secretary-General the majority have been making it clear that by 'development' they want far-reaching, structural attention to the potentially catastrophic North-South trade and other economic inequities and the deficiencies of the Bretton Woods financial institutions analysed in this book.

What all this may mean for the United Nations System as it crosses through its 50th anniversary may well depend upon another factor that is new, and refreshing. After decades during which the world community of non-governmental organisations (NGOs) held the UN at arm's length as only another impossibly complicated and adversarial bureaucracy, NGOs throughout the world have clearly decided that it is vital for their goals and that they must have a say in it. In chapters 8 and 9 Barbara Adams and Maximo Kalaw analyse the growth of this demand for the empowerment of 'We, the Peoples of the United Nations'.

Opportunities for action

Major anniversaries always tend to be called 'historic turning-points'. The United Nations' 50th really does merit such description, because it coincides with three truly history-changing developments. All three are turbulent, but just as the word 'crisis' in Chinese also conveys 'opportunity', we should remember how often turbulence ultimately proves healthy if wisdom is present.

The real problems of humankind are no longer subject to suppression and distraction under empires or cold war. History is now making its full claims. Unleashed with greater force because of their long neglect, they are very dangerous. The costs of continuing to neglect them and then trying to cope with their consequences in conflict and mass human misery will prove quite insurmountable. The stark lesson must be driven home in tired and myopic circles of orthodox power that these problems cannot be tackled by any one or group of states, only by genuine multilateral action having the support of the full world community; only through a strengthened United Nations System.

The second unprecedented development is that the era of bluff and bluster by a handful of apparently powerful states is clearly ending. No sooner were we informed that we were in 'the age of a single super-power', than that power itself began to plead inability to cope with such responsibilities (while of course trying to retain the illusion). In former Yugoslavia and elsewhere, one after another these former giants have been evincing growing signs of pre-occupation with domestic problems and inadequate funds. This is nothing but healthy, provided that it results in a genuine democratisation of the UN, and in a new and honest sharing of responsibilities.

We are not there yet, by a long measure. We are, indeed, in a new stage where one or more powers deny the UN vital equipment when it is most desperately needed, but seek to borrow the UN mantle for brief attempts to look as though they could still act like giants, alone. They need to be told that the UN Charter is not for rent as theatrical costume. The best leadership they can now offer is through joining democratically with the rest of the membership in shared peacekeeping and humanitarian burdens where they promptly offer their special logistical and other resources. They will gain infinitely more respect from the rest of the world once they really join it.

The third historic development is a growing restiveness among ordinary peoples everywhere, and an unstoppable momentum for human rights – all human rights, not only individual civil and political, but economic and social. The connections are being made between once remote diplomatic negotiations and masses of ordinary people, as when hundreds of thousands of ordinary Indian farmers demonstrated against the conclusions of the GATT 'Uruguay Round' ... or when representatives of the one in every 18 of us who is a member of an indigenous nation walked the length of the Western hemisphere to meet together at its centre. As to the largest human rights issues on our planet, a world for so long dominated by men (with such indifferent results) is now reverberating to the demands of more than half of humankind, and will never again be the same for this. And young people from one end of Earth to the other find chords of wonderful solidarity, in common human social issues, through their worldsong. Everywhere, the ordinary people of Planet Earth intend now to be heard.

This book should equip the caring citizen with new knowledge and insight, and the conviction that the United Nations and the needs of *all* its peoples are far too serious matters to be left to governments alone.

Charter of the United Nations

WE THE PEOPLES OF THE UNITED NATIONS DETERMINED

to save succeeding generations from the scourge of war, which twice in our lifetime has brought untold sorrow to mankind, and

to reaffirm faith in fundamental human rights, in the dignity and worth of the human person, in the equal rights of men and women and of nations large and small, and

to establish conditions under which justice and respect for the obligations arising from treaties and other sources of international law can be maintained, and

to promote social progress and better standards of life in larger freedom,

AND FOR THESE ENDS

to practice tolerance and live together in peace with one another as good neighbours, and

to unite our strength to maintain international peace and security, and

to ensure, by the acceptance of principles and the institution of methods, that armed force shall not be used, save in the common interest, and

to employ international machinery for the promotion of the economic and social advancement of all peoples,

HAVE RESOLVED TO COMBINE OUR EFFORTS TO ACCOMPLISH THESE AIMS

Accordingly, our respective Governments, through representatives assembled in the city of San Francisco, who have exhibited their full powers found to be in good and due form, have agreed to the present Charter of the United Nations and do hereby establish an international organisation to be known as the United Nations.

Article 1

The Purposes of the United Nations are:

1. To maintain international peace and security, and to that end: to take effective collective measures for the prevention and removal of threats to the peace, and for the suppression of acts of aggression or other breaches of the peace, and to bring about by peaceful means, and in conformity with the principles of justice and international law, adjustment or settlement of international disputes or situations which might lead to a breach of the peace;

2. To develop friendly relations among nations based on respect for the principle of equal rights and self-determination of peoples, and to take other appropriate measures to strengthen universal peace;

3. To achieve international co-operation in solving international problems of an economic, social, cultural, or humanitarian character, and in promoting and encouraging respect for human rights and for fundamental free-

doms for all without distinction as to race, sex, language, or religion; and
4. To be a centre for harmonising the actions of nations in the attainment of these common ends.

Article 2
The Organisation and its Members, in pursuit of the Purposes stated in Article 1, shall act in accordance with the following Principles.
1. The Organisation is based on the principle of the sovereign equality of all its Members.
2. All Members, in order to ensure to all of them the rights and benefits resulting from membership, shall fulfil in good faith the obligations assumed by them in accordance with the present Charter.
3. All Members shall settle their international disputes by peaceful means in such a manner that international peace and security, and justice, are not endangered.
4. All Members shall refrain in their international relations from the threat or use of force against the territorial integrity or political independence of any state, or in any other manner inconsistent with the Purposes of the United Nations.
5. All Members shall give the United Nations every assistance in any action it takes in accordance with the present Charter, and shall refrain from giving assistance to any state against which the United Nations is taking preventive or enforcement action.
6. The Organisation shall ensure that states which are not Members of the United Nations act in accordance with these Principles so far as may be necessary for the maintenance of international peace and security.
7. Nothing contained in the present Charter shall authorise the United Nations to intervene in matters which are essentially within the domestic jurisdiction of any state or shall require the Members to submit such matters to settlement under the present Charter; but this principle shall not prejudice the application of enforcement measures under Chapter VII.

Article 55
With a view to the creation of conditions of stability and well-being which are necessary for peaceful and friendly relations among nations based on respect for the principle of equal rights and self-determination of peoples, the United Nations shall promote:
a. higher standards of living, full employment, and conditions of economic and social progress and development;
b. solutions of international economic, social, health, and related problems; and international cultural and educational cooperation; and
c. universal respect for, and observance of, human rights and fundamental freedoms for all without distinction as to race, sex, language, or religion.

The United Nations System

ERSKINE CHILDERS

The United Nations System comprises the UN itself including its development and environment funds, and 15 Specialised Agencies listed in the diagram on page 23. As their names indicate, it works on every need of humankind. This section provides essential facts about the UN System, and some of the issues underlying problems discussed in this book.

Western media have long depicted the UN System as an incomprehensibly 'vast, sprawling bureaucracy'. It is in fact not as complicated as a medium-size national government, and the actual facts about its staff and budget demonstrate that in reality it is perilously under-resourced for its ever-increasing workload.

The heart of the System is the United Nations itself.

The United Nations

The United Nations is an international association of nation-states, each of which ratifies and is thereafter bound by its constitution, the Charter.

The Charter strongly expresses social-democratic values in the Preamble, Purposes and Principles, and Article 55, but it contains a basic flaw. Its eloquent iterations of goals for 'all peoples' in a democratic world institution are interspersed with provisions for the dominance of a small minority. It thus contains the basis for a continuous contest between a few states insisting on the rule of might, and the majority seeking a genuine world community. Even in 1945 this was a contest of five among 51; now it is five among 184 member states. If one allows for China's pronounced reluctance to be regarded as a member of the veto-wielding group, the representatives of 545 million people hold built-in special privileges vis-à-vis

5,000 million. Any of the 'Permanent Members' of the Security Council can veto any proposed amendment to the Charter, and thus any attempt to eliminate or reduce their special privileges.

The UN has six 'Principal Organs' so named in the Charter:

Article 108

Amendments to the present Charter shall come into force for all Members of the United Nations when they have been adopted by a vote of two thirds of the members of the General Assembly and ratified in accordance with their respective constitutional processes by two thirds of the Members of the United Nations, including all the permanent members of the Security Council.

• *The General Assembly* is the full-membership supreme decision-making body, functioning according to 'one nation, one vote'. Its many hundreds of resolutions since it first met in London in 1946 have helped to shape the modern world, including nearly 70 Human Rights instruments. The Assembly is the convenor of the UN's famous 'mega-conferences' (for example, the 1992 environment conference at Rio; the human rights conference in Vienna in 1993; the 1994 Cairo conference on Population and Development, and the Fourth World Women's Conference in Beijing in 1995), and it confirms the world programmes of action negotiated at these giant gatherings. Its decisions are not automatically binding on governments unless they are new treaties, such as the Law of the Sea or conventions for Human Rights that become binding when ratified. The Assembly also adopts 'Declarations'. Possessing a stature between resolutions and treaties or conventions, they signal a high degree of concern and resolve among members, and can lead to laws being adopted by states or can influence the content of national laws. [1]

The Assembly meets in New York and elects a President for a one-year term. Its regular session runs from September to December, beginning with a 'General Debate' in which many Heads of State and Government present their views of the world and of what the UN should do about it. Nowadays, sessions often have to be resumed during other months. The

---

1 An example, of bearing on the peacekeeping discussion in this book and of the General Assembly asserting itself in such matters vis-à-vis the Security Council, is the Declaration on Fact-Finding adopted in 1991 (Resolution 46/59).

Assembly has standing Committees (also full-membership) to deal with different parts of its agenda. They receive and draft final decisions on the numerous reports flowing to the Assembly from three UN Councils, as well as bodies directly responsible to it, like the International Law Commission.

• *The Security Council* has 'primary responsibility' for the maintenance of international peace and security, which the UN's members as a whole 'confer' upon it, the Charter also stipulating that it must act according to the Purposes and Principles of the UN. It currently has 15 members. Five are 'Permanent Members' (China, France, Russia, the United Kingdom and the United States) who insisted on being so named in the Charter, and on never needing to be elected to the Council. Ten 'non-permanent members' are elected by the General Assembly for two-year terms, reflecting the geographical spread of overall UN membership. Decisions of the Council are binding upon all UN members. The 'Permanent Five' also have powers of veto over such decisions.

The Charter directed the 'Permanent Members' to set up a working Military Staff Committee, among other matters to plan a system of arms regulation to ensure 'the least diversion for armaments of the world's human and economic resources'. They have not done so.

The Security Council is 'so organised as to be able to function continuously'. Nowadays it meets about a hundred times a year, with twice as many informal consultations. UN members as a whole have been profoundly dissatisfied with the tendency of several of the powers to treat the Council as their privy club, and the General Assembly is reviewing these issues of transparency along with the Council's size, membership, permanency or its elimination, and the veto issue.

• *The Economic and Social Council* (ECOSOC) is also a Principal Organ. It was intended to prepare macro-policy proposals for the General Assembly, and to co-ordinate the activities of the Specialised Agencies and funds. ECOSOC currently has 54 members elected by the General Assembly for three-year terms to reflect the whole UN membership. It meets each year for five weeks. It has a large number of subsidiary bodies, like the Human Rights Commission. It has an enormous workload, which now includes overseeing the implementation of the huge 'Agenda 21' on sustainable development, adopted at the 1992 UN Conference in Rio de Janeiro and monitored for it by the new Commission of ECOSOC on Sustainable Development (CSD). ECOSOC votes by majority.

ECOSOC has been in a state of attempted 'revitalisation' for many years, unable to fulfil its mandates in global macro-economic (trade, money, finance) policy formulation because the industrial powers refuse to negotiate such policies in the UN. The Council's difficulties are compounded by the restriction of its annual meeting-time to even less than in earlier years, when it had one-third of its members and far fewer reports to consider.

• *The Trusteeship Council* operates under the authority of the General Assembly. It was set up to provide international supervision of Non-Self-Governing Territories. Since it now has no ongoing functions left to perform, it is one obvious candidate for re-fashioning to undertake new roles.[2]

• *The International Court of Justice* (the World Court) is 'the principal judicial organ' of the UN. It operates under its own Statute, which is a part of the Charter. Its 15 Judges are nominated through national groups of their peers; they are then elected for nine-year terms by absolute majorities of both the General Assembly and the Security Council. The Seat of the Court is at The Hague (Netherlands).

All UN member-states are supposed to comply with a decision of the Court in any case to which they are a party, but some have ignored its findings.[3] The Court can be asked for an advisory opinion on any legal question – including alleged abuse of the Charter – by either the General Assembly or the Security Council. Many want the Secretary-General also to have this requesting authority (see further below).

Only States may be parties in cases taken by the Court. The UN does not yet have a Court of Human Rights to adjudicate for individuals and community groups but, as a chapter in this book details, the UN's Human Rights machinery is increasing its ability to hold governments accountable. A new Commission on Crime Prevention and Criminal Justice is now beginning its work. The Security Council (some say acting beyond its mandates) recently established a Tribunal to hear allegations of War Crimes in former Yugoslavia.

• *The Secretariat*, the civil-service administration headed by the Secretary-General, has its seat at New York, but parts of it are at Geneva (for exam-

---

2 For discussion of converting the Trusteeship Council into a Council on Diversity, Representation and Governance see Erskine Childers with Brian Urquhart, *Renewing The United Nations System* (Uppsala, Dag Hammarskjöld Foundation, 1994).

3 An example was the United States ignoring the findings of the World Court against its mining of Nicaraguan harbours.

ple, the staff of UNCTAD, and the Human Rights Centre) and there is a UN Office at Vienna. Smaller staffs are stationed in the Regional Commissions (of ECOSOC) at Addis Ababa, Baghdad, Bangkok, Geneva, and Santiago. There are UN Information Centres in some 53 capitals, many serving several countries. The total regular staff of this UN, world-wide, numbers about 9,000 (3,200 in professional grades, 5,800 support staff). That is less than the civil servants of the city of Winnipeg in Canada.

The Secretary-General is the head of the Secretariat and thus of a Principal Organ, and is the chief administrative officer of the UN. She or he is appointed by the General Assembly on the recommendation of the Security Council, which is subject to veto by any of its Permanent Members. (Constitutionally, this can not prevent the Assembly from rejecting a candidate endorsed by the powers, but it has never yet done so.) The Charter does not stipulate any process for the Council's choice of nominee to the General Assembly. At present, the Secretary-General serves for five years, renewable. No woman has yet been appointed.[4]

The full extent of the role of a Secretary-General has often been controversial in the view of one or more of the major powers. One key issue is whether the Secretary-General must invariably act as merely 'the servant of the Security Council' – or whether the office, heading as it does a Principal Organ, has its highest responsibility to the world community as a whole, and as a 'guardian of the Charter'.[5]

UN funds

Governments have created various development and humanitarian bodies of the UN down the years, like the Children's Fund (UNICEF), the Development Programme (UNDP), the Population Fund (UNFPA), or the High Commissioner for Refugees (UNHCR). These funds are not autonomous, even if their behaviour sometimes suggests otherwise, nor are they 'specialised agencies'; they are UN subsidiaries set up by the General Assembly

---

4 For full discussion of the lack of proper selection procedure and details of gender bias in appointments to all executive-head positions in the UN System, see Brian Urquhart and Erskine Childers, *A World In Need Of Leadership: Tomorrow's United Nations, Development Dialogue 1990:1-2* (Uppsala, Dag Hammarskjold Foundation, 1990).

5 In a lecture at Oxford University on 12 May 1986 (UN Release SG/SM/3870) Mr. Pérez de Cuellar said, 'Situations can and do arise when the Secretary-General has to exercise his powers to the full, as the bearer of a sacred trust and as the guardian of the principles of the Charter'. In the 1990 Gulf Crisis, however, he did not challenge the uses of the Charter by major powers and, since so many weak member-states were under intensive economic intimidation, the only 'guardian' readily available remained inert.

and under the responsibility of the Secretary-General.

Long-standing problems of 'co-ordination' among them have not been resolved as this book is published. Governments created the five major development funds (UNDP, UNEP, UNFPA, UNICEF, and WFP) as well as other, smaller ones like UNIFEM, at different times and without sufficient correlation. They are separately governed, financed and operated, they have separate country programmes, and several of them work in the same fields but with little or no co-ordination. For humanitarian assistance, governments have allowed as untidy a tangle to develop: UNICEF, UNHCR, the World Food Programme, often WHO, with UNDP supposed to hold the ring at country level, and since 1992 a UN Under-Secretary who is supposed to co-ordinate all this globally but without overriding authority.

These problems have arisen to some extent because Secretaries-General have left the funds very much to their own devices; but above all because governments simply have not taken care with their separate decisions about them. They blame the secretariats for 'not coordinating' but they, the governments themselves, compel them to compete with each other for voluntary contributions. They also allow their national ministries or offices that liaise with the funds to advocate their separateness.

UN financing

The UN is financed from two sources: assessment of members according to a scale adopted by the General Assembly; and voluntary contributions, ie, to development funds.

The assessed budgets

The UN Secretariat, and the workings of the intergovernmental organs outlined above, are financed by a 'Regular Budget' adopted by the General Assembly every two years, since 1986 on the basis of consensus. This budget is supposed to be paid for by the obligatory contributions of all members in assessments decided by the General Assembly according to a formula of 'capacity to pay' (national income, population, level of debt, etc). Separate budgets for UN peacekeeping operations are also financed by assessment, but on a slightly different scale.

Not surprisingly, industrial countries are assessed larger money amounts as larger percentiles of the total budget. Thus, for the main Regular Budget the US is assessed 25%; Japan 12.45%; Germany 8.93%; Russia 6.71%; France 6% and Britain 5%, Brazil 1.59%, India 0.36%, Nigeria 0.20% and so on, down to the poorest developing countries which each contribute 0.01%.[6] The combined Regular and Peacekeeping budgets of the UN in

1993 totalled about $4.1 billion. That is scarcely more than the budgets of the Fire and Police forces of New York City.

Under the Charter no member state may withhold any part of its assessed contribution for political reasons, or if it dislikes some aspect of UN administration. For many years, however, the United States has refused to contribute its full assessment unless the membership adopts various administrative reforms and/or drops various programmes approved by the majority. In addition the US, Russia, and other countries have not fully paid in their peacekeeping assessments. And since all members have to pay in actual US dollars which have to be earned in trade, many developing countries also fall behind.

The combined effect is calamitous: in recent years arrears owed to the UN as late as the third quarter of any budget year have amounted to three-quarters of its entire budget for that year. As of June 1994, the organisation was owed over $3 billion. Governments refuse to allow the UN to borrow so much as one dollar even for a week. Recent proposals for resolving this perennial teetering on the brink of bankruptcy include charging interest on late payments, and that members meet the UN's peacekeeping costs from their defence budgets.[7] Outside official circles, interest is growing in additional financing sources, such as the taxing of arms sales or international travel; perhaps even a United Nations Lottery.

Voluntary funding

The development and humanitarian funds are financed by voluntary contributions in 'Extra-Budgetary' accounts.[8] The great bulk of these contributions comes from governments, though UNICEF receives a significant amount from citizen donations and UNHCR can also do so.

This method of financing is not free of controversy, chiefly because it has led to an unhealthy 'donor-recipient' attitude in, and pressure for special influence from, the countries contributing major amounts. Here, too, gross misperceptions are at work: developing countries contribute land,

---

6 Leaders and editorialists in wealthier countries speak of them as 'contributing most', leading to endless pressure for special influence in the UN. This is a virtual violation of the Charter principle of relative capacity to pay, which is also the primordial basis of taxation in democracies – that it is just as difficult for a poorer citizen (or poorer UN member-country) to find its smaller money-amount as it is for a wealthier to find a larger amount. In the countries claiming to be 'paying most', any demand by wealthier citizens or corporations for special influence or weighted voting, or any refusal to pay taxes unless government changed its policy, would not be tolerated.

7 See the report to the Secretary-General of a panel of eminent financiers co-chaired by Shiguro Ogata and Paul Volcker, *Financing an Effective United Nations* (New York, Ford Foundation, 1993).

8 Administrative costs of UNEP and UNHCR are paid from the UN assessed, Regular Budget.

buildings, staff and salaries of their civil services and training institutions, and in addition cash for project budgets – usually aggregating to between 40 and 80 per cent of a project's total cost. In addition, developing countries contribute an aggregate of about 10 per cent of the central voluntary funds.

Nordic Governments have recently proposed that all funds should at least have their administrative costs met by assessment.

The specialised agencies

The years of the League of Nations saw the development of a good deal of co-operation between countries in a variety of international bodies specialising in such fields as agriculture, civil aviation, health, telecommunications, and so on. Some of these were already formal intergovernmental organisations, like the International Labour Organisation (ILO), created at Versailles after the first World War. As World War II ended, governmental and professional-technical supporters of the existing and newly planned bodies pressed for them to be separate from the proposed United Nations, fearing that their technical collaboration might be endangered if politicians failed in the UN as in the League.

These 'sectoral' groups began working for the creation of quite distinct, separate international organisations. Thus, Ministers of Education were meeting from as early as 1942 to fashion what became UNESCO. Ministries of Finance (or Treasury) were fashioning what became the International Monetary Fund and the World Bank (often called the 'Bretton Woods institutions' after a 1944 conference at that place in New Hampshire); and Ministries of Agriculture were drafting the constitution of what became the FAO, even before the UN Charter was signed.

Governments were thus influenced to a crucial collective decision, against a single, integrated United Nations and in favour of what Belgium described as 'a new system of a planetary type: a central organisation, the United Nations, around which gravitated independent agencies linked with the former by special agreements'.

Each of the Specialised Agencies has its own charter, membership, assembly and other organs, and its own policies, programmes, budget, and secretariat, with an executive head (usually called Director-General) elected by its member governments. ILO has a tripartite membership of governments, workers, and employers, but most of the other agencies are vertical offshoots of corresponding national ministries – ie, WHO of Ministries of Health, ICAO of national civil aviation authorities, FAO of Ministries of Agriculture, and so on. Delegations from member countries to the governing bodies of these agencies are composed of officers and technical specialists from these national counterparts.

If, however, it was to be a loose system the UN's founding governments at San Francisco did intend it to be led and coordinated by the new United Nations. A key assumption in this design was that very largely the same governments would be members of the UN as of each of these agencies, and would therefore themselves ensure common policies. But at San Francisco governments went further: they stipulated the leadership roles for the UN in the Charter itself. The General Assembly was to undertake studies in all fields (with expert assistance from ECOSOC), and was to formulate and adopt global macro-policies, then co-ordinate those policies and their implementation by the agencies. The Charter even stipulated (and still does) that the UN General Assembly should review the budgets of the agencies, with the overall objective of arriving at one consolidated budget for the whole System, which governments could adopt in one place at one time. The General Assembly's first session in 1946 also approved as a principle that the agencies' headquarters should be located at the seat of the UN.

This, then, was supposed to be the essential shape and working of the new United Nations system, as governments quickly created, alongside ILO, the Food and Agriculture Organisation, the World Health Organisation, and UNESCO for education, science and culture. With these four big agencies other technical organisations were created anew or existing bodies were brought into special agreement with the UN, until there are today 15 such specialised agencies (see box on page 23).

Totally missing from this list is the International Trade Organisation (ITO), whose charter was actually drafted but was rejected by the United States Congress. The GATT (General Agreement on Tariffs and Trade) was only to be a transitional compact, but lasted until 1994, never formally being made a UN Specialised Agency.

Governments, indeed, soon began to default more generally on their detailed, self-assumed responsibilities to build a System. As demonstrated in various chapters in this book, the UN System today is nothing like as cohesive as its member-governments originally pledged to ensure.

In essence, governments did not and still do not act as single governments in the UN System; they fail to co-ordinate themselves in their home capitals. National cabinets do not debate out and adopt, and heads of government do not then instruct, common policy positions to be expressed throughout the System. Wide leeway is left to the different Ministries and their delegations to each specialised agency's governing body. This often results in a substantial bias against being co-ordinated by the UN, even

The Specialised Agencies

Agriculture	FAO:	The Food and Agriculture Organisation of the United Nations
	IFAD:	The International Fund for Agricultural Development
Atomic Energy	IAEA:	The International Atomic Energy Agency
Civil Aviation	ICAO:	The International Civil Aviation Organisation
Education, Science, Culture, Communication	UNESCO:	The UN Educational, Scientific and Cultural Organisation
Finance	IBRD:	The International Bank for Reconstruction and Development (The World Bank Group)
Health	WHO:	The World Health Organisation
Industry	UNIDO:	The UN Industrial Development Organisation
Intellectual Property	WIPO:	The World Intellectual Property Organisation
Labour and Employment	ILO:	The International Labour Organisation
Maritime affairs	IMO:	The International Maritime Organisation
Climate and Weather	WMO:	The World Meteorological Organisation
Money	IMF:	The International Monetary Fund
Postal Services	UPU:	The Universal Postal Union
Telecommunications	ITU:	The International Telecommunications Union

whilst the same governments' Foreign Office delegates in New York call for precisely this. Authorities in Northern governments are prone to say that third world governments 'can't co-ordinate'; but the former are no better at all, some say even worse, than the latter in these matters.

Not one agency headquarters was located beside the UN, for no reason other than adroit host-trading among some self-important countries. The System's headquarters are now scattered in nine cities in seven countries across two continents and one ocean. The idea of a consolidated budget evaporated through lack of firm direction by Prime Ministerial and Foreign Offices. The IMF and the World Bank early refused to accept any UN coordination.

There is no intergovernmental council representing the separate governing bodies. The UN Secretary-General does chair an 'Administrative Committee on Coordination' with the agencies' heads as members, but it meets only a few days each year and agency heads do not have to accept any UN leadership. Thus, the UN System at present lacks either an intergovernmental body for the System as a whole, or any kind of 'cabinet' for it.

All these problems can, however, be corrected, given the political will among member governments.[9]

The Staff of the System

The total number of civil servants employed on the same basis in the whole UN System is the best test of the standard media description of a 'vast, sprawling swollen bureaucracy'. Excluding only peacekeeping troops, and the IMF and World Bank because they are recruited and paid differently, the total staff of the United Nations System – all grades, world-wide, for all its activities in every field – currently numbers some 52,000. That is somewhat less than the District Health staff in the Principality of Wales in Britain.

Financing of the UN System

With the exception of the three capitalised or underwritten agencies (IFAD, IMF, and the World Bank), the standard budgets of the System's specialised agencies are financed like the UN, from assessments on members. In addition, however, they receive voluntary contributions from two sources: the UN development funds, to carry out projects, and directly from 'donor' countries by their funding of projects in the same fields as UNDP finances, but not coordinated by UNDP. This tangle of financing, all of it the decision of governments, is a further obstacle to coherence. The expenditure of the whole System, excepting only the IMF and World Bank and covering all fields of endeavour world-wide including development grants, humanitarian relief, and peacekeeping, was $10.5 billion in 1992. That would maintain Britons in alcoholic beverages for about 15

---

9 For proposals to resolve these and other problems of the System as it has been allowed to develop, see Childers with Urquhart, op. cit., note 3.

weeks; or provide Western teenagers with half the accessories they buy for their clothing in a year.

To promote 'better standards of life in larger freedom', to 'save succeeding generations from the scourge of war', and to help those ravaged by the consequences of neglecting its causes, governments in 1992 invested in the UN System less than $2 per human being on Planet Earth.

They spent about $150 per human being on armies.

1. The UN's neglected brief
'The advancement of all peoples'?

NASSAU ADAMS

After now close to five decades of post-war history ushering in an era of unprecedented expansion of world income and prosperity, the gap in incomes and standards of living between the rich countries and the poor continues to widen. During much of this period, and particularly during the early years, there were high hopes that, with goodwill on all sides, co-operative international action could be effectual in bringing the poor countries into the mainstream of world economic development, and thereby helping to bridge the gap. The newly established international institutions, with their lofty aims and their grand purpose, were expected to play an important role in this regard. These hopes have not been borne out, however, and what we have witnessed instead is that large parts of the world have become increasingly trapped in poverty and destitution, while others continue to grow in affluence.

The current state of poverty in the South can be measured by reference to average income of the South as a whole, to the situation of individual developing countries, or to that of the large masses of the poor in these countries. By any of these measures the result is not bright. In 1989 average income in the South as a whole amounted to $911, less than 5 per cent of the nearly $18,000 average reported for the developed countries. This represents a substantial worsening in relative terms in the four decades since the 1950s, when average income in the South was estimated at 8 per cent of that of the North.[1] Seen in reference to individual developing

---

1 Figures for 1958 are based on estimates by Simon Kuznets showing the average for developed countries in that year of $1392 and for developing countries of $115. See Simon Kuznets, *Modern Economic Growth: Rate Structure and Spread*, Yale University Press, New Haven and London, 1966, Table 7.1.

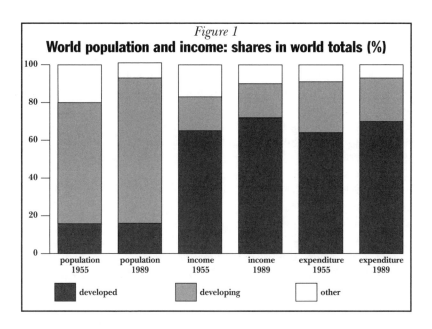

Figure 1
World population and income: shares in world totals (%)

countries the present gap appears even wider, with no fewer than 57 of such countries, accounting for over two-thirds of the total population of the South, now recording average incomes of less than one-fortieth (or 2.5 per cent) of the average for the developed countries. And masked by even these low averages is the vast sea of poverty, destitution, hunger and want that prevails among large masses of the populations in most of these countries. (Figure 1 highlights the growing income gap from the perspective of the respective shares of developed and developing countries in world population and income.)

This state of affairs is a cause of grave concern. Even more alarming is the fact that the situation has become distinctly worse in recent years. Over the past ten to 15 years there has been widespread deterioration in incomes and a sharp rise in poverty in large parts of the developing world, leading to an accelerated widening of the gap between rich and poor. Significantly also, the international development climate has shifted in ways which no longer provide even that minimal commitment to the development effort that prevailed in earlier years. To add to the woes, the ranks of the poor and the developing world have newly been swollen by a number of erstwhile communist countries of Eastern Europe and the former Soviet Union now struggling to adapt to a new beginning.

In the rich countries of the North an attitude of complacency prevails. A small group of the most powerful of these countries now controls the levers of world power virtually unchallenged. Convinced more than ever before that the course it has set is the right one, it has put the ship on auto-pilot (having turned over the controls to the workings of what passes for the free market) and seems determined to stay the course. But the passage is not turning out to be smooth. In the North there is growing disquiet as economic growth falters, unemployment mounts, homelessness spreads, and ethnic tensions and xenophobia raise their heads. And in the South the ride is, of course, proving to be even more stormy, and will inevitably worsen if the present course is held.

There is therefore no reason for complacency, no reason to take literally musings that we have now reached the end of history.[2] More likely, in fact, that we are at an important turning point in history, and that the course chosen now and in the immediate future will set the parameters and determine the character of the world of tomorrow. It is therefore high time to take a new look at the international development climate, at the institutions that are supposed to provide the framework for this development, and at the policies that prevail and how these need to change if the prospects of a brighter and more secure future for all are to be assured.

The institutional setting

The end of the second world war saw the establishment of an array of institutions for international co-operation of far-reaching scope and breadth never before seen or contemplated. These covered arrangements for co-operation in a wide range of areas, foremost among which were those primarily economic or political in nature. At the centre of the whole system stands the United Nations, whose Charter expresses the most noble aims of humankind, and whose aims, objectives and purpose cover almost the entire spectrum of political, economic and social issues. The United Nations was to be a global organisation whose structure would give it all-embracing authority to deal with the problems of international co-operation in their widest aspects.

In the economic domain, the main concern was to establish secure and stable conditions for the realisation of what was most conspicuously lacking in the inter-war years: economic prosperity and full employment growth. The focus was on three main areas considered vital for achieving these goals, namely: monetary and financial co-operation, trade co-operation, and macro-economic policy co-ordination. Also included in the agen-

---

2 See Francis Fukuyama, *The End of History and the Last Man*, Avon Books, New York, 1992.

da, though more as an afterthought than as an original basic ingredient, was the promotion of the economic development of the non-industrial, underdeveloped, and at the time largely colonised, areas of the world occupying the large land masses of Africa and Asia, the Pacific and Caribbean islands, and parts of South America.

Plans for dealing with the problems of monetary and financial co-operation led to the establishment soon after the second world war of the Bretton Woods institutions: the International Monetary Fund (IMF) and the International Bank for Reconstruction and Development (World Bank). On the other hand, plans for the establishment of an International Trade Organisation (ITO) to deal with the problems of trade co-operation did not materialise, though it came within a hair's breadth of doing so with the formal adoption in 1948 of a Charter for an International Trade Organisation, often referred to as the Havana Charter, in honour of the city in which the negotiating conference was held. Instead, the post-war world had to be content with a more limited scheme for trade liberalisation, the General Agreement on Tariffs and Trade (GATT). For the other two areas mentioned above, macro-economic policy co-ordination and the economic development of the underdeveloped areas of the world, the United Nations itself was to play the key role. Other specialised agencies (apart from the IMF and the World Bank) were also envisaged, covering such issues as food and agriculture, health, education and culture. The UN, as the highest body, was to have an oversight and co-ordinating role in relation to these institutions.

The best of plans often fail to foresee the actual course of events, and as things were to turn out, the institutional machinery established for responding to the needs of the post-war world evolved in ways, and ended up playing roles, very different from those originally intended. This is so especially as regards the two Bretton Woods institutions, discussed in chapter 2. Thus the IMF did not evolve to become the major global source of international liquidity, the role originally intended for it, and early on shifted its focus from the stabilisation needs of the countries of the industrial North and the issues of the broader global economy to concentrate on the problems of the South and on the management of the North's economic and financial relations with the South.[3] The World Bank also did not evolve to play much of a role in the 'reconstruction' of the war-torn economies, which idea figured so prominently in its name, and like the

---

3 See Nassau Adams, *Worlds Apart: The North-South Divide and the International system,* Zed Books, London, 1993, Chapter 2.

IMF also started early on shifting its focus towards the South. Before long, both institutions had put their original purposes as key players in the global macro-economy behind them, and had come instead to find their principal *raison d'être* as instruments for the conduct of the these North-South relations.

There was to be a similar deception concerning the role of the United Nations in the area of policy co-ordination for full-employment growth, a matter in which the industrial countries of the North would be principally involved. Thus, after a token and half-hearted start, the effort was soon given up, and the ambitious role that the United Nations was to play in this important area of global economic management was quietly buried and soon forgotten.[4] The UN was also never allowed to play any significant role of oversight and co-ordination in relation to the IMF and the World Bank, and over the years the provisions of Articles 59 and 63 of the United Nations Charter became increasingly irrelevant for these two agencies.

A noteworthy feature of these developments is the extent to which the industrial countries of the North have succeeded in removing themselves from the ambit of these institutions. The result is that, instead of being essential components of the UN-System framework for the conduct of economic and social relations among *all* countries (as was the original intention), these agencies have largely become instruments for the conduct of the North's relations with the South, and for dealing with the particular problems of the South. The GATT is the only important exception to this rule. For the most part, the problems of the North, and of cooperation among the Northern industrial countries, are dealt with elsewhere than in these supposedly global institutions.

The early UN role

In the United Nations proper, however, there was growing pressure from the increasing numbers of new independent states for greater attention to their needs and for implementation of the UN's economic and social mandates. It soon became the great crossroads and the central arena for fervent discussion of the problems of the South.

Programmes of technical assistance figured prominently in the earliest UN efforts in this area, though the question that attracted most attention in the early years concerned development finance, an issue on which de-

---

4 See Nassau Adams, *Loc.cit.*

veloping countries saw the most pressing need for international action. In this they were encouraged by the 1951 report of a group of experts on 'Measures for the Economic Development of Under-Developed Countries', which called for an 'International Development Authority' to make capital available to underdeveloped countries on a grant basis. Such an agency would supplement (or supplant) the World Bank, whose structure and lending policy were considered too burdensome to respond to the needs of the poor underdeveloped countries.[5] The ensuing debate led to the proposal in 1953 for a Special United Nations Fund for Economic Development (SUNFED), a facility that would differ markedly from the World Bank in that control would be shared equally between 'major contributors' and 'other members', and finance would be available largely as grant or on 'soft' terms.

The protracted and bitterly contested debate on this proposal led in the end to the establishment in 1959, as a weak compromise, of the United Nations Special Fund (subsequently reconstituted as the United Nations Development Programme – UNDP) as the principal channel for UN technical assistance to developing countries. It also led to the creation in 1960 of the International Development Association (IDA) as a soft-loan window of the World Bank, also a weak compromise given the limited and uncertain nature of the resources that were to be made available through it, and the fact that it would operate as an agency of the World Bank and under its rules, with control and decision-making resting exclusively with the main contributors.

Developing countries also pushed hard during the 1950s for international action to alleviate the adverse effects on their economies of unstable and declining primary commodity prices. Various concrete proposals for UN action were put forward. Based in most cases on detailed technical studies and on the findings of UN-appointed expert groups, they were extensively debated and the subjects of intense lobbying and voting in the General Assembly (GA) and the Economic and Social Council (ECOSOC). But always, the opposition, led by the US, was unrelenting. The objections were often clothed in technical language (arguing, for example, that such action would distort trade, foster inefficient allocation of resources, and lead to unwanted surpluses). However, it was not difficult to see that there were ulterior motives, especially as in the developed countries themselves primary producers were simultaneously enjoying the benefits of policies to

---

5 'Measures for the Economic Development of Under-Developed Countries', Report by a Group of Experts appointed by the Secretary-General of the United Nations, May 1951.

counter the effects of price instability and price declines very similar to those to which the technical objections were raised.

UNCTAD and the pressures for change

The 1960s saw a fresh vigour in the drive by the developing countries to bring about, through UN actions, new international policy measures supportive of their needs. This new vigour was inspired by a growing awareness, and an increased assertiveness, on the part of the countries of the South, and triggered by a sharp rise in their numbers[6] in the UN System and a consequential increase in their political importance. A growing sense of solidarity among the newly independent states, which also helped to set the stage for this new drive, soon achieved concrete political expression, first as the Afro-Asian bloc, largely anti-colonial in outlook, to be followed by the more cosmopolitan Non-Aligned Movement, and eventually by the Group of 77, the coalition of developing countries that was to spearhead the emerging clash with the North for changes in the international economic order.

The emphasis was now on the wider issues of international trade and economic development, and the pressure was for a UN conference on the subject focusing on the needs of the South. The idea of such a conference was vigorously opposed by the North, but the pressure led in the end to the convening, for eight weeks during 1964, of the landmark United Nations Conference on Trade and Development (UNCTAD), described by a contemporary observer as 'the largest and most comprehensive intergovernmental conference ever held'.[7]

Although the conference did not achieve much of immediate benefit in terms of practical policy measures, it did achieve a major result in that it gave birth (in the face of strong opposition from the developed countries) to a major new UN body, UNCTAD (bearing the same name as the original conference), devoted to the ongoing discussion and negotiation of international policy issues important to the South. The new body, equipped with its own secretariat and empowered to reconvene the plenary conference every three years to continue the negotiations, soon became a crucial

---

6 In the six years up to 1962, decolonisation resulted in the creation of some 34 newly independent states. All became members of the United Nations, swelling that organisation's membership by a half in these few years.

7 See Richard N. Gardner, 'The United Nations Conference on Trade and Development' in Richard N.Gardner and Max F. Millikan, *The Global Partnership*, Praeger Publishers, New York, 1968, p.99.

source of data and analysis and the main focal point for the evolving North-South dialogue. The conference also provided, for the first time, a hint to the underdeveloped countries of what could be achieved in the international arena by group solidarity, sheer numbers, and the purposeful pursuit of negotiating objectives.

Towards the NIEO

The decade of the 1970s was to see a much more determined bid by the South to force the North into serious dialogue and negotiation aimed at achieving the kinds of changes they sought. The success of OPEC in hiking prices and in seizing control of their oil industries so long dominated by the North was the catalyst which set the stage for this bid. The commodity price boom in the early 1970s, and the idea, widely discussed at the time, that the world was now entering an era of permanent shortage of raw materials, also played their part, strengthening the feeling in the South that they occupied a position of strategic importance that would allow them to extract worthwhile concessions from the North.

The boldness with which the South, through the now well established Group of 77, put forward and pressed for early discussion and adoption of their daring proposals for a new international economic order (NIEO) went beyond anything before contemplated. And such was the nature of the times that, at the Sixth Special Session of the GA in April 1974, the draft Declaration and Programme of Action on the NIEO submitted by the developing countries were, with some amendments, adopted without dissent. Also part of the NIEO package was the Charter of Economic Rights and Duties of States, adopted at the 29th regular session of the GA in the autumn of 1974. The latter, however, was adopted by vote, the developed countries having by then regained some of their composure and become able to register their opposition.

But while the developing countries could, with their numerical strength and in the circumstances of the time, secure formal adoption of their proposals for a NIEO, it was quite another matter when it came to implementation. Thus the fact that the industrial countries may not have registered their votes against the NIEO demands, and may have acquiesced in their adoption by consensus, did not by any means presage a genuine willingness on their part to see them implemented. This became more than evident as soon as the pressures eased, and as the North began to see more clearly how the crisis could be handled. From there on it was a question of procrastination, stalling for time, and just plain inaction.

Where the issue was one of new rules and principles governing international economic relations, as was the case for a good part of the NIEO, there was little more to be said, and for the developed countries it was then just a question of ignoring these pronouncements in actual practice. Where it concerned measures to be taken by developed countries individually, for example in achieving aid targets, there was also little more that needed to be said, since it would be those countries that would, in time, decide whether and to what extent implementation would take place. Only where the NIEO called for specific *international* action, such as for changes in existing institutions or for the creation of new institutions and mechanisms, did implementation demand further negotiation leading to binding commitments. The main fora for these negotiations were the 7th Special Session of the GA in September 1975, the Conference on International Economic Co-operation (CIEC) which took place intermittently in Paris between 1975 and 1977, and the fourth UNCTAD conference in Nairobi in May 1976.

The negotiations at the 7th Special Session resulted in some relatively minor concession on IMF policies, vague promises to consider other more basic proposals bearing on this institution, and a decision to shift to the forthcoming UNCTAD conference consideration of the whole set of issues bearing on raw materials (prices, terms of trade, market stabilisation agreements, etc) which were so central to NIEO demands. The CIEC, to which great hopes were once attached, became in practice something of a side show, and eventually petered out without achieving any useful results. The main focus was therefore on the UNCTAD conference, which was to achieve distinction, not only for the high hopes it spawned, but more importantly, as it turned out, because it would go down in history as the high water mark in the whole process of North-South confrontation and dialogue that had been gathering force over the years to reach such intensity during the 1970s.

The conference itself was a major international event, well attended at the highest level, and very much the centre of media and public attention. The centre-piece of the conference was an ambitious proposal for a multi-commodity stabilisation programme backed by a special commodities fund, and given the high hopes on all sides for a positive outcome to the conference, there was a great deal of pressure for an accommodation on this issue. Thus, despite the misgivings, and indeed underlying opposition, the conference ended with agreement on the outlines of a scheme along the lines proposed, the details of which were to be negotiated subsequently. But this was a case of formal agreement without any meeting of minds on essentials, and the negotiations which followed only served to expose this fact. Consequently, after nearly three years of hectic but mostly fruit-less negotiations, pursuit of the original objectives was for all practical pur-poses abandoned. And it may with justification be said that the abandon-ment, by the turn of the decade, of the objectives of the commodities pro-gramme signalled the extinction of the last flicker of hope for a NIEO. It would also usher in a new era where the North-South issue would take on a wholly different aspect.

Why did the NIEO debate, which at its heights had generated such ex-citement and high hopes, and which for a while gave rise to so much fren-zied negotiating activity, fizzle out so completely after a few brief years, with little to show for it, and such that by the early 1980s the very concept was all but forgotten? It would take us much too far afield to try to answer this question here. But we can mention a number of factors that bore on the issue. These include: an over-optimistic assessment by the South of their strength deriving from control of their raw material resources; a number of tactical errors on their part (and of tactical triumphs by the North) in reacting to the unfolding events of the 1970s;[8] and perhaps most important of all, the rise, partly as result of the events of this period, of conservative governments in the North committed to a ferocious free-mar-ket philosophy and determined to roll back the trends of the recent past. The result was a crystallisation in the North of a total lack of sympathy for the aims of the developing countries as expressed in the North-South dia-logue and the NIEO, and a resolve to put an end once and for all to pres-sures from the South for achieving such aims. The fact that the main thrust of NIEO demands called for interventionist measures to regulate and control the market mechanism, now anathema to the new conserva-tive philosophy, only served to add fuel to this resolve.

The debt crisis and its aftermath

The debt crisis which erupted in the early 1980s provided the backdrop for the great change in the character of North-South relations that was to take place. When the crisis broke (following the steep rise in international

---

8 For the South, the most obvious tactical error was to expend too much energy in trying to force systemic changes on an unwilling North on the basis of a perceived shift in the balance of eco-nomic forces, to the neglect of the crucial question of how best to adjust to the economic distur-bances of the period (in particular the sky-rocketing of oil prices and the convulsions in the com-modities markets), unappreciative of the fact that it was how effectively this latter task was han-dled that would ultimately determine their ability to realise their broader aim of forcing changes on the North. Both the oil importers and the oil exporters were guilty of this neglect.

interest rates and the collapse of commodity prices), the scene was set for the playing out of one of the most frightening nightmares imaginable in the developing countries affected. Faced with an acute temporary shortage of foreign exchange to meet their abruptly inflated debt charges and to cover normal import needs, developing debtor countries found themselves suddenly thrown at the mercy of an international financial system, under tight Northern control, that would show no mercy at their plight and would insist on every last pound of flesh.

Working largely through the channels of the Bretton Woods institutions – the IMF and the World Bank – the system was used, with callous determination, to impose a harsh burden on the developing countries affected. Under the guise of debt relief, debt obligations were ruthlessly enforced under conditions leading to widespread impoverishment, hunger and starvation, and in some cases to virtual economic collapse, a situation for which it is difficult to find a parallel even in relations between victor and vanquished after war. They also suffered the humiliation of becoming the virtual wards of the Northern-controlled financial institutions which dictated, and in many cases largely administered, their economic policies. Africa and Latin America and the Caribbean were the regions most acutely affected. Average income levels in some of these countries fell by 15 to 20 per cent in the first few years of the crisis, and given the nature of the case, it was the poorest sectors of the communities that suffered most. Long-term development potential was also permanently damaged because of the induced deterioration of physical and social infrastructure.

It was a traumatic experience that these countries were forced to undergo. And remarkably, after all these years of debt relief and associated policy conditions, and despite all the suffering, the South, instead of seeing the burden of debt lightened, now faces, a decade later, a debt burden more that twice as heavy as when the crisis first broke (see Figure 2).

Thus, by ensuring the continuous build-up of a growing mountain of unserviceable debt, the process of debt relief is itself laying the basis for continued outside control of these countries in the years ahead. These countries are thus caught in what can only be referred to as a debt trap. And in the process, the aims of the new Northern resolve have been attained: the South has been stripped of any will to confront and to challenge, talk about changes to the system has been silenced, and the North-South dialogue, once so prominent on the international agenda, now scarcely deserves mention.

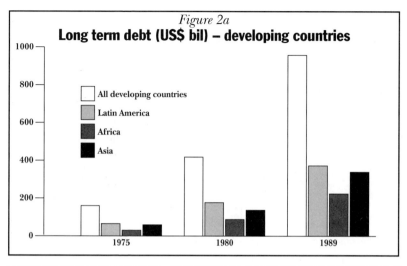

Figure 2a
Long term debt (US$ bil) – developing countries

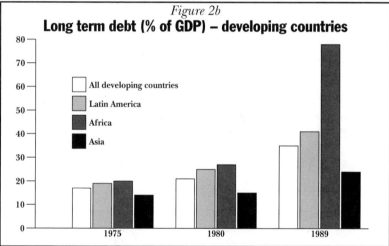

Figure 2b
Long term debt (% of GDP) – developing countries

The income gap: trends and policy implications

In the wake of the debt crisis the economic prospects facing developing countries took a turn for the worse, contributing to the further widening of the income gap. This is well illustrated in Figure 3, which shows a pathetic picture for growth during the 1980s, compared with the two previous decades. The graph makes it is easy to see why for the South the 1980s have been referred to as the 'lost decade'. In fact, for many individual countries the losses suffered in that decade have more than wiped out the

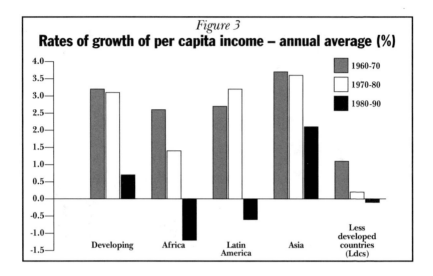

Figure 3

Rates of growth of per capita income – annual average (%)

gains made during the two previous 'Development Decades' when pressures for change to meet the needs of the South were being felt and, however partially and tentatively, being responded to.

For the great majority of developing countries, the single most important issue that presently stands in the way of a more favourable prospect for long-term growth concerns the debt. Unless something is done about it, the future will remain bleak indeed. To continue with what has been passing as debt relief, with the accompanying build-up of debt while economic growth is being stultified, can only perpetuate poverty and dependence. Much better to write off unserviceable debt and allow the debtor countries space to breathe and to develop, than to continue with the pretence that the debt can eventually be paid and in the meantime keep the debtor countries in bondage and poverty.

Commodities

Another issue which remains important concerns commodity prices. While it is true that for the South as a whole dependence on primary commodities has fallen substantially over the past several decades, there is still a large number of developing countries, particularly among the poorest and weakest, who depend heavily on primary commodities for their export earnings, and for whom commodity prices are, often literally, a matter of life and death. Thus more than a half of all African countries depend on primary commodities for over 80 per cent of export earnings, and in many

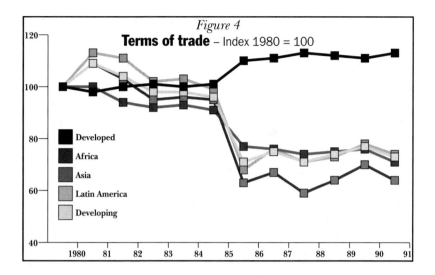

Figure 4
Terms of trade – Index 1980 = 100

Developed
Africa
Asia
Latin America
Developing

cases just two or three commodities dominate the export picture. For the other geographic regions the dependence on primary commodities is not generally as great, but it is still substantial. The downward trend in commodity prices since the beginning of the 1980s is thus a matter of grave concern, especially when seen in the light of the rising prices of manufactured goods imported by developing countries, and the resulting deterioration in their terms of trade (See Figure 4).

The link between the commodities issue and the wider issues of debt and development is brought out by the relevant figures for Africa. In 1980 the total debt for Africa amounted to $87 billion, and by 1986 this debt had grown to $185 billion, but between 1981 and 1986 Africa had 'lost' a cumulative total of $80 billion from the deterioration in its terms of trade, equivalent to the total debt in 1980 and to the bulk of the increase in the debt up to 1986. Since then the commodities picture has not improved much, if any. The issue is therefore one that cannot continue to be ignored.

The policy environment

All this brings us to the paramount question of what future for the developing countries, and for the income gap, given present trends and policies. As to the latter, the significant fact is that the policy framework of the 1980s still dominates, and in place of what used to be a reluctant, tentative but constructive effort by the North to respond to pressures for change to meet the needs of the South, we now inhabit a world where such pressures no longer make themselves felt, and there is therefore no need to respond. Instead, all must now accept the Northern-defined system as packaged and presented, with no questions asked. The question therefore is whether this idealised free-market, free-enterprise, free-competition, non-regulated, TNC-dominated free-trade system which is now taking hold meets the needs of the South and points the way for them to the promised land of economic growth and catching-up.

The experience to date does not lead to much optimism on this score. Undoubtedly there will be individual countries (and perhaps sectors and groups within individual countries) who are uniquely placed and will prosper in the present policy environment. But for the vast majority of developing countries caught in the trap of poverty, debt and underdevelopment, this is not a likely outcome. They face instead a grim prospect, continually buffeted by what passes for others as free competition but which for them is a far from level playing field. For them, a new emphasis on some of the issues highlighted in the North-South dialogue of earlier years, such as resource transfers, low cost financing, debt write-offs and commodity prices will be essential if they are to escape from the trap of perpetual poverty and to begin the process of catching up.

The South still matters

There can be no doubt that the post-1980 world has witnessed a sea change in the attitude of the North towards the South and towards the whole question of international co-operation for development. The North-South dialogue, which played such an important role in the years up to the 1980s, was largely sustained by an implicit understanding that the North had a certain responsibility for the development of the South. That this dialogue got started and remained vibrant for so long is proof enough that both sides were conscious of this understanding. What exactly was to be regarded as the source of this responsibility remained unclear. Some would see it as a kind of compensation for the exploitation of the colonial past. Others would stress the moral aspects, the shared humanity, the principle of solidarity (of being your brothers' keeper), the underlying instability of an increasingly polarised humanity, and the wider benefits of living in a more harmonious world. These arguments are all relevant and remain so. What has changed, however, is the perception in the North that the South no longer matters, that the North no longer needs the South to anywhere near the extent previously thought, and that the development of the South need no longer be a major concern of the North. Hence the collapse of dialogue and the withdrawal from involvement in development.

This is a short-sighted and mistaken view. The world is becoming increasingly inter-linked and interdependent and is shrinking in size in psychological if not in geographic terms, thanks to the phenomenal advances in transportation and communications which is reducing the world to a truly global village. Equally important is the mutual concern about the global environment referred to below (see page 43-44). All this has brought the peoples of the world closer together in terms of common concerns, shared experience, greater awareness about each other and their lifestyles, opportunities for physical contact, etc. With the population dynamics obeying their own laws (see page 45), it is easy to see that the neglect of the development of the South is a recipe for disaster. One form that this will take will be a wave of unwanted migrants as teeming impoverished masses from the South slip through porous (or even heavily fortified) borders to seek a better life in the North. Planners in the North, already aware of this risk, may think that they can guard against the danger, but as the sea of poverty expands and the tide rises, it is unlikely that the largely coercive methods contemplated will suffice. Much better and more efficacious in the long run to accept the broader responsibilities which befall the rich, to embrace the implications of a common humanity, and to accept the need for international action aimed at making economic expansion and progress possible everywhere. This is the way forward, not a niggardly insistence on repayment of unserviceable debt which keeps the debtor countries in bondage and poverty, and which can only plant the seeds of future conflict.

The UN's changing role in the post-1980s

The changes in the pattern of North-South relations which took place in the 1980s had their repercussions on the functioning and roles of the international institutions. The way in which they impacted on the Bretton Woods institutions, greatly increasing their power and influence in the developing world, is evident from the earlier discussion. These changes also had their effects on the workings of the United Nations, and the part of the organisation that was perhaps the first to feel the full impact was UNCTAD.

From its inception UNCTAD had been at the vanguard of the North-South debate and a rallying point for efforts by the South to bring about change in the international system. Thus it was within the UNCTAD framework that the Group of 77, guided and prodded by the UNCTAD secretariat, put forward and fought for the implementation of proposals in such areas as commodities, preferences, compensatory financing, terms and conditions of financing, monetary reform, debt relief, and a code of conduct for transfer of technology, in all of which the North has had to take notice and engage in negotiations, and to a greater or lesser degree, often make concessions. In all this the UNCTAD secretariat had always played a catalytic role, making full use of its capacity to initiate technical studies, to gain political support for important proposals by having them first vetted and endorsed by specially convened meetings of independent experts, and to maintain close liaison with the developing countries in pushing for action in the inter-governmental machinery.

It was not surprising, therefore, that a high priority should attach to bringing UNCTAD to heel. What was more surprising, but quite understandable in view of the debt crisis, was the spectacle of the developing countries sitting increasingly silent, with folded arms, while UNCTAD was tightly reined in and transformed into a pale shadow of its former self. This took place during the 1980s, which saw a process of 'rationalisation' in which the competence of the secretariat to initiate studies and prepare documentation was greatly circumscribed, its capacity to convene meetings of independent experts removed, and the scope and frequency of inter-governmental meetings greatly reduced. Henceforth, UNCTAD would no longer be capable of leading the debate on the North-South front, and would no longer be championing the cause of the South, nor would it be able to make bold proposals in such areas of interest to the South as commodities, compensatory financing, financial flows, monetary reform and debt. Instead, UNCTAD was allowed to find new outlets for its energies in providing technical assistance to developing countries, a safe non-confrontational activity, with emphasis on such issues as the computerisation of customs documentation.

Reducing the UN's own capacities

Paralleling these changes in the work and character of UNCTAD has been a restructuring of the work of the UN in the economic and social fields. This restructuring has been underway since the early 1990s, following the assumption of office of the new Secretary-General. An important purpose of this restructuring has been to de-emphasise the UN's work in the area of economic analysis and policy, including development policy, while putting greater emphasis on operational activities, including technical assistance. One of the earliest and perhaps the most significant step in this restructuring has been the abolition of the post of Director-General for

International Economic Co-operation and Development. The significance of this step lies in the fact that the creation of this post was one of the few concrete outcomes, and certainly the most noteworthy, of the efforts of the developing countries during the NIEO negotiations to secure a stronger UN presence in support of international economic co-operation and development. And while it is true that for various reasons the post had not been effectively used to secure this presence, it still retained the potential. That this post, which was created by the General Assembly with great ado after prolonged consideration and negotiation, could be so summarily abolished by the new Secretary-General spoke volumes for the changed times. Also noteworthy is what has happened to the Centre for Transnational Corporations, a unit established during the 1970s under pressure from the South to help them better deal with the increasingly powerful Northern-dominated TNCs. This unit was effectively disbanded in the restructuring and its staff sent to join the now debilitated UNCTAD.

The other part of the restructuring has taken place outside the United Nations proper, as the Bretton Woods institutions (the IMF and the World Bank) and the GATT (to be succeeded by WTO) have increasingly been encouraged to fill the gap in the fields of economic policy analysis and development strategy now vacated by the UN. In the process, the UN has been losing its role as a forum for discussion of global economic policy issues, including the issues of development strategy and policy. Apart from the new emphasis on technical assistance, peace-keeping is where UN activities are now overwhelmingly focused.

This restructuring is in line with the new dominant thinking in the North. This prefers to see work on international economic policy issues undertaken by institutions under their traditional tight control, which they are confident will reflect their views and portray their thinking. The fact that these institutions (in contrast to the UN) have ready access to funds for carrying out their activities has greatly facilitated their tasks in taking over these functions.

Environment and UNCED – 1992

The impact of these changes in the currents of North-South relations can also be seen in the way in which the North now takes the lead in defining the issues on the UN development agenda, in contrast to the 1960s and 1970s when it was the South which did so. This is well illustrated by the recent UN Conference on Environment and Development (UNCED), held in Rio de Janeiro, Brazil, in 1992, the most important UN conference on development-related issues for over a decade, about which it is useful to say a few words. It was the North that took the initiative in calling for this conference and in setting the conference agenda, driven by the perceived need for international action on issues they considered important.

The background was the growing pressure to stem the damage to the environment resulting from existing patterns of economic growth, coupled with the knowledge that while a good deal of the damage to the local environment could be handled at the national level, there were also important cross-country effects that required action at the international level. These involved issues ranging from pollution of international water-ways, the seas and the atmosphere, to the threat of global warming and of the depletion of the ozone layer endangering life on the planet. But while it was the North that had made the giant strides in economic growth that was largely responsible, on a global scale, for the environmental damage that now threatened the planet, the way in which the agenda for the conference was approached made it seem that responsibility was to be more evenly shared. The prominence given to the new-found concept of 'sustainable development', directed particularly at the developing South, made this seem especially so. The tropical forests issue, which came close to dominating the conference, dramatised the South's concern in this re-gard. Here the South was being asked to preserve their tropical forests for the wider benefit of mankind, at the cost of their own development efforts, even as the North continued with business as usual, not only in pursuing economic growth but also in continuing to monopolise control of the in-ternational economic system.

And while there was much talk in pre-conference circles about massive new aid to the South as *quid pro quo* for their contribution to the global en-vironment effort, in particular in preserving their tropical forests, there was never any serious prospect that such aid would be forthcoming. To add insult to injury, the Global Environment Facility (GEF), the mech-anism for financing environment related activities in the South agreed on at the conference, has been placed in the World Bank, where the Bank can now add environmental conditionalities to those already imposed on developing countries. The recent negotiations on the governance of the GEF, held in Cartagena (Colombia) in December 1993 and in Geneva in March 1994, ended in a compromise agreement which has not changed much, since notwithstanding the well-founded opposition of developing countries, the GEF remains firmly within the ambit of the World Bank. The quest for sustainable development based on just and equitable part-nership between North and South had certainly not been realised.

Coping with the challenges ahead

The fact that the Cold War is now over and the world no longer faces the constant threat of nuclear holocaust gives rise to a great sigh of relief, a major cause of world-wide anxiety and preoccupation over the past decades having been removed from our midst. We can obviously sleep better at nights because of this. But unfortunately the end of the Cold War has not brought a golden age, and there are other issues which, if not as immediately menacing and glaring, nonetheless pose serious threats and are cause for grave concern. These are not necessarily issues which are new, although some of them may well be relatively so (as, for example, the environment issue). Whether new or not, however, they all call for appropriate institutions and policies to achieve acceptable solutions.

One issue which is not new, and which continues to pose both a grave threat and a major challenge, is the growing income gap between rich and poor countries and the spread of poverty and destitution in large parts of the world as others grow in affluence. The nature of the income gap and of its likely future trend, given present policies, has been alluded to in earlier discussion. To obtain a clearer idea of the problem and of the threats to international stability that it poses, however, we must look beyond the income gap and at the underlying population dynamics. Between 1960 and 1990 the world's population doubled, from 2.6 to 5.3 billion, and demographers estimate that in another 35 years it will come close to doubling again, to reach 8.5 billion by 2025. The bulk of this increase is taking place not in the rich countries, but in the poor ones, whose share of the total is increasing rapidly: from 70 per cent to 76 per cent between 1960 and 1990. It is expected that between now and 2025 95 per cent of global population growth will take place in the poor countries. Now if anything is known about population growth, it is that it falls as incomes increase and economic aspirations rise. Hence there is no mystery about the population dynamics. But the longer-term implications are staggering, not the least for the rich countries themselves, who will eventually have to confront the problem of the growing sea of poverty around them.

Current international policies for dealing with this issue, if 'policies' is the correct term, are those largely of neglect, of the pretence of going back to the basics of the free market in which the weak must compete on equal terms with the strong, of continued insistence on repayment of debt which it is clearly beyond the capacity of the poor and bankrupt debtor countries to repay, and of an excessive and unholy reliance on the Northern-controlled financial institutions for the implementation of these policies. These institutions have now accumulated great political power, able to sway policy even in non-economic areas. In the process the role of the UN in areas of international economic policy has been greatly reduced. To cap it all, an elite group of leading industrial countries has now put in place its own private mechanism, outside the UN or other established fora, for assuming the role of an executive directorate overseeing world economic policy. This is the Group of 7, at whose annual heads of government meeting pronouncements are made on world economic policy of far-reaching scope, with implications of vital importance to the South and to their development prospects.

This trend towards elitism, towards concentrating all discussion and policy making in a small group of powerful countries, with little or no scope for feed-back from the less powerful, must be reversed, and a wider and more democratic system of participation introduced. This is especially important now in light of the growing realisation that we live in a highly interdependent world, and that there are important issues of international scope that it will be beyond the capacity of a small group of even the most powerful states, acting alone, to resolve.

One such issue concerns the environment. As already noted, important changes in lifestyles and patterns of economic growth are also needed if environmental catastrophe is to be avoided. But since what each individual person or country does for his or its private benefit contributes to the global impact which could be disastrous for us all, there is a huge chasm between private benefit and the ultimate, wider costs, and this has somehow to be bridged if collapse of the whole system is to be avoided. This presents an international problem of great complexity. It is one, however, that cannot be solved by simplistic rhetoric about leaving everything to the free play of market forces that now seems to dominate policy. It is also one that is unlikely to be solved while a few rich and privileged states monopolise positions of power and exclude others from participating in decisions and influencing policy.

The Rio summit, which broached for the first time the environment issue in its broadest aspects, failed to come forth with any meaningful programme for a solution to the problems identified. This reflects as much the complexity of the issues dealt with as the lurking suspicions and resentments arising from the glaring imbalances in power and privilege among the participants. All this suggests that the direction in which international policy making has been moving in recent years is not one that is conducive to achieving realistic long-term solutions to the important problems that the community of nations now faces.

Another area which is crying out for international action of some kind concerns the role of the increasingly powerful transnational corporations (TNCs). With the diminishing importance of geographic distance as a factor in business organisation and management (due largely to the on-going revolution in information and transport technology) the globalisation of economic activities is now a growing reality. This has been spurred on in no small way by the trend towards the liberalisation of cross-border trade in goods and finance capital. The result has been an enormous increase in the power and influence of the TNCs who have profited from these developments, and many of whom now operate on what can only be described as a global basis, sometimes controlling vast resources that exceed the incomes and budgets of all but the largest and richest states. Increasingly, they control the resources, the technology and the know-how which drives the economy, and they dispose of financial resources in amounts far in excess of the capacity of central banks to cope.

But as their powers and influence grow with globalisation, so their activities tend to escape the control of national governments, not the least because of their importance and the ease with which they can take their favours elsewhere. But there are no international laws or conventions to control or otherwise circumscribe their activities either. There is clearly a gap here that needs to be filled,[9] and given the crucial role of these firms, and the enormous powers they wield for good and for mischief, the question of a multilateral framework of rules to govern their activities is surely one that demands a place on the international agenda. This will of course be resisted by the leading industrial countries whose governments identify, perhaps too closely, with their powerful TNCs. But the efforts of the mightiest of these countries, the United States, to impose its own national laws over the world-wide operations of its TNCs, even in contradiction to the national laws of the countries in which they operate, illustrate the nature of the problem.

It is time to recognise that there has to be a wider and broader-based intellectual input into the definition of the agenda and the discussion of the issues for there to be any real progress towards a solution of the problems faced by the international community. This will require both a rever-

---

9 One can readily think of examples where this gap gives rise to activities disruptive of good order, for example where competition for the favours of TNCs leads to the setting aside of environmental safeguards, or where labour laws are breached for similar reasons, etc. There is also the question of competition policy, highly valued in domestic legislation, but which does not apply to TNCs outside their home base.

sal of the trend towards the increasing concentration of policy analysis and policy making in a few Northern-dominated institutions, and a greater democratisation of these and other international institutions. Otherwise policy will continue (and increasingly so) to reflect the narrow preoccupations, viewpoints and interests of a few economically powerful states that represent an ever shrinking share of mankind, and fail to take account of a broader viewpoint essential for long-term solutions to global problems.

Challenges to change through the UN

In the light of all that has been said above, it is not difficult to indicate the types of institutional changes that are now most needed. Foremost among these is the need to bring the UN back into the picture in the area of economic and social policy making. The UN is the universal organisation endowed with overall authority for dealing with the great issues that face the international community. Such issues include not only those of a purely political nature, but equally those of economic and social character as well, and the United Nations Charter expressly recognises the authority of the UN in all these areas. There is therefore no reason for diffidence in calling for a restoration of the UN's standing in the field of economic policy making, including the strengthening of its oversight role in respect to the financial institutions and the other specialised agencies.

This will require the reconstitution or strengthening of secretariat structures dealing with such policy making (possibly restoring the post of Director-General for this purpose) and a rebuilding of the UN secretariat's professional capacity in this area – if not back to the uniquely high standards that prevailed in the early UN years, then at least so that it can hold its own against the other institutions. To achieve this, more than high salaries and an energetic recruitment drive will be needed. The status of the UN in this area of work will itself need to be raised so that the secretariat's work can have the required impact on international policy and decision making. For this, the methods of work of the GA and the ECOSOC will need to be reexamined.

This line of thought also suggests the need for a fresh look at the question of the recommendatory and decision making powers of the UN. Under present arrangements, only the Security Council has binding decision making powers, and that only on political and security matters. No provision presently exists for such decision making by the UN in respect to economic and social matters. But this may need to change. In the world in which we now live, where the major issues facing the international community include the growing income gap and the spread of mass poverty, the pressures arising from imbalances in population growth, and environmental degradation that could threaten the planet, what might seem purely economic and social issues are clearly latent and potentially explosive security matters, and it would be wrong to maintain that the international community must wait until matters have reached the stage of threatening security before its decision making powers can be invoked. This is especially so in view of the recent trend towards the control of decision making in the Security Council by a conclave of the five permanent members, and sometimes by only a restricted number within this group.

In looking to the future, quite revolutionary ideas may need to be considered. One such could involve the introduction of a system of international taxation to eradicate the worst forms of mass poverty, promote the development of the poor countries, and carry out other tasks of international scope. The tax could be levied directly on individual countries (based on some appropriate formula), on specified international transactions (such as trade in goods, cross-border financial flows and capital movements, international airlines travel, etc), or on other agreed bases. To those who think that this smacks too much of world government and utopia, it is useful to reflect on where the world is now heading, and to bear in mind that in view of the power now concentrated in the Security Council, the Group of 7, and the IMF, we are really not that far from a form of world government anyway.

UN Charter Article 57
1. The various specialised agencies, established by intergovernmental agreement and having wide international responsibilities, as defined in their basic instruments, in economic, social, cultural, educational, health and related fields, shall be brought into relationship with the United Nations in accordance with the provisions of Article 63.

2. Such agencies thus brought into relationship with the United Nations are hereinafter referred to as specialised.

UN Charter Article 59
The Organisation shall, where appropriate, initiate negotiations among the states concerned for the creation of any new specialised agencies required for the accomplishment of the purposes set forth in Article 55.

UN Charter Article 63

1. The Economic and Social Council may enter into agreements with any of the agencies referred to in Article 57, defining the terms on which the agency concerned shall be brought into relationship with the United Nations. Such agreements shall be subject to approval by the General Assembly.

2. It may co-ordinate the activities of the specialised agencies through consultation with and recommendations to such agencies and through recommendations to the General Assembly and to the Members of the United Nations.

2. The IMF and World Bank
Managing the planet's money

AMIR JAMAL

Born of the ravages of the second world war, and named after the place of their conception in New Hampshire, the Bretton Woods institutions comprise the International Monetary Fund (IMF), the International Bank for Reconstruction and Development (commonly known as the World Bank) and the limited scheme for trade liberalisation, the General Agreement on Tariffs and Trade (GATT). This last is due to metamorphose as the World Trade Organisation on 1 January 1995 as the outcome of seven years' multilateral trade negotiations, and is discussed in the following chapter.

The advanced industrialised countries, with their allegiance to the free market, find the Bretton Woods institutions, at least ostensibly, serving their interests well. The less industrialised developing countries have increasingly accepted as inevitable the need to co-exist with the Bretton Woods institutions. However, many in the developing world are restless, being critical of IMF/World Bank policies to promote 'liberalisation' of their economies at great social cost. The remaining poor countries, for the most part, find themselves bending over backwards to comply with a range of conditions imposed on them by structural adjustment policies. And this on top of indebtedness out of all proportion to their wealth and their rate of economic growth.

It is amazing that the IMF and World Bank fail to appreciate the immense and costly social unrest caused by their insistence on what they perceive as sound macro-economic management combined with liberalisation: two prescriptions that add up to the so-called 'structural adjustment'. They are instigating the very reverse of progress just when the most urgent need is to harness the willing cooperation of the majority of the population. They are pre-eminent in determining the destiny of these wretched countries.

Evolution of the IMF and World Bank

Why were these institutions created in the first place? The professed concern of the founding fathers was to build stable trade and economic relations. Empire had provided Britain, France, the Netherlands and Belgium, amongst others, with the opportunity to accumulate capital though privileged access to raw materials and other minerals, as well as preserved markets for their manufactures. Indeed, inexorable expansionism had landed them in bloody and otherwise costly wars. The lessons were well and truly learned. Standard specifications used by all sectors of society within the colonial powers were, *de facto*, being exported to the South via architects, doctors, engineers and other professionals. Indeed, the colonial administrators insisted on this, thereby ensuring that construction and hardware merchants, pharmacists, transport and utility organisations were supplied by the metropolitan country concerned. Why not capitalise on this?

Meanwhile, the United States, with a history of massive immigration from Europe and the slave trade, had escaped destruction on its own soil in the two world wars. This had given it ample time and opportunity to accumulate economic power superior to any other country. It could not afford to remain aloof when the crumbling empires were still able to cash in on their standard specifications and other links forged in the past. While Europeans competed to gain a foothold in one another's preserved through all means, including the beggar-your-neighbour policy of competitive devaluation, they were contributing to making the US dollar the strongest currency.

The two unconscionably costly wars had also resulted in a political backlash in the North. 'No more wars' for the sake of commerce surfaced as the increasingly prevailing sentiment as the second world war was nearing its end. The decision makers in the US were determined to overcome the isolationist reflexes of American society. Already, in order to avoid being drawn physically into the second world war, they saw the importance of providing the military and logistical wherewithal to the British by means of an arrangement that became known as lend-lease. This involved military hardware and software being either lent or leased to the allies on an indefinite basis. Those who were able to repay did so some time after the the end of the war, at the invoiced prices but in greatly devalued currency. No interest was charged.

The US and UK, the two dominant powers in the immediate aftermath of the war, went about conceiving and putting in place institutions that were aimed at reconstructing war devastated market economies of the

North. At the same time they were concerned with the priority need of establishing exchange rates and international trade disciplines based on the principle of Most Favoured Nation.

The spirit of free enterprise giving full play to market forces had to be preserved. The US and UK, the two countries which for a short time filled the North's power vacuum, moved into action. Two individuals close to their respective establishments, social scientists and thinker economists in their own right – Dexter White for the US and John Maynard Keynes representing the UK – were to lead negotiations as discreetly as possible, with the purpose of constructing the post-war edifice to promote common perceived interests. Thus the Bretton Woods institutions were born. It was inevitable that other Western countries would fall in line, as they were beneficiaries of US munificence.

It is worth underlining that the enlightened disciples of the market needed the Bretton Woods system to ensure a dynamic if somewhat unruly organisation based on the gains of centuries past. It is quite clear that the Bretton Woods institutions were never equipped to understand the deep-rooted causes of underdevelopment, let alone to examine them closely enough to realise the Herculean tasks that faced humankind. The assumption that membership of these institutions will make up for lost time can charitably be described as myopic. The equilibrium of asymmetry based on power play is here to stay.

Bretton Woods mandates

The IMF

The mandate of the IMF was to carry out surveillance of the member states, to ensure that they maintained stable exchange rates and to provide a temporary facility that could enable a member state to overcome cyclical balance of payment deficits. Its Board of Executive Directors, headed by its Managing Director, carries the mandate and reflects the economic weight of its members with the US having the dominant voice. This was justified by the fact that it was the US Treasury's undertaking, by means of a simple letter to the Managing Director, to maintain a fixed gold-dollar parity that underpinned the ability of the IMF to enforce stable exchange rates, and which by the same token enabled the IMF to accumulate gold reserves as part of the quotas subscribed to by the member states. Obviously the IMF was in the eminent vantage position of purchasing gold at relatively low prices. In due course this enabled the IMF to develop much greater clout than it actually needed to carry out its mandate. But it never secured the collective political will of the major shareholders to maintain surveillance of their own economic management.

The IMF gold reserve was to play, in the ripeness of time, a decisive role in enticing developing countries to become party to the IMF's amendment of its article, which required it to maintain fixed exchange rates. By 1971/72 this was totally ignored by the US and others because it was no longer convenient to comply with it.

The World Bank

The World Bank, as its full name suggests, was mandated to assist the reconstruction and development of the advanced market-economy countries, by lending real resources to them at manageable rates of interest. Its Board of Executive Directors, chaired by an Executive President, reflects, like the IMF, the relative economic weight of the member states, with the US leading. The recent rise of the German and Japanese economies have given these countries greater weight than was the case in the early days. It does not seem to have made any difference to the Bank's policies, which are now almost exclusively directed at developing countries, and more recently at what are called the 'economies in transition' of the CIS (parts of the former USSR now independent political entities). No country which is not a member of the IMF can become a member of the World Bank. There are over 160 states belonging to the IMF and about the same number are members of the World Bank.

The GATT

The limited third leg of the Bretton Woods institutional set-up, the General Agreement on Tariffs and Trade (GATT), was a quick improvisation when the US refused to ratify the 1948 Charter for an International Trade Organisation (ITO), often referred to as the Havana Charter. The US at that time did not wish to place its agriculture, livestock and horticulture in a multilateral arena. Nor was it willing to take responsibility for ensuring remunerative prices for primary commodities. This was mainly for strategic reasons but also to avoid the potential direct burden on its resources, which would have had to be borne at the expense of domestic farmers and mine-owners. It was able to achieve its aims by way of 'waivers', which it demanded and was given in the provisional GATT agreement.

It is instructive to grasp the meaning of 'provisional' in this context. The GATT is financed by member states who subscribe in direct proportion to their respective shares in international trade. In theory each member state, rich and poor, has an equal voice. In practice the story is rather different:

the Director-General has extensive powers, and it is his sole responsibility to appoint staff officials; the bilateral deals by the major trading partners are effectively rubber-stamped in the GATT Council of Representatives; and powerful member states are able to twist the arms of weaker members by threatening unilateral restrictions under one excuse or another. Needless to say, the Director-General invariably comes from an advanced industrialised country. In 1993 the bid for the post from a developing country's nominee, with all the required experience and credentials, predictably failed because of the contrived disunity of developing member states.

How have the Bretton Wood institutions performed?

Two distinct phases can be identified in the functioning of the Bretton Woods institutions.

The first phase
The first phase related to the pursuit of the founders' goals: namely, the creation of larger trading and investment space by rejuvenating the war-torn market economies, forestalling the rise of fascism and keeping the so-called Iron Curtain at bay.

The IMF and World Bank succeeded in large measure in realising the aims of the founders so far as war-devastated Western Europe was concerned. The economies of Western Europe and Japan registered a prolonged period of sustained growth in the first quarter century after the Bretton Woods institutions were established. In addition, a group of developing countries, particularly in south-east Asia, were able to take advantage of Europe's growth despite the restrictive business practices of the advanced industrialised countries. This was largely due to the developed physical and social infrastructure and significant investment in industry, mining and services left behind by the colonial rulers, albeit for their own largely strategic reasons. On top of this was the culture of hard work and savings of the societies concerned. A further element was the communist incursions into south-east Asia which the North could not ignore, at the height of the Cold War. It called for deployment of resources and training of domestic manpower. The stage was set for those economies to take off.

For a brief springtime the industrialised countries manifested enlightened self-interest and established in 1960 the International Development Association (IDA), an affiliate of the World Bank. This had a mandate to give long term interest-free loans to the poorest developing countries. Another affiliate of the World Bank, the International Finance Corporation (IFC), was expected to stimulate private enterprise by providing partnership equity to domestic entrepreneurs for a temporary period, at the end of which it would sell its shares either to the partner or to another domestic investor ready to hold those shares. It is a moot question as to what role the IFC will play in future now that its more powerful affiliates have thrown their weight behind free enterprise all the way.

In 1965 Part IV was adopted, becoming an integral part of GATT in June 1966. This allowed special and preferential treatment to developing countries in the markets of the industrialised countries. However, those developing countries that were successfully competing in the export of textiles were to be placed in the straitjacket of the Multi Fibre Agreement (MFA), which put a ceiling on what the signatory developing country can sell to its consumers. Because of this restriction, the already competitive developing countries that were exporting textiles were prevented from sustained expansion of their textiles industry. This left the field open to the already industrialising countries to develop technology applicable to the textiles industry, thus providing the industrialising countries with increasing capital surpluses for diversification into linkages. Such scope was throttled for the developing countries concerned.

Also in the early 1960s, with a strong intellectual leadership provided by Raul Prebisch, a group of all developing countries, then including New Zealand, forged sufficient cohesion to achieve a UN General Assembly resolution to set up a permanent UN Conference on Trade and Development (UNCTAD). It held its first meeting in 1964.

Despite all of this, the Bretton Woods institutions remained sacrosanct with mandates whose origins were outside the UN. Their constitutions and policies remained their own exclusive domain.

The second phase

It was the Vietnam war that marked the second phase. The United States financed its increasing involvement by borrowing enormous sums from the Federal Reserve and the banking system. Concurrently the oil prices upsurge meant greater costs throughout the US economy, and payment for the higher-cost oil in still more dollars. As confidence in the value of dollar declined, pressure increased on gold, which was demanded at the official dollar parity rate. The US, followed by other industrialised countries, resorted to exchange rate adjustment, but was no longer able to sustain what by then was an artificial dollar-gold parity. A letter from the US Treasury to the IMF Managing Director withdrew the US underpinning of the parity. The role of the IMF suddenly eroded, because it was no longer able to exercise surveillance over member states' compliance regarding fixed exchange rates.

Strictly speaking, the behaviour of the monetary authorities with 'hard' currencies was illegal in international law, being in breach of a binding international agreement. The industrialised North wanted the fig-leaf of retrospective respectability through a formal amendment of the offending article concerning fixed exchange rates. In negotiations in Kingston, Jamaica, the developing countries as a group commanded a little over 15 per cent of the total IMF quotas and were therefore in a position to exercise a negative veto. They could thus have obtained substantial concessions from the industrialised countries prior to giving their consent. But the developing countries succumbed to the offer of an absurdly paltry Trust Fund, to be financed by means of the sale of a tiny portion of the IMF gold reserve. They failed to take a unified position. The Kingston deal enabled the adoption of the needed amendment to the articles at the 1976 IMF/World Bank joint boards annual meeting in Manila.

The industrialised countries wasted no time in setting up the Interim Committee of 20, dominated by the advanced market economy countries, with a mandate for policy-making on behalf of the IMF. At the same time, as a palliative to developing countries, the Development Committee of the World Bank was established as a talking shop, with no policy-making mandate. (It is worth noting how useful it is to describe most potent international instruments as 'Provisional' or 'Interim', no matter how long they continue to function and deliver the required goods.) All that the developing countries could do was to set up their own Group of 24 (G24) to influence the work of the Interim Committee. G24 membership rotates every four years. It has hardly made any dent on the Interim Committee. Having killed two birds with one stone, distancing UNCTAD more or less finally from the Bretton Woods institutions on the one hand, and on the other softening the mood of developing countries, the stage was set to prevent the developing countries from uniting and using the 'negative veto' in order to demand major concessions from the North.

The IMF's powers of surveillance over the economies of the rich member states had already been diluted by the monetary implications of financing the Vietnam war, as well as by the possession of large amount of dollars by oil rich countries. Private banks were awash with Euro-dollar and Petro-dollar deposits. The IMF, with the resources of its main quota-holders dried up, had no option but to appear to make a virtue of necessity and encouraged indiscriminate lending. Many developing countries that were already indebted found it tempting to borrow almost unconditionally from private banks. That the chickens would come home to roost not a day too soon was the remotest of their preoccupations.

From the Vietnam war on, the global economy had become hostage to private banks and credit institutions to an unprecedented extent. Once exchange rates began to float, the banks found themselves speculating on exchange rates. Money, always believed to be a unit of value and a medium of exchange, had now itself become a tradeable commodity. Unprecedented amounts of capital funds flew in and out, bearing no relation to the needs of balance of payment settlement or genuine productive investment.

Holding the South hostage

A stable monetary and financial system has been totally disrupted. The damage wrought on developing countries, quite apart from landing them in heavy indebtedness, calls for serious objective and scientific research covering the past two decades. Still today the IMF and the World Bank resort to appalling devices in order to keep the poorer and poorest countries on a care and maintenance regime.

It is all very well for the IMF to point out, time and again, that it is not a development institution. The fact of the matter is that, in close collaboration with the World Bank, some 70 countries are its hostages, simply because there is no other planet to which they can migrate.

The structural adjustment programmes presently being pursued in these 70 countries at the behest of the World Bank owe their inspiration to the IMF and its concern for macro-economic management. The IMF could never succeed in compelling the rich countries to practice sound macro-economic management. Indeed, it is the IMF's very default in this area that has brought about the unprecedented turmoil in the global financial and monetary system. By devising programmes for developing countries which allowed private banks to reduce their exposure, and thus their lending, to indebted poor countries, the IMF achieved a reverse flow of funds from the poor to the rich of $130 billion between 1983 and 1992.

The sacred tenet of the IMF is that the efficiency of economic performance is to be judged by the velocity of circulation of money in the economy in question. This is all very well as a yardstick for judging the performance of industrialised countries with all the intra-inter-sectoral linkages in place. The circulation of money, based on the dictates of interest rates, has to be rapid enough. In poor developing countries, however, where so many such linkages are either weak or non-existent, to use velocity of money circulation as a yardstick of efficiency is to polarise most effectively the society subjected to a structural adjustment programme. Obviously money will circulate much faster in urban areas, and the poor financial managers will be hard put to rely on responses from the rural sector that will help to qualify for the certificate of efficiency from the IMF. Not surprisingly, the World Bank's structural adjustment programmes stress macro-economic management, with this essential attribute being part of the deal.

The easiest option for the financial managers of poor developing countries is then to agree severe cuts in budgetary allocations to education and health, vital sectors where there is a high public demand.

The actual purchase of produce can then be safely left to dealers with loans from the commercial banks, with the full burden of high interest rates passed on to the producers. They could not possibly save enough to meet their daily needs, let alone to invest in health-care clinics and even basic primary education. The IMF and World Bank are saying that tomorrow will take care of itself even as tomorrow is being destroyed, with growing numbers of sick and ignorant. Unmanageable political realities are being created which will almost certainly lead to explosions similar to Rwanda's tragedy.

The way forward

The question that hangs on humanity is, how long can this total disparity between the rich and the poor carry on? And tied to this, how long can the Bretton Woods institutions remain footloose, not even answerable to the UN?

The proposals that follow are just some of the basic tasks to be performed by the Bretton Woods institutions and member states under the legal and moral injunctions of the UN. This is not just an ethical imperative. It is truly in the enlightened self-interest of people in the rich, industrialised countries, their children, and their children's children. If no committed endeavour is made now, the UN and Bretton Woods institutions will go their separate ways to become irrelevant to humanity.

For sure, these institutions will not reform themselves in any fundamental respect from within. The UN will have to restructure itself, but it is not clear how much it can do given the reality of today's global power structure. In the final event it boils down to politically enlightened visionary leadership arising in a collegiate spirit to protest. In the meantime, there is more than enough work to be done by concerned groups and individuals all over the planet. They know it. That is promising enough. Just.

Proposals

1. The UN must reform, giving priority to moral concern for the rapid development of the poor so that global convergence takes place before it is too late. The UN must designate the three Bretton Woods institutions as its prime instruments to carry out the mandate though an entrenched article of the Charter. Such an article should be so fixed that it can only be amended through a unanimous vote or after a given period of, say, 30 years.

2. The three Bretton Woods institutions – the IMF, the World Bank and the GATT/World Trade Organisation (WTO) – with a mandatory obligation to place development at the top of their commitments will need to work complementarily in three critically decisive areas:

a. The IMF must be allowed to restore its credibility as a global institution fully accountable to the UN. It should no longer be an accessory to the commercial banks and money markets, whether public or private. It must be enabled to put in place an international unit of reserve that truly reflects global natural resources endowment, stable cost-plus value of commodities and international financial, monetary and technological resources. It must be given the constitutional right to require excess liquidity in the hands of credit institutions at its disposal, according to professionally-backed prudential criteria. A collectively held IMF-managed liquidity could be partially recycled into a long-term and highly concessionary facility at the disposal of fragile and vulnerable developing economies. The interest payment to the concerned commercial institutions should be duly subsidised by the IMF surpluses and a proportion of subscribed quotas. The IMF must make a professional effort to analyse weaknesses in physical and social infrastructures with a view to levelling the velocity of money circulation between town and country.

Furthermore, the IMF must abandon, once and for all, the turning of compensatory financing into debt. By definition, compensation is for a permanent loss of income. The age-long downward curve of terms of trade of commodities is well within the knowledge of the IMF. The permanent 'negative multiplier' effect, each time a permanent loss of surplus value is incurred, has had calamitous consequences for the wretched countries concerned.

The IMF must also take the bull of endemic structurally created indebtedness by the horns, in close collaboration with the World Bank, other international financial institutions, commercial banks and governments. War-devastated Europe's needs were fully realised by those concerned. Today's devastation of economies, forcibly restrained on the sidelines, helpless observers to the South's one-way outward flow of resources and Northern accelerated accumulation technology and capital, deserves nothing less, to put it charitably.

b. The World Bank has no time to lose in bringing about a total reorientation of its policies toward developing countries and societies. The International Development Association (IDA), created with all good intentions to provide long term easy finance, has had a false start in as much as it relied on World Bank staff experienced in the reconstruction of western Europe, with little understanding of the weak infrastructure of many an underdeveloped economy. To graft on to such a body politic advanced technological specifications, to maintain the projects and programmes with commensurate imports, and to assume that commodity production for exports *ipso facto* meant that a base existed for modernising food production, with little regard for climatic and soil conditions, for health or energy, or for vocational skills training. All this was a clear invitation to frustration and despair.

A new fresh start is needed, employing a small band of extension-service oriented professional staff, with a commitment to enabling people in both urban and rural settings to do things for themselves. The programmes must be securely devised to maximise human potential, creating small entrepreneurs serviced appropriately by credit institutions. There should be no obsession with linkages with sophisticated external money markets; instead, the emphasis should be on the belief in the potential of a firmly based domestic and regional network.

c. The GATT/World Trade Organisation (WTO) should stop patting itself on the back for having 'trained' sophisticated developing countries in the art, law and science of external trade. In a developing country context the GATT/WTO's first priority is to cooperate with others, both agencies and individuals, in mutually reinforcing internal marketing networks and assisting in the siting and planning of urban and rural market places. This would encourage a broader range of improved quality goods through production and marketing competitiveness. The GATT/WTO has an obligation to accept a pattern of tariff protection to suit individual needs, whereby it could move in the direction of phased lowering of tariffs in the interest of competitive external marketing as the opportunity arises. It also has an obligation to respect concern for a secure revenue base, remembering that the Southern options are few. It must help developing countries to be vigilant concerning restrictive business practices against added value production. The GATT/WTO should also, in cooperation with the UN's World Intellectual Property Organisation (WIPO), develop on-going access to technology whose patent protection may have recently expired but which seems relevant, in a given context, to a number of developing countries.

Finally, the GATT/WTO, instead of remaining an amused onlooker, should become a positive and progressive contributor to the General Scheme of Trade Preferences (GSTP). This scheme was first placed on the table at a pre-UNCTAD meeting in Arusha in 1979 and agreed in Belgrade in 1989, when 48 countries signed. A number of those who did not sign, such as Colombia and Morocco, are new seeking accession. Under the scheme, the industrialised countries agreed to give according to the specific preferences of particular developing countries. The scheme thus promoted regional, inter-regional and inter-developing countries' trade and exchange. It should be actively supported by the IMF in helping finance the GSTP trade and exchange, without fear of being held back by short-sighted advanced industrialised countries eager to maintain their head-long lead over their new competitors-to-be. Indeed, the GATT/WTO should seek a positive contribution from the IMF in the financing of the GSTP operations. If the IMF is genuinely interested in the steady, environmently-friendly international division of labour, the long-term interests of the progeny of the advanced countries, just as much as those of the developing countries, demand this overdue contribution.

3. The UN and the Bretton Woods institutions – early comers on the world's technological stage – must manifest in their policies and programmes ecological and environmental balance, for sustainable and equitable development and for improved quality of life in material and moral content. If resolute leadership is not enacted, the much less fortunately en-

dowed latecomers on the scene should not be penalised for falling into the trap made by the North.

4. Even the most underprivileged country has an overriding responsibility to ensure that human rights are an integral part of its cultural, religious, social and economic concerns, and that its highest tribunal is constitutionally endowed with responsibility to mete out reward and punishment. Furthermore, building up a capacity for fiscal rectitude, for human resource development and for health care must be at the core of its own social and economic development policy.

5. Global democracy is unattainable without adequate equitable international taxation.

3. World trade
Free for whom, fair for whom?

MYRIAM VANDER STICHELE

On 15 April 1994, new agreements on international trade among 111 countries were signed in Marrakesh (Morocco). They were the result of seven years of negotiations called the 'Uruguay Round' under the General Agreements on Tariffs and Trade (GATT). The final agreements included the decision to replace the GATT by a new multilateral body, the 'World Trade Organisation' (WTO).

International trade and competition have always played an important role in international politics. Now, economic rivalry has replaced the ideological East-West rivalry. It is the very time when a new world trade organisation should become part of the UN System. Since the WTO is not, it is a further stage in a long process in which, contrary to the original design of the UN, decisions and rules on international trade, and the international economy in general, have been kept away from the world organisation.

International trade management in the post-world war peace

In the 1940s, the founders of the UN wanted to manage international trade as an important element in international politics to avoid another world war. In their view, the second world war had been caused in the 1930s by countries in economic depression that transferred their economic problems to other countries. They had tried to solve their employment and balance of payment problems through successive devaluations which enabled them to export their goods more cheaply. At the same time they increased protectionism against (cheaper) imports. Another cause of the depression had been the collapse of primary commodity prices. No international authority had been able to monitor these trade movements, let alone coordinate and intervene in trade policies.

After the war the International Monetary Fund and the World Bank were created to deal with international macro-economic coordination. But they were designed to be complemented by an International Trade Organisation (ITO), because it was understood that balance of payment problems, exchange rate stability, monetary policies, finance, employment, development policies and trade policies are all related.

The new UN Economic and Social Council (ECOSOC) was to coordinate the work of the IMF, the ITO and World Bank in the UN system, with the other UN specialised agencies and with member-governments. For reasons explained elsewhere in this book ECOSOC did and does not fulfil its functions. Financial problems affecting the expansion of trade – short-term shortage of foreign exchange reserves due to balance of payments problems, and exchange rate instability, which can lead to devaluations – were assigned to the International Monetary Fund. But after the dollar was de-linked from the gold standard in 1971, little became of the IMF's function of stabilising exchange rates. The IMF and World Bank have achieved little in international economic coordination.

The creation of GATT instead of the ITO

The intended UN system of international macro-economic coordination was, however, rendered incomplete from the beginning in the area of trade. The International Trade Organisation (ITO) was supposed to be the 'third pillar' of the system to eliminate trade barriers and protectionism. In 1948 the 'Havana Charter' for the ITO was adopted at Havana. It embodied the recognition that trade and balance of payments were playing an important part in many countries' national economies. Drawing on pre-war experiences, the ITO would have taken an integrated approach to international trade, incorporating broad-ranging aspects related to commercial policy such as national employment, development, commodities (price stabilisation), business practices which restrict free trade (RBPs), and even the flow of productive capital and transfer of know-how on equitable terms.

In 1950, however, the US Congress, and consequently other countries, failed to ratify the ITO, and it was never created. The main reason was its very comprehensiveness, in the factors it was designed to regulate and its authority to supervise and enforce the application of its international rules. This would have limited autonomous national commercial policies and the economic domination of the industrialised countries, too much for the politicians and business of the North to endorse.

As the ITO could not be set up, only one part of it was created in 1948: the General Agreement on Tariffs and Trade (GATT), to deal with commercial policy, the reduction of tariffs and trade barriers, and the abolition of trade preferences among a limited number of countries. The GATT was only supposed to be applied on a provisional basis, as a contract with legal rights and obligations between its signatory governments.

The GATT and Northern interests

The GATT was created in a world where trade was dominated by the colonising industrialised countries. Therefore, the GATT was mainly a 'rich man's club', and remained so. The industrialised countries were able to use GATT to advance their interests through liberalising trade in goods of interest to them. They especially saw advantages in its contractual basis and in the possibility to impose sanctions on countries that did not abide by the GATT rules. This differed from UN declarations and conventions which were voted through by a majority (by the 1960s the majority being that of developing countries), and which could not be enforced through sanctions. In GATT, until the 1980s, the decision-making practices allowed the industrialised countries to negotiate mainly among themselves, with little regard for developing countries and long-term global economic coherence.

It is not surprising, therefore, that different efforts and proposals in the decades following the creation of GATT did not succeed in setting up the ITO or another comprehensive trade body, or in converting GATT or changing its provisional status. Moreover, the link between GATT and the UN became almost non-existent in practice.

GATT 'Rounds'

The tariff reduction agreement that was made at the start of the GATT was periodically reviewed in what were called 'Rounds'. During these negotiations, which lasted for several years, the GATT countries bargained among each other, country per country and product per product, to further reduce tariffs. Tariff reductions that were agreed between two of them were automatically extended to the other GATT members on the 'most favoured nation' principle.

Until the eighth round started in 1986, textiles, agriculture and some other non-industrial sectors were not covered by the GATT agreements. On the one hand this allowed the North to protect its own agriculture with subsidies, to the detriment of exporting developing countries. On the other it enabled the North to export its agricultural overproduction with subsidies at depressed prices. Many local producers in developing countries could not sell their agricultural products any more, in turn making those countries dependent on Northern food imports.

In the same pattern, since 1974 the textile industry of the North was protected against cheap imports from the South by the Multi-Fibres Agreement (MFA). Through this import quota system, a developing country could only export the amount of textiles which it was allocated by the industrialised countries.

Given the nature and complexity of trade, the GATT also gradually covered more trade 'rules', such as on dumping (exporting products at less than production cost), legitimate use of subsidies (to avoid unfair competition), or 'technical' barriers to trade (such as exaggerated health norms). All members had to abide by these rules but they remained quite vague, their implementation left very open to national interpretation.

The prevailing view in industrialised countries is that the GATT largely contributed to their post-war wealth, and that trade liberalisation, through GATT rounds amongst others, has been a key instrument of economic growth.

Over the years, more developing countries also became members of the GATT. However, during the rounds of negotiations they basically had to wait on the sidelines for the major trading powers to agree on concessions, which then became binding on them as well. Moreover, many products of importance to developing countries were not covered by GATT. For instance, coffee and oil are the most traded products but they are covered by mechanisms outside the GATT.

UNCTAD's limited role in international trade

Some aspects which were supposed to be part of the ITO and which were not taken up by the limited functions of GATT were dealt with by different UN specialised agencies. An example is the International Labour Organisation (ILO) which deals with improving workers' conditions. But the most prominent UN agency on trade has been the UN Conference on Trade and Development (UNCTAD).

The first conference (UNCTAD I) took place in 1964 after strong pressure from the increasing number of developing countries in the UN. UNCTAD's aim was to promote international trade and development, especially between countries at different stages of development. An UNCTAD secretariat was created to promote its functions between the periodic conferences.

Trade disadvantages for the South

The developing countries wanted UNCTAD to help resolve the many problems they encountered in expanding their trade and trade revenues in an international system that was operated and dominated by the interests of the industrialised countries and supported by GATT. Key impediments were:

- Developing countries did not receive remunerative prices for their commodities, like coffee, tea, bananas, and cacao. They had not been allowed to industrialise during the colonial era, so commodities were their main export products.
- When they tried to improve their earnings by first processing their commodities, these exports came up against Northern 'tariff escalation': the more their commodities were processed the higher the tariff imposed on them by Northern countries.
- At the same time developing countries experienced the vicious circle of constantly deteriorating terms of trade. The prices of industrialised countries' products rose; they had to export more and more commodities to earn the same amount of foreign exchange to pay for and import the technology they needed to develop their economies – and in turn their export capacity.

'Trade not aid'

UNCTAD thus became a crucial forum for the South, where developing countries tried to argue for 'trade not aid' and to establish a New International Economic Order (NIEO, discussed elsewhere in this book).

UNCTAD was able to achieve a few results in the first period of its existence. It initiated International Commodity Agreements to try to stabilise prices of coffee, tin, cacao, and other products, some of which became independently functioning agreements (such as the London-based International Coffee Agreement started in 1962). An effort to create a 'Common Fund', which aimed to assist commodity exporting countries and their attempts to diversify their export products, largely failed because of unwillingness by the industrialised countries to provide the money. In the 1980s the prices paid for these commodities in the North declined yet again with disastrous effects, especially on African economies.

Other issues and sectors that UNCTAD dealt with were the transfer of technology, finance and technology, restrictive business practices (RBPs), trying to advance the creation of the ITO, providing technical assistance to expand trade, and overviewing the world trade system.

The industrialised countries, however, had secured that UNCTAD would not touch on the autonomy and the functions of GATT and the IMF and World Bank. One of the few areas where UNCTAD negotiations led to changes in the GATT system was a new GATT chapter on trade and development in 1965, and the agreement on a General System of Preferences (GSP) in 1970. The GSP would allow industrialised countries to reduce duties on certain imports from developing countries without having to give the same market openings to the industrialised nations. This was an exception to a basic GATT principle whereby a member-country has to give the same trade access to all GATT members. The GSP, however, covered mainly industrialised products which were only of interest to a limited number of developing countries.

The pressure that developing countries exercised also resulted in GATT incorporating the principle of some special and differential treatment for them. In practice this meant that developing countries would not have to implement all the agreed GATT rules and tariff reductions, or would receive a longer transition period before implementing them.

But UNCTAD was not able to tackle the structures of the world trade and the world economy. Its functioning was blocked by continuous efforts by the North to deny it any negotiating or binding authority, while the South tried to use its voting majority to persuade the North to change the international economic system and its adverse terms of trade, and to give more aid.

Cartagena, 1992

The North won. At UNCTAD VIII in Cartagena in 1992, all negotiation functions of UNCTAD were eroded; its existence was once again placed in question; and all links with GATT in the Uruguay Round negotiations were avoided.

The outcome of UNCTAD VIII was as the industrialised countries wanted, and a reflection both of trade discussions in other North-dominated international fora and of the further weakening of development policies. As a result, the South consented with the North, instead of the usual North-South debates. The dominant emphasis was now on the national policies of *developing* countries instead of the impact of industrialised countries' policies upon them. And the South was compelled to accept the thesis of solving economic and trade problems through the 'free market system' instead of regulation. UNCTAD's main function would henceforth be analysis, consensus-building on some trade related issues, and technical assistance. No commitments were made at Cartagena by the North, only vague declarations.

In these ways it was possible for the North to keep crucial decisions on trade in institutions *of* the North. These are, essentially: the Group of Seven (G-7) richest countries who meet once every year at heads of state level; the Organisation of Economic Cooperation and Development (OECD), where discussions influence the promotion and coordination of economic issues of interest to the industrialised countries (for instance in the Uruguay Round negotiation); and, most important of all, in GATT.

GATT and world trade

The eighth Round of GATT negotiation started in September 1986 at Punta del Este, and thus became known as 'the Uruguay Round'. It drastically changed international trade regulation. New sectors were introduced and membership was considerably increased, which did allow developing countries to have a little say in the negotiations.

By the beginning of the 1980s, the industrialised countries realised that several sectors had become much more important in their economies, and increasingly for their trade. The services sector (transport, communication, banking, tourism, etc), intellectual property right protection (copyrights, patents, etc), and foreign investment were now important parts of their economies (60 per cent for services) and increasingly their trade.

In order to facilitate market access for services, and protection for intellectual property rights, industrialised countries wanted to regulate these 'trade-related' sectors multilaterally within the GATT. Developing countries first fiercely opposed this move. They would be required to give concessions in sectors which they had not yet developed; they needed protection to develop them and to implement their development policies. The industrialised countries then brought agriculture on to the negotiating table, because their agricultural subsidy system had become too costly. They also conceded to eliminate the MFA's textile import quota system. The Uruguay Round negotiations then got off to a slow start.

It took seven years, three years more than foreseen, to finalise these negotiations, during which many countries participated for the first time. When the Uruguay Round was signed on 15 April 1994, 111 countries were members of GATT. Developing countries had realised that they had to participate in GATT because it was the only international trade forum in which the North was willing to operate and to negotiate concessions based on reciprocity. Badly in need of export markets, they had to try to break through the protectionism of the North in order to pay off their debts, as well as to succeed in their structural adjustment programmes, which the IMF insisted be based on the 'free market' and exports.

The developing countries did not negotiate collectively as in UN fora; indeed they now had increasingly diversified interests to defend. They were able to avoid some of the worst possible outcomes, especially the countries with large markets, such as Brazil and India. But they conceded more than they received in return, because they were still not involved as equal partners in the real decision-making. The worst case was the agricultural deal between the United States and the European Union, which had blocked the negotiations all along and then had to be accepted by the other negotiating countries within one week of the final deadline. This US-European agreement clearly did not have in mind either food security or the majority of the population dependent on agriculture in developing countries.

The industrialised countries were able to achieve a lot of concessions in the sectors of interest to them: a liberalisation framework in services; internationally enforceable 'trade-related' intellectual property rights; and rules and tariff reductions in industrialised goods which were especially of interest to them. In sectors in which the North can hardly compete with developing countries – agriculture and textiles – it managed to a large extent still to protect its interests, for example in the long time-frame provided for dismantling the MFA's quota restrictions on Southern textile exports to the North.

The Uruguay Round fulfilled the desire of the industrialised countries to suck more and more 'trade-related' sectors into the GATT which they control, and to enforce the new regulations through trade sanctions, without a link with the UN. For instance, the UN World Intellectual Property Organisation (WIPO) had been discussing intellectual property rights regulations which would also take development aspects into account. Since its proposals in the 1970s and 1980s would not always benefit the industrialised countries, all discussions in WIPO were blocked, and then undermined by the binding new Uruguay Round rules.

Another trend that appeared clearly during the Uruguay Round negotiations was the great influence that big corporations had in the negotiation positions of the industrialised countries, and in the final result of the Round.

Current situation of world trade

The fundamental condition of world trade at the time of the Uruguay Round, and the domination of the industrialised countries at the end of the long provisional system of the GATT, can be seen in the figures below for shares in world trade.

The developed market economies provide now almost three quarters of world trade, and have increased their share in value terms over the decades, at the expense of most of the developing countries.

Nevertheless, in 1993 34 per cent of trade among GATT members was constituted by developing countries. In 1992, 45 per cent of the exports of the European Community went to developing countries, much more than to North America and Japan together.[1] In the early 1990s, trade among developing countries, especially in east and south-east Asia, has been one of the most dynamic components of world trade, while the economies of the industrialised countries stagnated.

The new world trade picture for developing countries

The picture for the South in world trade today is one of greater diversification of circumstances, showing some gains for some groups of countries amid continued severe disadvantages.

The newly industrialised countries (NICs) in south east Asia have been able to take an increasing part in world trade mainly by upgrading their exports in a long-term strategy of diversification and greater input of complex technology. In severe contrast, African and other least developed countries continued to be marginalised because of their high dependence on commodity exports.

Prices for commodities have continued to fall and are at a record low. After the commodity agreements broke down because of unpayable intervention mechanisms, the industrialised countries only wanted to tackle the commodity problem with 'market solutions'. But the tariff escalation for processed commodities noted earlier remained after the Uruguay Round negotiations. The very low prices have affected quality and supply and recently led to some new attempts at intervention schemes by the producer countries for commodities such as coffee and cacao.

The unit values of manufactures exported by developing countries as a whole have equally continued to decline relative to those of manufactures exported by developed countries. Only by increasing their export volumes were developing countries able to register improvements in their income terms of trade. In the given context of depressed industrial economies, such increases tend only to depress prices further.[2]

---

1 P. Sutherland at Forum de l'expansion in Paris on 19 Oct. 1993.
2 UNCTAD, *Trade and Development Report 1993. Overview.* UN, New York , 1993, p. 20.

Percentage share of world exports and imports[1]

	1950	1970	1991
Exports			
World	100	100	100[4]
Developed market economy countries of which	60.8	70.9	72.4
EC[2]	33.1	43.2	45.6
N. America	21.7	18.9	15.4
Japan	1.4	6.1	9.2
Developing countries and territories of which	31.1	18.4	22.8
Lat. America	12.4	5.5	3.9
Asia	13.1	8.1	16.5
Africa	5.2	4.1	2.0
LLDCs[3]	2.8	1.6	0.4
heavily indebted countries	10.9	5.8	4.5
Former socialist countries	8.1	10.7	4.8
Imports			
World	100	100	100[5]
Developed market economy countries of which	64.9	71.6	72.9
EC[2]	32.3	37.8	40.6
N. America	19.9	17.3	17.3
Japan	1.5	5.8	6.7
Developing countries and territories of which	27.2	17.9	22.6
Lat. America	10.1	5.5	3.7
Asia	11.1	7.8	16.3
Africa	5.4	3.4	2.0
LLDCs[3]	2.4	1.6	0.7
heavily indebted countries	9.2	5.7	3.9

1 Source : UNCTAD, *Handbook of International Trade and Development Statistics 1992*, New York 1993, p. 28-29.
2 EC : figures used for 1950, 1970 and 1991 refer to same 12 countries, ie Belgium, Denmark, France, Germany, Greece, Ireland, Italy, Luxembourg, Netherlands, Portugal, Spain, UK.
3 LLDCs = economically least developed countries
4 *Ibidem*, p. 2 : value of world exports in million $: 3 424 700
5 *Ibidem*, p. 3 : value of world imports in million $: 3 542 800

Since the 1980s, trade has taken an increasingly important place in most developing countries' economies. In order to repay their debt, many developing countries have undertaken structural adjustment programmes (SAPs) towards export-led growth economies. Central in these SAPs have been reforms towards a market economy, and trade liberalisation to improve economic performance through competition with the 'world market' and integration with it. In the 1990s, the former Soviet-bloc countries have joined these economic reforms.

This has increased the dependence of the reforming countries on growth and openness in the economies of the industrialised countries. The latter's trade liberalisation, meanwhile, has been modest, or has been compensated for by many more openings created for them in new sectors by developing countries during the Uruguay Round. Industrialised countries have been using indirect forms of protectionism which the GATT could hardly tackle.

Increasingly, developing countries are treated on what Northern authorities call the 'same level playing field', ie they have to compete on almost equal terms with the industrialised economies. In this world of 'efficient allocation of resources', developing countries with other economic developments or difficult geographical circumstances might be easily marginalised or become totally dependent on aid. Or, as Ambassador Barnett of Jamaica put it at UNCTAD VIII, 'Everybody speaks about expansion of markets, but what do you do if you are on a small island?'

Increasing complexity of trade

Together with enormous advances in technology and communication, trade has resulted in increasing globalisation of the world economy and integration by more and more countries. As capital has been allowed to flow freely, firms are setting up production units abroad instead of exporting to those countries. Trade and foreign development investment (FDI) are, in important part, in the hands of multinational firms. For instance, trade between units of multinationals constitute one third of world trade. The concentration of corporate power is also due to the fact that more complex and expensive technology and communication systems now contribute significantly to competitiveness, making it more difficult for small enterprises, or economies, to play a role. Intellectual property rights secured by one company on products and technology are increasingly the most important trade competition asset for the industrialised economies, and especially the United States.

Regional trade blocs

Free trade is not only negotiated on a multilateral or bilateral basis. Countries within different regions in the world have liberalised among themselves, at a quicker pace than at the multilateral level. The world therefore seems increasingly divided into three blocs:

1. the US, Canada and Mexico (North American Free Trade Agreement - NAFTA), ultimately aiming at a free trade area in the whole of America ('Initiative of the Americas');
2. the European Union, with free trade agreements with the European Free Trade Association (European Economic Area - EEA) and Eastern and Central European countries, ultimately aiming at a European free trade zone; and
3. Japan with its strong economic links in Asia.

These regional trade blocs have allowed the industrialised countries to strengthen their dominant power and to be more competitive vis-à-vis the other regions. However, such blocs have also led to increasing concentration of firms and have not (yet) led, in the case of the European Single Market, to the proclaimed increase in jobs.

In Latin America (through, for example, Mercosur - the Common Market of the South), the Caribbean, Asia and Africa, regional economic groupings have also accelerated, but the benefits of regional blocs for developing countries are mixed. Results have been disappointing where there has only been trade liberalisation and no economic policy cooperation, where the countries basically export the same products onto the world market, or where the region has been dominated by one big economically powerful country.

A regionalisation of economies can be more sensitive to ecological, cultural and democratic demands. But without multilateral rules, each bloc could develop its own means to hamper the development of other regions.

Towards trade wars?

Regional trade blocs have also sharpened trade conflicts in the context of the dominating new ideology of free trade and competition. Since the end of the Cold War, international competitiveness and expanding trade have topped the national economic and foreign policy agenda of many countries, and are even considered as 'national economic security' matters. Alongside this, 'managed trade' has been practised, especially by the US. This means that the government intervenes to ensure that products can be exported to a given country, sometimes under threats of trade sanctions or other measures unilaterally decided by that intervening government. In this way countries in the South were forced to open their markets or to introduce legislation on intellectual property rights. All this has already led to many disputes about unfair trade practices or state intervention. Some of these 'trade wars' are being waged among the major trading powers in the North – the US, EU and Japan – because their export strategies to get out of their recession and their unemployment problems increasingly compete.

The multilateral trade dispute settlement mechanisms under GATT have so far proven inadequate to deal with these conflicts. It is not certain that the new World Trade Organisation will be able to deal better with unilateral trade measures which are incompatible with its rules. The United States, for instance, is determined also to use bilateral and regional policies alongside the multilateral rules to further its trade interests.

Towards the future

Today, international trade and competition seems to have become an aim in itself, with few corrective mechanisms to distribute the benefits of trade and achieve higher employment, better standards of living and environmentally sound development. Competition in the form that it is currently applied does not only lead to 'more efficient' economies, but also to conflicts, marginalisation of 'uncompetitive' countries and population groups, and a concentration of economic power in the hands of multinationals (the yearly turnover of some transnational corporations is higher than the Gross Domestic Product of some national states) – which could result in less efficiency.

There is a lack of global tools to deal with these problems. But globalisation and trade liberalisation have increased awareness of how trade is touching on all the related areas, as was foreseen by the founding fathers of the UN in the intended system with the IMF, World Bank, and the ITO. For instance, trade unions in the North now argue that many of their workers' jobs are being lost because the lowering of tariffs allows imports of goods produced at very low wages or under unacceptable working conditions. Clauses on workers' rights linked to trade are pushed on the international agenda, but this is a sensitive and complex issue.

Politicians in North and South have declared that they will place multilateral rules on competition on the future trade negotiation agenda of the WTO. This would inhibit world-wide corporate monopolies, cartels, mergers, state subsidies and public monopolies as well as trade restrictive practices (such as setting prices or agreements to divide markets among companies).

What has already been officially discussed is the interrelationship between international trade and the environment. The problem here is that developing countries fear that higher environmental standard norms will undermine their export capacity and become a hidden form of protectionism by the North.

All these new trade-related issues are being pushed on to the new agenda of the new WTO. The challenge will be whether and how these matters will be dealt with in the United Nations, where they originally belonged: will the trade aspect prevail or will the issues be dealt with from different angles in a coordinated way.

Acknowledging WTO/ITO differences

To understand the importance of the UN in future trade matters the nature of the new 'World Trade Organisation' (WTO) needs to be clarified. The Uruguay Round has created the WTO following a proposal of the European Union and some other countries, but with hardly any official negotiations and debate. The purpose was to give the GATT a permanent structure that would include the new sectors in the Uruguay Round agreements (agriculture, services, intellectual property rights and investment).

The WTO will not only be an executive 'umbrella organisation', as EU officials presented it. It will also provide 'the forum for negotiations among its members concerning their multilateral trade relations in matters dealt with under the WTO agreements'[3] and administer the dispute settlement mechanism. In other words, as the North wishes, the WTO could become the only forum for future negotiations and agreements on more and more trade-related issues, instead of the United Nations.

Some pretend that the WTO is the new ITO, but there are substantial differences in scope, principles, functions and methods of work as well as relations with other international organisations:

• The organic link with the UN and especially ECOSOC – and therefore the link between world peace and its socio-economic basis – is omitted.
• There are no instruments to incorporate trade-related areas which the ITO was supposed to deal with. The WTO will continue the GATT

---

3 Art.III of the Agreement establishing the World Trade Organisation.

and Uruguay Round practices and agreements, ie with a strong bias towards free trade, and based on economic bargaining power by which the country offering most market opportunities can bargain most benefits.
• Its decision-making and implementation procedures lack the necessary checks and balances, and democratic principles of accountability and equity.
• While trade is operated by companies the settlement of international trade disputes can only be done through governments.

The aim of creating the WTO was to give trade a higher status in international economic policy by putting it at the same level as the IMF and the World Bank, and to strengthen multilateral rules against unilateral trade actions. One of the few functions that the WTO is assuming from the originally planned mandates for the ITO is cooperation with the World Bank and the IMF in order to achieve greater global policy coherence. However, the structure and function of the WTO will not enable it to deal with the challenges of a globalised and integrated world economy where international trade policy is increasingly linked with investment, technology, debt, money and finance as well as social, environmental, political and cultural aspects that are situated outside traditional trade problems. Neither will the coordination with the IMF and World Bank be able to provide enough analysis, synthesis, and consensus to deal with these complex matters in an integrated way so that all countries and groups of society can benefit.

Trade and related issues: what the UN should do

The WTO provides for 'appropriate arrangements for effective cooperation with other intergovernmental organisations that have responsibilities related to those of the WTO'. No more details are given. UN agencies performing different functions on trade-related matters should use this Article[4] to establish an active relationship with the WTO. UN agencies still have a role in the trade sectors that are not covered by the WTO, such as regulation of trade in arms and toxic waste, agreements to deal with problems in commodity markets and prices, and the erosion of cultural diversity through trade liberalisation. (The erosion of cultural diversity is an alarming but unexplored area for UNESCO as, even in economic terms, it might undermine the long-term potential for economic creativity and

---

4 Article V of the Agreement establishing the World Trade Organisation.

diversification.) All UN agencies should increase their capacity to analyse the trade-related aspects of their sector and bring their analysis into the WTO. This would enable checks and balances on a strong and trade-biased WTO where the aim of social, economic, environmental and cultural well-being is insufficiently incorporated.

The importance of the UN and its agencies lies also in its secretariats. These can issue independent studies to give guidance on effective global trade, and encourage equitable rules. Trade negotiations under GATT/WTO are too dominated by national and corporate interests. In a complex trade world, such negotiations result in short term and fragmented policies, trade conflicts and economic power-games, domination by interest groups which have little concern about the effects on others, and actual trade by TNCs on which governments and people have no control. The UN should be providing a global and long-term policy perspective against the national and corporate interests which governments defend in the GATT/WTO.

Adjusting to globalisation will be painful in North and in South. Cooperation, as promoted in the UN Charter, might well be better than competition to ease pains. The UN is well-placed to look at long term solutions and to question how current international trade is contributing to human wellbeing. The UN might well find quite different solutions to the current form of free trade and competition (such as more selective intervention and differentiation in rules). UNCTAD should therefore implement its original mandate of assessing the functioning of the global trading system. It should evaluate the Uruguay Round agreements and the WTO system, its impact on the world trade system, on the global economic, social and environmental system, and on national economies and development. Proposals for corrections of the WTO system could be discussed in UNCTAD and negotiated in the WTO.

The UN has provided a more adequate voice to concerns from developing countries and is a better forum for achieving real consensus. The decision-making power structures of the GATT and the Bretton Woods institutions have so far failed to sufficiently discipline Northern governments towards truly global policy coherence. By not taking all legitimate countries' interests into account, the marginalisation of many developing countries and especially their populations from the mainstream world economy might in the future be a cause of huge conflict.

The United Nations should promote the original integrated approach of the ITO, and decide on ways to do so within the UN System itself. The UN should dare to link issues which have been kept in their separate compartments, such as trade and debt, or trade and culture, on discussion and ne-gotiating agendas to obtain comprehensive issue packages. In this respect, there is no need to construct new super organisations since the UN system already constitutes a true world forum. But the UN needs to adapt to new realities of economic activity and to the challenges of the future. It needs to bring the IMF, the World Bank, and a trade organisation also constitut-ed as a UN specialised agency into an appropriate high-level forum where all macro-economic world problems are considered and tackled in their real interrelationships. Ideally, the UN should negotiate the issues compre-hensively and integrate the trade-related results in the WTO.

Need for a bottom-up approach in the UN

One reason that the UN has failed to play a role in international trade pol-icy development is its top-down approach, whereby the international UN secretariats play an important role, and decisions are then taken by gov-ernments. The population – 'We, the peoples' – are little informed and in-terested because neither they nor their parliamentarians are involved in the decision-making. Only a very few interest groups, business firms, and NGOs at present see the usefulness of dealing with UN decisions in trade.

The result of the current globalised economy is that decisions on trade-related areas in one place (or corporation) of the world will increasingly have positive or negative effects elsewhere. International decision-making on trade is a key instrument to ensure that legitimate and diversified inter-ests of all countries and their different groups of population are taken into account. But it will have to be based on democracy, good governance and long-term self interest.

There is a real danger of a world in which there would be two kinds of economies, one being the globalised export- and consumption-oriented economy which is driven by competition and reaps all the economic bene-fits, the other being the marginalised economies of poor countries and populations which cannot compete in the world and have to struggle to meet their needs. If this transpires it will have all kinds of negative conse-quences on individuals and societies, with serious possibilities of conflict internationally and nationally.

Communications (especially the media), education and consultation have important roles to play in increasing understanding and support for decision-making which can result in trade that benefits not only a few. In-ternational institutions with equitable and accountable structures also have an important role so that, in the end, the decision-makers take up their re-sponsibility and make binding trade rules.

The UN therefore needs urgently to undertake steps to democratise its international decision-making, to allow for active consultation at international level with all sectors of societies, and to make its decisions more accountable. Such an enlarged dimension to the United Nations is also needed because states will not remain the most important actors in world trade (trade liberalisation has contributed to that). State regulation will be undermined by transgovernmental, transnational and non-governmental actors. International consultations should therefore not only include parliamentarians but also many different actors in research, professional and business networks, political parties, trade unions, social movements, and NGOs.

In this way the UN would greatly contribute to improving a global vision and spirit of interdependence, beyond national and corporate interests. It would also hugely assist the full world community in forging coherent economic strategies for the benefit of all peoples.

4. Human rights
Fundamental freedoms for all

KATARINA TOMAŠEVSKI

In discussing the problems and prospects of United Nations human rights work it is much easier to criticise it than to make it function well. The reason is the inherent conflict between two roles of governments – as violators and as protectors of human rights. The main method of effective human rights protection is self-policing by governments, individually and collectively. Their reluctance to commit themselves to universally binding human rights standards and to supra-national supervision of their observance *in practice* explains the lack of a neat, logical and well-functioning UN human rights system. Indeed, the fact that virtually all governments cooperate with the UN on human rights issues, that most are party to the main human rights treaties, and that more than half of them have been held accountable for violations, represents a genuine success. This was, is and will remain a slow, painstaking and piecemeal process, where progress is determined by the collective will of governments.

Were it possible to conduct a public opinion survey on organisations which people associate with human rights it is likely that Amnesty International would rank much higher than the United Nations. Indeed, the human rights work of the UN is not widely known, nor is it recognised as such by those who perceive it solely as exposing and opposing human rights violations. The UN accomplishments in holding governments accountable for human rights violations are seldom publicised; programmes aimed at assisting governments to establish national human rights protection even less so. The creation of the United Nations High Commissioner on Human Rights is intended to redress this invisibility. But will it also translate into enhanced human rights protection? It is all too easy to answer in the negative: an inter-governmental structure seems unsuited to sanctioning governments for human rights violations. However, this very inter-governmental structure has allowed, or at least tolerated, the mush-rooming of human rights activities. Sifting through human rights docu-mentation, one finds that 60 governments were named in the 1994 annual report on torture,[1] also 60 in the report on disappearances,[2] and 74 in the annual report on extrajudicial executions.[3] Thus almost one-third of gov-ernmental representatives who take part in discussing how human rights should – and should not – be dealt with by the United Nations have the unpleasant task of responding to allegations of violations for which their own governments are held accountable.

This has not, of course, emerged overnight. The UN human rights work evolved from defining what human rights are, to determining what consti-tutes their violation, and to condemning governments that are violating human rights. It has recently developed further to procedures to prevent violations and programmes of expert and technical assistance to new, or changed, governments.

Background: defining what human rights are

The first task of the United Nations was to lay down the main substantive human rights standards in order to develop a globally applicable yardstick; understandably, it was important to define *what* before the United Nations could proceed to *how.* Even more important is the fact that governments, regardless of what people may think and the law may say, both make and break human rights, hence their acquiescence in both 'what' and 'how' is crucial to make human rights viable. The particular feature of human rights is that their respect does not occur spontaneously, improved obser-vance of human rights does not just happen. Human rights therefore con-stitute obligations for governments. The UN Charter was the first to affirm explicitly equal rights in its preamble, and proclaimed human rights to constitute one of the main purposes of the United Nations, specifically, 'to achieve international co-operation … in promoting and encouraging re-spect for human rights and fundamental freedoms for all without distinc-

---

1 United Nations Commission on Human Rights – Torture and other cruel, inhuman or degrad-ing treatment or punishment, Report of the Special Rapporteur, Mr. Nigel S. Rodley, UN Doc. E/CN:4/1994/31 of 6 January 1994.

2 United Nations Commission on Human Rights – Report of the Working Group on Enforced or Involuntary Disappearances, UN Doc. E/CN.4/1994/26 of 22 December 1993.

3 United Nations Commission on Human Rights – Extrajudicial, summary or arbitrary executions, Report by the Special Rapporteur, Mr. Bacre Waly Ndiaye, UN Doc. E/CN.4/1994/7 of 7 December 1993.

tion as to race, sex, language or religion'. Through the Charter all members of the United Nations are legally bound to strive towards full realisation of all human rights and fundamental freedoms. Human rights were thereby elevated from a noble aim to an obligation of all governments. It is important to add here that the United Nations never did – nor could – oblige itself to ensure that governments are indeed complying with their human rights obligations. Rather, words like 'encourage' and 'promote' reflect awareness of its inability to enforce compliance. It should not be forgotten that the UN has never promised more than it could deliver.

Human rights were reaffirmed in the Universal Declaration of Human Rights in 1948. This Declaration defined human rights as the 'common standards of achievement for humanity'. Although it expressed universally accepted standards as these were perceived at the time, it was not a legally binding document. The next step was therefore to translate human rights into obligations for governments. The drafting of an international treaty to convert the provisions of the Universal Declaration into legal obligations was a long and conflict-prone process. Firstly, the aim to draft one treaty had to be abandoned. The conceptual integrity of human rights was a victim of the Cold War, and human rights divided into two treaties: the International Covenant on Civil and Political Rights (ICCPR) and the International Covenant on Economic, Social and Cultural Rights (ICESCR). The Western countries, led by the USA, argued for the supremacy of civil and political rights, which often amounted to denying that economic and social rights were, or could become, human rights. The Soviet-led communist and/or socialist bloc argued that economic and social rights should take precedence over civil and political rights, which often resulted in the denial of civil rights and political liberties. Secondly, this protracted process lasted until 1966, when the two Covenants were adopted, and it took ten additional years for them to come into force – it was neither easy nor fast. It took more than 15 years to negotiate the text of these two Covenants, and ten more years until a sufficient number of governments ratified them so that they could come into force. The *Chronology of main human rights instruments* pages 85 and 86 provides a listing of milestones in standard-setting.

Chronology of main human rights instruments

1945   United Nations Charter
1948   Universal Declaration of Human Rights
1948   American Declaration of the Rights and Duties of Man
1948   Convention on the Prevention and Punishment of Genocide
1949   Geneva Conventions
1949   Convention on the Suppression of Traffic in Persons
1949   Convention on the Right to Organise and Collective Bargaining
1950   European Convention for the Protection of Human Rights and
        Fundamental Freedoms
1951   Convention on the Status of Refugees
1951   Equal Remuneration Convention
1952   Convention on the Political Rights of Women
1953   Protocol amending the 1926 Slavery Convention
1955   Standard Minimum Rules for the Treatment of Prisoners
1956   Supplementary Convention on the Abolition of Slavery
1957   Convention on the Nationality of Married Women
1957   Abolition of Forced Labour Convention
1958   Discrimination (Employment and Occupation) Convention
1959   Declaration of the Rights of the Child
1960   Declaration on the Granting of Independence to Colonial Countries
        and Peoples
1960   Convention against Discrimination in Education
1961   European Social Charter
1962   Convention on Consent to Marriage, Minimum Age for Marriage and
        Registration of Marriages
1963   Declaration on the Elimination of All Forms of Racial Discrimination
1965   International Convention on the Elimination of All Forms of Racial
        Discrimination
1966   International Covenant on Economic, Social and Cultural Rights
1966   International Covenant on Civil and Political Rights
1966   Protocol relating to the Status of Refugees
1967   Declaration on the Elimination of Discrimination against Women
1968   Proclamation of Teheran
1969   American Convention on Human Rights
1969   Declaration on Social Progress and Development
1973   International Convention on the Suppression and Punishment of
        Apartheid
1974   Universal Declaration on the Eradication of Hunger and

Malnutrition

1974 Declaration on the Protection of Women and Children in Emergency and Armed Conflict

1975 Declaration on the Rights of Disabled Persons

1975 Declaration on the Protection of All Persons from Being Subjected to Torture and Other Cruel, Inhuman or Degrading Treatment or Punishment

1977 Protocols Additional to Geneva Conventions

1978 Declaration on Race and Racial Prejudice

1979 Convention on the Elimination of All Forms of Discrimination against Women

1981 African Charter of Human and Peoples' Rights

1981 Declaration on the Elimination of All Forms of Intolerance and of Discrimination Based on Religion or Belief

1984 Convention against Torture and Inhuman or Degrading Treatment or Punishment

1986 Declaration on the Right to Development

1989 Convention on Indigenous and Tribal Peoples in Independent Countries

1989 Convention on the Rights of the Child

1991 International Convention for the Protection of Human Rights of All Migrant Workers and Their Families

1992 Declaration on the Rights of Persons Belonging to National or Ethnic, Religious and Linguistic Minorities

1992 Declaration on the Protection of All Persons from Enforced Disappearance

1993 Vienna Declaration and Programme of Action

United Nations membership 1946-1993

1945 Argentina, Australia, Belarus, Belgium, Bolivia, Brazil,Canada, Chile, China, Colombia, Costa Rica, Cuba, [Czechoslovakia], Denmark, Dominican Republic, Ecuador, Egypt, El Salvador, Ethiopia, France, Greece, Guatemala, Haiti, Honduras, India, Iran, Iraq, Lebanon, Liberia, Luxembourg, Mexico, Netherlands, New Zealand, Nicaragua, Norway, Panama, Paraguay, Peru, Philippines, Poland, Russia, Saudi Arabia, South Africa, Syria, Turkey, Ukraine, United Kingdom, USA, Uruguay, Venezuela, [Yugoslavia]

1946 Afghanistan, Iceland, Sweden, Thailand

1947 Pakistan, Yemen

1948 Burma

1949	Israel
1950	Indonesia
1955	Albania, Austria, Bulgaria,Cambodia, Finland, Hungary, Ireland, Italy, Jordan, Laos, Libya, Nepal, Portugal, Romania, Spain, Sri Lanka
1956	Japan, Morocco, Sudan, Tunisia
1957	Ghana, Malaysia
1958	Guinea
1960	Benin, Burkina Faso, Cameroon, Central African Republic, Chad, Congo, Côte d'Ivoire, Cyprus, Gabon, Madagascar, Mali, Niger, Nigeria, Senegal, Somalia, Togo, Zaire
1961	Mauritania, Mongolia, Sierra Leone, Tanzania
1962	Algeria, Burundi, Jamaica, Rwanda, Trinidad and Tobago, Uganda
1963	Kenya, Kuwait
1964	Malawi, Malta, Zambia
1965	The Gambia, Maldives, Singapore
1966	Barbados, Botswana, Guyana, Lesotho
1968	Equatorial Guinea, Mauritius, Swaziland
1970	Fiji
1971	Bahrain, Bhutan, Oman, Qatar, United Arab Emirates
1973	Bahamas, Germany
1974	Bangladesh, Grenada, Guinea Bissau
1975	Cape Verde, Comoros, Mozambique, Papua New Guinea, São Tomé and Principe, Suriname
1976	Angola, Samoa, Seychelles
1977	Djibouti, Vietnam
1978	Dominica, Solomon Islands
1979	St Lucia
1980	St Vincent and Grenadines, Zimbabwe
1981	Antigua and Barbuda, Belize, Vanuatu
1983	St Kitts and Nevis
1984	Brunei Darussalam
1990	Liechtenstein, Namibia
1991	DPR Korea, Estonia, Korea, Micronesia, Latvia, Lithuania, Marshall Islands
1992	Armenia, Azerbaijan, Bosnia and Herzegovina, Croatia, Georgia, Kazakhstan, Kyrgyzstan, Moldova, San Marino, Slovenia, Tajikistan, Turkmenistan, Uzbekistan
1993	Andorra, Czech Republic, Eritrea, The Former Yugoslav Republic of Macedonia, Monaco, Slovak Republic

The changed membership of the United Nations, illustrated in *United Nations membership 1946-1993* on pages 86 and 87, explains to some extent the slow and unsystematic evolution of human rights. In the early days, the United Nations had 51 members, less than one-third of the today's 184. The first wave of independence in the 1960s brought about the first challenges of the ideologically divided bipolar world, but also added another division into South and North. It is important to add that individual complaints for human rights violations were first introduced into the UN system as part of the process of decolonisation. With the end of the Cold War and the disappearance of West-East confrontation, the divisive line has moved again to North-South and development has emerged as the new battlefield. The current challenge to the UN is thus to introduce human rights safeguards into development, which structurally takes human rights much beyond the existing United Nations bodies that have 'human rights' in their mandate.

With the benefit of hindsight one can easily explain the importance of the right to self-determination as the basis of decolonisation – the majority of today's members of the United Nations were colonies at the time the UN came into being. It is also easy to understand obstacles to its further application – no government is willing to lose a part of its territory so that a new country can emerge. The gaining of political independence in the 1960s led to demands of economic independence in the 1970s, which on the human rights agenda culminated in the right to development. Self-determination and development remain the twin bottlenecks of human rights standard-setting. Looking further back into history, into what is commonly referred to as the Western concept of human rights, the emphasis on individual freedom and not equality, on individual liberties and not collective rights, explains unsolved controversies. Freedom from abuse of power by governments remains the core of effective universal human rights standards, while calls for governmental investment into reducing inequalities – internationally, nationally and locally – remain largely unheeded.

The second wave of independence, evidenced by the increase of United Nations membership in the 1990s, has revealed the potential – and the danger – inherent in the right to self-determination. Self-determination was originally defined as the right of peoples, and 'peoples' remain undefined. Invoking self-determination thus stumbles into the obstacle of uncertain subjects of that right, and the obvious unwillingness of governments to open the way for fragmentation of states. Because self-determination has been used (many would say abused) in practice to justify armed conflicts, human rights have again been taken beyond the area earmarked 'human rights' into peace-making and peace-enforcement, which was originally envisaged as the main area of UN work, at least by major powers.

Mushrooming standards: non-law, soft law, hard law

Determining what is, and what is not, a universally recognised human right is a tedious exercise. The obvious appeal of elevating claims to rights has led to a proverbial proliferation of 'rights' for which lobbyists (be they governments or NGOs) can quote some United Nations document which says that something is a right. Thus it is possible to find evidence that some body has proclaimed the right to tourism, to freedom of sexual expression, freedom from genetic mutation, or to democracy. The ease with which such 'rights' find their way in to United Nations 'non-law' documents originates in the fact that such pronouncements do not create effective entitlements for anybody, nor do they impose any obligations upon governments. Difficulties in nudging governments to accept human rights language in issues that imply changed rules of conduct – such as development, population policies or environment, which have fought their way from non-law to 'soft law' – testify to the importance of process. While a single United Nations meeting can adopt a resolution proclaiming a new right, the drafting of an international treaty whereby governments impose obligations upon themselves takes ten or 20 years of negotiations. Results of these negotiations become 'hard law'. International human rights law defines human rights and specifies the nature and scope of each right and freedom in turn. These rights constitute the corresponding obligations of governments. Human rights are better described as an art rather than a science. Much effort is needed, even for human rights contained in 'hard law', to attain their observance in practice. In the advocacy of those rights for which only a political agreement of governments exists, that is, 'soft law', such as developmental or environmental rights, for example, obtaining changes in governmental conduct is obviously even more difficult.

Those who expect human rights to conform to theory and to be conceptually consistent are often disappointed that norms represent a patchwork. The operative principles of international law-making require governments to agree upon any and every form of self-restraint. Nevertheless, the acceptance of human rights as universal and inherent makes them subject to international scrutiny. Governments no longer have the ultimate say in judging how they treat their 'own' population. The international community, embodied in the United Nations, monitors the compliance of governments with their human rights obligations. This has been grudgingly accepted by all governments in principle; in practice, procedural devices to avoid being held to account range between invoking national sovereignty, silence, or blanket rejection of alleged violations.

Human rights entail two types of governmental obligations: to prevent abuses of power, and to create conditions for the realisation of human rights and fundamental freedoms. Prohibitions have been defined quite well, but norms which require governments to undertake specific measures, rather than to refrain from a prohibited action, were and are more difficult to elaborate and monitor. Because they ought to be applicable universally, the existing differences in the capacity of countries to implement their obligations impede precise definitions. This is coupled with the proverbial unwillingness of governments to commit themselves to more than they are compelled to. The credibility of human rights is further jeopardised when wishful thinking is converted into the language of rights. For example, everybody has the right to the continuous improvement of living conditions, which forms part of hard law, but hardly any government in the world is able to guarantee such a right, even if it were fully committed to do so. Much more attention is paid to what governments should not do. This emanates from the Western/Northern focus on civil and political liberties, but is also a result of the relative ease with which breaches of prohibitions are monitored: it is much easier to determine whether a government is killing off its opposition than whether it undertook whatever it could to prevent its population from starvation. Assertions that civil and political rights require only governmental restraint, while economic and social rights necessitate only governmental investment, have created much confusion: both categories involve both types of obligations. The myth that civil and political rights are costless is dispelled against evidence of the effort necessary to establish and sustain a judiciary, or to pay, train and discipline the police.

The interplay between these two types of obligations can be easily explained with respect to gender discrimination. The challenge to inequality is inherent in the very notion of human rights, thus the core principle is that all human beings have equal rights, which are properties inherent to human beings. Thus not only should women be accorded rights equal to those of men, but they should be equally able to enjoy all these formally accorded rights. This requires that other-than-legal obstacles be identified and eliminated. Eliminating *de facto* discrimination is much more difficult than enacting laws which recognise equal rights for all. The 1993 Vienna Conference[4] has created a precedent by integrating equal rights of women into the main body of its final document(s), but the translation of this rhetoric into holding governments accountable for denying women their equal rights in practice has yet to happen. The 1994 Asian and Pacific NGO Symposium on Women in Development summed up its critique of the Vienna final document by saying: 'To the millions of people all over the world who are victims of human rights violations, it brought little hope. It is silent on the role of the state as violator of human rights.'[5]

Implementation: self policing by governments

Human rights are often criticised for being state-centred, which they indeed are. Non-state entities, be they warlords or transnational corporations, have yet to be fitted into this state-centred human rights system. In theory, one can develop beautiful people-centred designs, demand that responsibility for violations be individualised, and lament on the discrepancy between theory and practice. The practice remains that the main purpose of human rights – to prevent abuse of power – is necessary for those who wield power to police themselves. Even where the effective control is exercised by warlords or transnational corporations, the practice of human rights follows its basic assumption 'that the State, through the Government, ... is genuinely capable of exercising real control throughout its territory'.[6]

The most widespread – and the least publicised – method of monitoring governmental human rights performance is reporting. Seven human rights treaties envisage a system of international supervision, which obliges states' parties to report on their implementation and enables supervisory bodies to monitor their performance. The eighth one, dealing with human rights of migrant workers, was adopted in 1991 but is not yet ratified by a single government. The number of parties to each of them is given in the *Number of countries bound by human rights treaties that entail reporting* on page 92. One can easily see that the rights of the child and elimination of gender discrimination enjoy the support of the largest number of governments. Children, women and the disabled are proverbially deemed the least political

---

4 The Vienna Conference was held in June 1993, with 174 governments and 1,700 non-governmental organisations participating. Originally planned during the brief period of enthusiasm following the end of the Cold War, the Conference proved to be much more divisive than anybody had expected, not only at the inter-governmental level but also at the non-governmental one. Its results did, however, show clearly how much agreement and disagreement is contained in this apparently simple term 'human rights'.

5 Workshop on Women's Human Rights, Asian and Pacific Symposium of NGOs on Women in Development, *Law and Society Trust Fortnightly Review*, vol. 4, No. 71, 1 February 1994, p. 16-17.

6 'United Nations – On the relation between development and the enjoyment of all human rights', study prepared by Highboard Wieland Conroy, UN Doc. A/CONF.157/PC/60/Add.2 of 5 April 1993, para. 77.

Number of countries bound by human rights treaties that entail reporting

Convention on the Rights of the Child	152
International Convention on the Elimination of All Forms of Racial Discrimination	132
Convention on the Elimination of All Forms of Discrimination against Women	131
International Covenant on Economic, Social and Cultural Rights	126
International Covenant on Civil and Political Rights	124
International Convention on the Suppression and Punishment of the Crime of Apartheid	94
Convention against Torture and Other Cruel, Inhuman or Degrading Treatment or Punishment	68
International Convention for the Protection of Human Rights of All Migrant Workers and Their Families (not yet in force)	2

parts of the human rights agenda. Nothing in human rights can really be apolitical, as evidenced by large numbers of reservations to both the Children's and Women's Convention. These testify to yet another layer of governmental reluctance to fully commit themselves to the observance of equal rights for all.

The reporting procedures established by these seven treaties provide an insight into the governmental views on human rights, their efforts to implement human rights obligations or the lack thereof, and their reactions to criticism by monitoring bodies (as governments submit their human rights records to international supervision). Reports are assessments of the state of human rights by the government itself and information is hence authoritative, but not necessarily accurate. The monitoring bodies rely primarily on information from governments which, of course, do not advertise violations for which they are likely to be held accountable. Monitoring bodies consist of experts acting in their personal capacity (but elected by governments), who may and do rely on their knowledge of countries under study, which broadens sources of information. Informal submission of information by human rights NGOs has become accepted practice. The system is paralysed when governments do not report and negative correlation exists between the scope and severity of human rights problems and governments' reports. This is illustrated in *Countries with the largest number of overdue reports under human rights treaties* on page 93.

Countries with the largest number of overdue reports under human rights treaties

Guyana	20	Haiti	11
Guinea	18	Laos	11
Liberia	16	Nepal	11
Zaire	16	St. Vincent & Grenadines	11
The Gambia	14	Tanzania	11
Gabon	13	Vietnam	11
Somalia	13	Cameroon	10
Jamaica	12	Congo	10
Libya	12	El Salvador	10
Mali	12	Niger	10
Sudan	12	Romania	10
Togo	12	Sierra Leone	10
Uganda	12	Suriname	10
Central African Republic	11		

Note: Countries with ten or more overdue reports under the seven human rights treaties which entail reporting are listed according to the number of overdue reports for each countries. Countries with the same number are listed alphabetically.
Source: Status of the international human rights instruments and the general situation of overdue reports. Report of the Secretary-General, UN Doc. HRI/MC/1991/3 of 25 September 1992.

Reporting is likely to change in the near future because of in-built multiplication of information that governments have to send: they have to repeat the same and similar contents in their various reports and answer the same and similar questions before each monitoring body. Changes have already been initiated (for example, basic information is submitted in the form of a core document to all monitoring bodies) and undoubtedly will go much further. One innovation which is increasingly demanded, and found its way into the final documents of the Vienna Conference, are optional protocols to the main human rights treaties so to enable individuals to seek remedies. This was first applied to the ICCPR and its monitoring body, the Human Rights Committee, has created impressive jurisprudence. Despite the general unwillingness of governments to allow individuals to pursue their complaints of human rights violations internationally when domestic remedies prove inadequate, almost a third have allowed it, as illustrated in *Parties to the Optional Protocol to the International Covenant on Civil and Political Rights* on page 94.

Parties to the Optional Protocol to the International Covenant on Civil and Political Rights (ICCPR)

Algeria	Estonia	Peru
Angola	Finland	Philippines
Argentina	France	Poland
Australia	The Gambia	Portugal
Austria	Hungary	Russian Federation
Barbados	Iceland	St. Vincent and
Belarus	Ireland	Grenadines
Benin	Italy	San Marino
Bolivia	Jamaica	Senegal
Bulgaria	Korea, Rep.	Seychelles
Cameroon	Libya	Slovak Republic
Canada	Lithuania	Somalia
Central African Rep.	Luxembourg	Spain
Chile	Madagascar	Suriname
Colombia	Malta	Sweden
Congo	Mauritius	Togo
Costa Rica	Mongolia	Trinidad and Tobago
Côte d'Ivoire	Nepal	Ukraine
Cyprus	Netherlands	Uruguay
Czech Republic	New Zealand	Venezuela
Denmark	Nicaragua	Zaire
Dominican Republic	Niger	Zambia
Ecuador	Norway	
Equatorial Guinea	Panama	

The Human Rights Committee has managed to enhance international protection of human rights in many important ways: it reversed the burden of proof and thus enabled individuals to obtain remedies when governments violated their human rights and refused to furnish evidence which – by definition – is in the possession of the government. It broadened remedies against discrimination to economic and social rights, and also prevented the death penalty from being carried out when due process of law had not been respected. Generally, it has shown *in practice* that supra-national human rights protection does not remain confined to Europe, but can be put into practice globally.

UN human rights structure: institutionalised 'ad-hocism'

What is called the United Nations human rights system really represents a patchwork of diverse bodies and procedures. Even the listing of numerous committees, working groups, special rapporteurs and special procedures requires enormous patience and the uninitiated are bound to get lost in the labyrinth. Finding the answer to the obvious question – why does it have to be so complicated? – strains the patience still further. It is difficult indeed to explain that, despite the human rights rhetoric in the United Nations Charter and the Universal Declaration of Human Rights, the organisation was not intended to carry out human rights work as defined in the way it is seen today, namely addressing violations. It developed very slowly, against much opposition inherent in its inter-governmental structure. The proverbial United Nations rule 'if you cannot commit yourself, committee yourself' results in the creation of new bodies for each new topic. The range of issues on the human rights agenda and organisations schemes for addressing them is illustrated in the *Overview of the 1994 United Nations Commission on Human Rights* on page 96.

The fact that governments have to submit their reports on the same topics under different treaties and to different committees is obvious duplication. Politically and legally, this has to be so because each treaty has an overlapping, but not identical list of governments that are party to it, and all these would have to agree to any modification of the reporting procedures. In practice it could be different if it had a strong secretariat, which could take over a great deal of reporting and relieve governments of this cumbersome task. The secretariat, however, the Centre for Human Rights, is plagued by multi-layered problems. The most often quoted one, the lack of resources, is evidenced in the minuscule part of the United Nations budget earmarked for human rights (0.8 per cent) and in the small size of staff (the professional staff was actually reduced from 81 in 1982 to 79 in 1992), who are burdened with the myriad of tasks which this institutionalised `ad-hocism' inevitably produces. Alongside reporting procedures established by human rights treaties, virtually every new topic creates another questionnaire to governments, the responses to which are then presented as a report to some human rights body. Responses are fewer and fewer, sometimes limited to a dozen, and studies based on them are frequently a mere reproduction of these responses. This, nevertheless, creates much work for the secretariat, as the human rights agenda has encompassed issues as diverse as mercenaries and AIDS, environment and impunity, privatisation of prisons and sale of children. The number of reports exceeded

Overview of the 1994 United Nations Commission on Human Rights

THEMATIC MANDATES	COUNTRY MANDATES
WORKING GROUPS	WORKING GROUPS

- contemporary forms of slavery
- enforced or involuntary disappearances
- draft declaration on right and respon-
  sibility to promote human rights
- indigenous populations
- arbitrary detention
- right to development
- draft optional protocol to the
  Convention against Torture
- draft optional protocol to the
  Convention on the Rights of the Child
	- Special Committee on Israeli Practices

SPECIAL RAPPORTEURS	SPECIAL RAPPORTEURS

- extrajudicial executions
- racism, racial discrimination and
  xenophobia
- torture
- traditional practices affecting the health
  of women and children
- states of emergency
- religious intolerance
- mercenaries
- sale of children
- right to property
- human rights and the environment
- impunity of perpetrators of violations
- internally displaced persons
- right to adequate housing
- population transfer
- violence against women
- independence and impartiality of the
  judiciary
- consequences of armed conflicts for
  children
	- Afghanistan
	- Burma
	- Burundi
	- Cambodia
	- Cuba
	- El Salvador
	- Equatorial Guinea
	- Guatemala
	- Haiti
	- Iran
	- Iraq
	- Palestine
	- Somalia
	- South Africa
	- Sudan
	- former Yugoslavia
	- Zaire

SECRETARIAT	SECRETARIAT

- civil defence forces
- mass exoduses
- co-operation with UN human rights
  bodies
- forensic science
- Third Decade to Combat Racism and
  Racial Discrimination
- International Decade of the World's
  Indigenous Peoples
- decade for human rights education
	- Albania
	- Cyprus
	- East Timor
	- Georgia (Abkhazia)
	- Papua New Guinea (Bougainville)
	- southern Lebanon

60 in 1992 and yet more are being added; special procedures increased from 4 in 1980 to 30 in 1992; governmental requests for assistance grew from two in 1985 to more than 70 in 1992.

An important reason for this institutionalised ad-hocism are the operative norms of the United Nations system. The lowly priority for human rights inevitably stems from the fact that the main actors, governments, are the target of criticism. One procedural device to avoid such criticism is to increase the number of studies and reports that do not 'name names'. This incremental broadening of the human rights agenda multiplies tiny secretariats for each item and sub-item, without any horizontal co-ordination. Thus the mountains of documentation (read probably only by language editors) do not provide for the possibility of cross-referencing. To find information relevant for the human rights of women it is necessary to sift through piles of documents produced for and by each different body. Even for violations of human rights of persons deprived of their liberty – who were and are the most frequent target – there is no overview. The constant addition of agenda items lengthens the meetings and shortens the time available for discussing each item. Speaking time for NGOs who, more often than governments, 'name names' by exposing on-going violations, is constantly shortened. Adherents of conspiracy theory could easily read into all this an attempt to inflate the human rights currency so that devaluation becomes inevitable. Because human rights were introduced into an inter-governmental structure gradually, through the choice of topics and countries where governments could be nudged into a grudging acceptance, no master plan has ever been made. Hopes that the Vienna Conference on Human Rights would accord human rights its deserved priority turned to frustration. The Conference called for 'immediate steps to increase substantially the resources for the human rights programme from within the existing and future regular budgets of the United Nations' and for 'increased extrabudgetary resources'.[7] Unable to agree either where resources should come from, nor how much is necessary, nor indeed what for, the Vienna Conference relegated the fate of human rights to the General Assembly. The Assembly agreed to the establishment of the High Commissioner on Human Rights, but not to an increased budget.

---

7 United Nations – Vienna Declaration and Programme of Action, UN Doc. A/CONF.157/23 of 12 July 1993, p. 14, para. 9.

The realm of the possible: responding to violations

The United Nations Commission on Human Rights started in 1947 by explicitly rejecting the proposal that United Nations could receive and act upon complaints for human rights violations. Only in the 1970s did it become possible to institute international complaints procedures, and individuals were able to pursue demands to investigate and condemn human rights violations by their own government before the United Nations. Critics of the international human rights system regularly emphasise that not all governments violating human rights are condemned, but seldom stress the importance of the profound change: the government is no longer the ultimate arbiter in its own case, it can be held accountable internationally for what it does to its 'own' people.

As Dag Hammarskjöld, UN Secretary-General in the 1960's, used to say, the United Nations had never been meant to take humanity to heaven but to save it from hell. Its human rights system was not designed to police governments, but only to assist them in policing themselves. It cannot deter or punish gross and systematic violations, and thus cannot ever become effective by this criterion. Its achievements have been to define violations and make them visible – mobilisation of shame is the only form of deterrence that United Nations can use. Manoeuvres by governments whose violations are being exposed affirm the truism *qui s'excuse s'accuse*. Because the United Nations systems can only act in response to information it receives, the initiative of victims of human rights violations, or on their behalf, is the first necessary step. Indeed NGOs rather than governments always take a lead in exposing and opposing violations. The focus on Latin American countries during the late 1970s and 1980s can to a large extent be attributed to the work of NGOs in the region. African countries were placed on the agenda only in 1990, also largely as a consequence of the increasing activity of African NGOs. The growth of NGOs in Asia is likely to change the human rights landscape in the 1990s.

The importance of the human rights work of the UN can be explained as follows: governments undertake and implement human rights obligations, and it is only governments that sit in judgement over the conduct of other governments. The work of the only global inter-governmental human rights system thus reflects the realm of the possible. The strength of the system is at the same time its weakness : the inter-governmental system cannot be anything but dominated by governments, and thus politicised, slow and expensive. The existing criteria and results of their application leave a lot to be desired. This inter-governmental human rights machinery is not perfect, but it is the only one there is.

International human rights law requires the observance of basic rights and fundamental freedoms by all governments. It is evident from the terms used that only the basic and/or fundamental rights and freedoms can be protected. There are different opinions about what is, or what should be, deemed basic and/or fundamental. Guidance is, however, contained in the human rights law itself – the right to life has priority over the right to paid vacations. The core notion is the indivisibility and interdependence of human rights, which prohibit their ranking or 'trading-off', that is, respect of some rights at the expense of others. The awareness that human rights entail redressing unequal opportunities is emerging very slowly. Earlier decades, largely due to the approach of the United States government, divided human rights into three generations, relegated economic and social rights to the second generation, and development and solidarity to the third and last one. The focus of human rights activism is still on purposeful governmental acts against individual life, integrity and liberty, not on governmental obligations emanating from access to the necessities of survival.

Not every violation can be an object of international concern and action. The United Nations can only be a corrective to the national systems for the protection of human rights. Hence international action takes place when the level of severity of violations justifies it. This is exemplified by the notion of gross and systematic violations. As developed and applied by the United Nations, it denotes the degree of severity, scope and perpetuation of violations which implies that they constitute the *policy* of the government; gross and systematic violations describe situations where violations amount to prevalence rather than mere incidence. Resolutions of the United Nations human rights organs, however, do not encompass all the countries which practise human rights violations as a matter of policy, nor are all the countries found in these resolutions pursuing a policy of violations.

The table *Human rights violations at the United Nations agenda* on pages 100 and 101 gives the list of countries placed on the UN human rights agenda for violations over the last decades. As the table shows, the UN started addressing violations in the late 1960s. The first case was South Africa in 1967, followed by Israel in 1968. These two, with the addition of Chile in 1974, dominated the first decade of the UN's work on violations. The table demonstrates that the number of countries that have been found in violation of human rights by the United Nations is much larger than that is usually presumed. It does not encompass all the governments

Human rights violations at the United Nations agenda

Country	Commission	Sub-Commission	1503 procedure
Afghanistan	1980-91, 1993-94	1981-88	1981-84
Albania	1988-91, 1993-94	1985-88	1984-88
Angola	1994	—	—
Argentina	—	(1978)	1980-84
Bangladesh	—	—	(1988)
Bahrain	—	—	1990-91, 1993
Benin	—	—	1984-85, 1988
Bolivia	1981-83	1980	1978-81
Bosnia and Herzegovina	1994	1993	
Brazil	—	—	1974-75, 1990
Brunei Darussalam	—	—	1988-90
Burma	(1989-90), 1992-94	1991, 1993	1979-80, 1989-91
Burundi	1994	1988	1974
Cambodia	1979-80, 1984-89, 1994	1978-88, 1991	1979
Central African Republic	—	—	1980-81
Chad	—	1993	1990-93
Chile	1975-90	1974-88	1975-79, 1981
China	(1993)	1989, (1993)	—
Colombia	—	—	1990
Cuba	(1988), 1990-94	—	—
Cyprus	1975-88, 1990	1974-88	—
El Salvador	1981-91, 1993-94	1981-92	1981
Equatorial Guinea	1979-85, 1989-90, 1992-94	1979-80	1976-79
Ethiopia	(1986)	—	1978-81
Gabon	—	—	1986
[Germany, D.R.]	—	—	1981-83
Grenada	1984	—	1988
Guatemala	1980-86, 1992, 1994	1982-86, 1989-93	1989, (1990)
Georgia	1994		
Guyana			1974
Haiti	1984, 1987-90, 1992-94	1988, 1992-93	1981-87, 1989-90
Honduras	—	—	1988-89
Indonesia (East Timor)	1983, (1993), (1994)	1982-84, 1987, 1989-90, 1992-93	1974-75, 1977-81, 1983-85
Iran	1982-94	1980-93	1974, 1983
Iraq	(1989), 1991-94	(1989), 1990-91, 1993	1988-89
Israel (Palestine)	1968-94	1968-93	—
Japan	—	—	1981
Kenya	—	—	1993

Country	Commission	Sub-Commission	1503 procedure
Korea, Rep.	—	—	1978-82
Kuwait	1991	1990	—
Lebanon	1985-94	1982-90	—
Malawi	1980	—	1978-80
Malaysia	—	—	1984
Mauritania	1982, 1985	1982, 1984-85	(1990)
Mozambique	—	—	1981
Namibia	1967-88	1967-88	—
Nicaragua	1979	1979	—
Pakistan	1985	1985	1984-85, 1988
Panama	1990	1990	—
Papua New Guinea (Bougainville)	1993-94	1992	—
Paraguay	1985	1983-85, 1989	1978-90
Peru	—	1992-93	1990
Philippines	—	—	1984-86
Poland	1982-84	—	—
Portugal	—	—	1974
Romania	1989-91, 1993	(1989)	—
Rwanda	—	—	1993
Somalia	1992, 1994	1991-92	1989-93
South Africa	1967-94	1967-93	—
Sri Lanka	1984, 1987	1983-84	—
Sudan	1992-94	—	1990-93
Syria	—	—	1989,1990-92
Tanzania (Zanzibar)	—	—	1974
Tibet	—	1989-91	—
Togo	1994	—	1993
Turkey	—	—	1983-86, (1990)
Uganda	—	(1979)	1975-81
United Kingdom (Northern Ireland)	—	—	1974
Uruguay	1985	1983-84	1978-85
Venezuela	—	—	1982
Vietnam	—	—	1975
Western Sahara	1981-87, 1989-90, 1993	1987	—
Zaire	1992-93	—	1985-89, 1990-93
[Yugoslavia]	1992-94	1992-93	—
[Yugoslavia/ Kosovo]	1994	—	—

Note: The first column refers to the consideration of specific countries under the human rights violations agenda item by the Commission on Human Rights, the second one to its Sub-Commission, and the third one to the 1503 procedure whereby 'a consistent pattern of gross and reliably attested violations of human rights' may be investigated for any country.

Square brackets denote countries which do not exist any more, while round brackets refer to those resolutions or decisions of the respective United Nations bodies which were not formally adopted due to some procedural reasons.

for which violations have been documented, but it includes 71 countries where violations have been exposed – this is more than one-third of the countries in the world, and more than the entire UN membership when the Universal Declaration of Human Rights was adopted in 1948.

Data in the table are derived from the resolutions and decisions of the three main bodies empowered to ascertain violations and recommend appropriate action. These are called 'political' organs in the UN parlance. The information included in the list represents results of the work of the Commission on Human Rights, its subsidiary body, the Sub-Commission (which bears the name of Sub-Commission for the Prevention of Discrimination and Protection of Minorities), and the 1503 procedure, which enables individuals to bring to the attention of the United Nations gross and systematic human rights violations in any of its members. It is important to note that these three procedures are not dependent on the ratification of particular human rights treaties by the government in question. Rather they are based on the availability of reliable information on the ongoing human rights violations in a country, on their gravity and scope, and on the willingness of the governments represented in the UN human rights bodies to condemn a particular government.

The United Nations is regularly blamed for condemning violations in too few countries. The proverbial triumvirate – South Africa, Israel and Chile – set the precedent and dominated the violations agenda for almost three decades. South Africa was the first in 1967; it was joined one year later by Israel, and in 1974 by Chile. Significantly, none of these three is likely to remain on the violations agenda any longer. Critics of the United Nations work in ascertaining and condemning violations have an easy target: that work is the least popular within the United Nations, is exposed to constant pressures, and understaffed. Critics forget that the fact that any government can be held accountable for the way it treats its population – inconceivable 30 years ago – represents the most important accomplishment of the international system of human rights.

Beyond violations: investing in human rights

International human rights politics is often accused of hypocrisy. The selective condemnation for human rights violations, evident in results of the UN work, is regularly cited as evidence. Condemnation as the main method of international human rights action is criticised as hypocritical as well: it focuses on violations while disregarding the fact that enjoyment of human rights can be impossible due to poverty or detrimental development policy. Human rights are confined to a small and highly politicised segment of the inter-governmental co-operation, whilst left out from its mainstream. The mainstream is, of course, guided by economic, political and ideological, rather than human rights objectives.

The United Nations does not provide much assistance to governments to implement their human rights obligations. Aid falls short of meeting the articulated needs, even in the narrow technical field of drafting laws and setting up legal libraries; trade jeopardises rather than facilitates enjoyment of human rights in the South. Nevertheless, human rights assistance has been criticised as the betrayal of what some see as its primary role of the United Nations in human rights, namely to expose and condemn violations: 'Increasingly unwilling to confront governments with reported human rights violations, the United Nations itself in recent years began to divert more and more of its limited human rights resources to "promotional programs".'[8] Examples of 'the crying lack of resources' (the professional staff required to deal with all human rights worldwide numbers 79 while the annual budget of the Centre for Human Rights amounted to $11 million in 1993) have often been included in reports which tried to advance UN human rights policy from just condemning violations to assisting in preventing their perpetuation. An expert looking into the elimination of slavery thus regretted the lack of response by donors and concluded: 'States act as if bodies concerned with human rights have nothing to do with bodies concerned with development assistance'.[9]

Resource requirements for the implementation of governmental human rights obligations are regularly disregarded. The problem is recognised with respect to economic and social rights, not for human rights as a whole, and not mentioned at all with respect to civil and political rights. It is admitted that economic and social rights are beyond the reach of the majority of countries in the world, and can only be realised gradually and progressively, but it is postulated that civil and political rights can and should be guaranteed fully and immediately. The United Nations Special Rapporteur on Torture dispelled this myth: 'The international community has not been aware that the realisation of political and civil rights is also dependent upon international co-operation. This may be partly due to the fact that political and civil rights are usually seen as obligations for the

---

8 United Nations, *Human Rights and U.S. Foreign Policy*, Lawyers Committee for Human Rights, New York, 1992, p. 43.
9 Slavery and slavery-like practices: Report on the mission to Mauritania, UN Doc. E/CN.4/Sub.2/1985/26, para. 44.

State to abstain from interfering in the private sphere of the individual. However, for the full enjoyment of those rights, a certain infrastructure is essential. Up till now, hardly any funds have been set aside to comply with requests for assistance in this field.'[10]

The human rights commitment of the West/North is often criticised as hypocritical as its interest in human rights goes no further than actions which do not cost anything. Human rights do not enjoy high priority in international development finance, and are virtually absent from trade and investment. It is hence noteworthy to quote the attitude of the government of the Netherlands: 'The industrialised countries cannot make a credible stand for human rights in the Third World if they do not display willingness to make sacrifices for the sake of a structural change in the existing imbalance between themselves and developing countries.'[11]

Human rights have recently been included in 'mainstream' United Nations operations, and this promised a much needed change. However, Human Rights Watch examined five UN field operations (Cambodia, El Salvador, Iraq, Somalia, and former Yugoslavia) and concluded that 'human rights have been treated as a dispensable luxury', criticised the UN for its failure to end gross abuses and establish a system of accountability, and attributed this failure to misguided neutrality, diplomatic caution, and the desire for a quick fix, where human rights are dispensed with so as to make possible the delivery of humanitarian aid or elections.[12]

New human rights battlefield: development

The ongoing battle about the global human rights agenda is best illustrated by the voting pattern of the UN Commission on Human Rights. Resolutions dealing with foreign debt are accepted by majority vote, with all Southern countries voting in favour, the Northern abstaining and the US voting against. Those dealing with the right to development fall into a similar pattern, as do those condemning the use of unilateral economic sanctions. A breakthrough will only be achieved when the Northern govern-

---

10 Torture and other cruel, inhuman and degrading treatment or punishment. Report by the Special Rapporteur. Visit by the Special Rapporteur to Argentina, Colombia and Uruguay, UN Doc. E/CN.4/1988/17/Add.1 of 23 February 1988, para. 23.

11 Memorandum presented to the Lower House of the States-General of the Kingdom of the Netherlands on 3 May 1979 by the Minister for Foreign Affairs and the Minister for Development Co-Operation.

12 Human Rights Watch, *The Lost Agenda. Human Rights and UN Field Operations*, New York, June 1993.

ments accept that human rights necessitate investment, that the 'crying lack of resources' hampers not only the UN work on human rights, but the realisation of human rights for most of humanity. As long as Northern governments pursue only condemnations and sanctions as the method of enhancing human rights, their commitment to human rights will continue to be seen as reaching no further than saving themselves money.

The current clash of ideologies pervading inter-governmental human rights politics counterpoises those advocating multi-party elections (which they call democracy) and those insisting on developmentalism (which they deem to constitute a precondition for human rights). Governments have lost much of their economic sovereignty, and obstacles of vested interests (often claimed as acquired rights) by those favoured by the status quo impede dialogue. Indeed, as Eduardo Galleano noted a long time ago, the international division of labour has caused some to specialise in winning, others in losing. The underlying reasoning of those doomed to lose relies on the assertion that authoritarian rule can create economic miracles. Those specialising in winning employ a great deal of human rights rhetoric, but refuse to acknowledge the simple fact that human rights necessitate large, long-term and sustained investment. In underdeveloped countries, some of this investment ought to come from abroad. It is, however, paradoxical that development has penetrated the human rights agenda much more than human rights have been accepted on the development finance agenda. Those wielding power over development finance have adopted electoralism, not human rights. The insistence on the rule of law in human rights stems from the fact that governance is exercise of power and should be subjected to safeguards so as to prevent its arbitrary use. Paradoxically, again, rule of law is disregarded both in electoralism and in developmentalism.

The right to development was accepted by the industrialised countries, even if only rhetorically, at the 1993 Conference on Human Rights, seven years after the Declaration on the Right to Development had been adopted by the majority of the General Assembly. In the existing international human rights instruments relating to development no mention is made of the fact that development is inherently conflict-prone. The realisation of human rights requires recognising conflicts between mutually opposed rights and designing mechanisms for conflict-solving. A good example is the (legal) right to property which regularly impedes access to land necessary for the survival of the rural landless. Rather than setting a procedure for coping with such inevitable conflicts, the existing human rights instruments embody guarantees of substantive rights for all, while omitting to provide guidance on how to deal with conflicting rights and conflicts of rights-holders; to make it even more complicated, rights claimed in development encompass states, peoples and individuals.

The ultimate aims of development may be more-or-less shared with those of human rights, but means differ a great deal. Much criticism of development was generated by the adverse effects of structural adjustment on conditions for the enjoyment of human rights. The dominance of freedom from governmental interference with individual liberty provides 'no mandate to support the individual beyond its duty to protect his opportunity to act freely, however useless that opportunity might be in fact'.[13] While human rights obligations reach far beyond governmental self-restraint, their precise definition is still lacking. As always, demands to protect human rights emerge in response to perceived violations; it is always easier to determine what governments should *not* do. Large-scale industrial projects, those involving relocation and resettlement, often entail human rights problems, and safeguards have to be incorporated into their design and implementation. With regard to development interventions that entail population transfer, the Sub-Commission on Prevention of Discrimination and Protection of Minorities found 'invariably serious consequences for the enjoyment of human rights'.[14] Clusters of human rights that are frequently affected in development include land rights, freedom of movement and residence (particularly safeguards against forced removal), labour rights, including child labour. United Nations human rights bodies have thus demonstrated that much can be accomplished by focusing on human rights violations which take place under the pretext of 'development' and striving to prevent them, rather than by concentrating on a grand scheme to define what human rights in development should be.

Governmental denial of collective rights

Despite the fact that after the Cold War the main challenges to peace come from within states, human rights have not progressed in defining rights and duties, freedoms and responsibilities of peoples, minorities, communities, groups, that claim specific collective rights as entities. The only area where a conceptual breakthrough has been made is that of

---

13 L. E. – Reasoning with the Charter, Butterworths, Toronto and Vancouver, 1991, p. 7.
14 On Prevention of Discrimination and Protection of Minorities – Human rights dimensions of population transfer, including the implantation of settlers and settlements, Resolution 1990/17 of 30 August 1990, preamble.

indigenous rights. This has indeed been the most creative area of the human rights discourse in the 1980s. One possible reason is its relative freedom from the Cold War politics. Indigenous organisations have changed the global human rights agenda by including collective and developmental rights, by arguing the necessity to move away from the individual and the state as the sole entities recognised in human rights. The evolving Draft Declaration of the Rights of Indigenous Peoples asserts 'the right of all peoples to be different, to consider themselves different, and to be respected as such', advocates 'control by indigenous peoples over development affecting them', and lays down basic rights of indigenous individuals and peoples.[15]

Nevertheless, full agreement amongst governments on the denial of collective human rights was clearly evidenced in the final documents of the Vienna Conference. Those who did not follow the vehement protests of NGOs against the intransigence of Western governments may miss the changed wording: it is indigenous people (not peoples) and persons belonging to minorities (not minorities) whose rights are promoted and protected.[16] This marked the boundary which human rights can cross easily in theory, but not yet in inter-governmental law-making, and dispelled the myth that Western governments are committed to (collective) human rights.

In 1948 the Universal Declaration of Human Rights postulated that the lack of protection of human rights compels people 'to have recourse, as a last resort, to rebellion against tyranny and oppression'. Arguments continue about the role of human rights in changing the unjust status quo, founded on the violation of the right to self-determination of peoples or on an exploitative economic system. Much criticism targets Western intransigence: 'One gets the impression that human rights is yet another marketplace of so-called free competition, a hidden way of protecting what has been achieved or what could be achieved by the more powerful'.[17]

After the Cold War, democracy is advocated as global panacea. Democracy is, following the Universal Declaration of Human Rights, conceived as the 'will of the people'; namely, governance is legitimate only when de-

---

15 United Nations – Discrimination against indigenous peoples. Report of the Working Group on Indigenous Populations on its eleventh session, UN Doc. E/CN.4/Sub.2/1993/29 of 23 August 1993, Annex 1, p. 50 et seq.

16 United Nations – Vienna Declaration and Programme of Action, UN Doc. A/CONF.157/23 of 12 July 1993, p. 7-8, paras. 19-20.

17 Ellacuria, I. – 'Historización de los derechos humanos desde los pueblos oprimidos y las mayorías populares', *Estudios Centroamericanos*, vol. 45, No. 502, August 1990, p. 590.

rived from the consent of the governed. People are, however, perceived as a single homogeneous entity consisting of atomised individuals. This favours majorities, but leaves out minorities that do not have voting power to protect their specific identity and who therefore need protection that is not dependent on a number of eligible voters. The gap left by the non-recognition of substantive human rights of groups, minorities, communities and peoples could be filled by laying down procedural rules for articulating, negotiating and settling such claims. The bulk of human rights work has focused on elaborating substantive standards, defining who is entitled to what, while procedures to articulate and negotiate different and often mutually opposed claims have yet to be elaborated.

Collective rights remain hampered by the jealous adherence to the nation-state and to the territorial integrity of the existing (nation-)states. We may know that nation-state is a fiction that does not bear factual analysis, but it remains unchallengeable. Any recognition of ethnic, religious, or linguistic minorities is seen by states as a step towards redrawing national borders, and is opposed by the many who fear loss of territory. Little progress has been made to move away from this obsession with territory as the symbol of statehood. Although scholarly writings have suggested numerous ways and means of recognising 'collectivities' within states through various types and levels of internal self-determination, claims for self-determination are regularly perceived as territorial claims. Peace-making remains confined to stopping warfare, but creativity in tackling underlying causes remains yet to be seen.

Moving forward: pressure for change

Human rights organisations have realised long ago that human rights are too important to be left to governments. Virtually all accomplishments in the UN human rights work were imposed upon governments: initiatives came from non-governmental organisations (NGOs) in response to perceived violations. Human rights developed in practice as the language of political criticism. Whether the immediate aim was public condemnation of a government, or standard setting to make prohibitions of abusing power explicit, NGOs regularly led and governments (sometimes) followed. Any and every proposed change of inter-governmental human rights policy stumbles into 'the paradox that is central to the human rights struggle: the main protector of human rights – the authority one must in the end rely on to enforce human rights standards – is also the main violator.'[18]

It is worthwhile recalling that 'we are the people' was a call to the peaceful revolution which preceded the dismantling of the Berlin Wall. Another peaceful revolution, the mass participation of NGOs at the Vienna Conference on Human Rights, called for the dismantling of walls around the inter-governmental human rights system. The sheer number of human rights NGOs at the Vienna Conference exceeded all expectations; they outnumbered governments at least four times. While various registers and directories usually list a few hundred, those registered in Vienna numbered 1529. The total number of registered NGO participants was 3691. The composition of the NGO community had changed dramatically: the largest number still coming from Western Europe (426), followed by Asia (270), Latin America (236), Africa (202) and North America (178). The high number, excellent organisation and effectiveness of Asian human rights NGOs was one of the most surprising and promising aspects of the conference.[19]

'We the peoples of the United Nations…'. Thus begins the Charter of the United Nations. It is paradoxical that a major scandal at the Vienna Conference on Human Rights was the deletion of the 's', where peoples were downgraded into people, thus demonstrating that governments are erecting yet another wall, previously deemed dismantled. The topic was the indigenous peoples of the world. The right to self-determination, the only collective right explicitly added to the listing of individual rights and forming the first part of both main human rights treaties (that on civil and political, as well as the one on economic, social and cultural rights), has effectively been de-recognised. Besides peoples under colonial rule there are hardly any left – so who are the peoples of the United Nations today? Who is the 'we' at the beginning of the Charter? When the Charter was formulated, the 'we' was less than a third of the current United Nations membership; the bulk of humanity was 'peoples' under colonial rule, due to await their independence for another 20 years.

The current soul-searching within human rights is taking place against profound changes: human rights became in the early 1990s a fashionable topic, particularly the issue of external monitoring. Because its results easily led to the cutting off of development finance, it is punitive. Much as missionaries ventured into developing countries long before they became

---

18 The Commonwealth Human Rights Initiative – *Put Our World to Rights. A Report by a Non-governmental Advisory Group chaired by Hon. Flora MacDonald*, London, August 1991.

19 Ludwig Boltzmann Institute of Human Rights – World Conference on Human Rights, Vienna, 14 to 25 June 1993, *NGO-Newsletter Number 4*, July 1993.

'developing', human rights missions proliferate in our times to document human rights violations. The right to determine what constitutes a violation is taken for granted, as is the right to undertake whatever action on the behalf of victims is deemed appropriate by external monitors. External monitoring in non-Western countries by Western NGOs has therefore been forcefully challenged, while their tendency to treat local NGOs merely as informants and to continue 'safari research' has come under severe criticism. The essential defining feature of NGOs used to be that of working for others, whether it was the eradication of slavery before the Second World War, or the freeing of political prisoners with Amnesty International in the 1960s. The human rights landscape has changed in the meantime and NGOs will have to change as well.

Another reason for change is the necessity to move beyond the exposing of violations. The prevailing tendency of international human rights bodies is, like NGOs, to state what is wrong, but to invoke the lack of resources when asked to help to put things right. This inaction goes, however, beyond resources and challenges the very essence of the universality of human rights: who has the right to determine what human rights entail? The voices of victims were heard loud and clear outside and below official Vienna Conference premises (the walls did not actually crack), and if the message 'we are the people' did not find its way into the final document it dominated the media coverage. The criticism of the UN human rights work thus increased, and the establishment of the High Commissioner for Human Rights may have been its one result.

Drastic changes of the UN human rights system to make it efficient and effective are easy to formulate but have thus far proved impossible to put into practice. As mentioned above, human rights are an art more than a science – no matter how good proposals for change are, they will only be put into practice if governments decide so. The best proposals aim to change the essential features of the United Nations. Indeed, supra-national human rights protection would be much more effective if guaranteed by judicial rather than political bodies: the best way to depoliticise human rights work internationally is to apply the same rule that has been adopted nationally, namely the rule of law. Separation of the judiciary from the legislature and the executive was designed a very long time ago and has survived because it is a sound principle. Because human rights address abuses of power and are therefore inherently political, strengthening the rule of law is crucial. Human rights would have a higher priority in law and in practice were it not for the fact that international law primarily regulates relations between, not within, states. The unwritten but operative rule for implementing changes within the UN human rights work is that only marginal changes are accepted; if proposals 'present a danger of real reform, they are carefully laid to rest'.[20] The creation of the High Commissioner for Human Rights well illustrates the process whereby an originally anticipated reform – making the UN human rights work visible and effective – was in practice transformed into a marginal change – a small office restricted by a minuscule budget, diplomatic rather than expert staff, and a carefully worded mandate. The High Commissioner has the task to make the right to development viable ('to promote and protect the realisation of the right to development'), but his mandate regarding conventional human rights work, namely violations of long-established and well-defined individual rights, is less clear. His task is 'to play an active role in removing the current obstacles and in meeting the challenges to the full realisation of all human rights and in preventing the continuation of human rights violations throughout the world.'[21] This was dubbed as 'Asian compromise'.[22]

The opposition to increased powers regarding human rights granted to the United Nations goes beyond the often described verbal duels between Western and Asian and Middle Eastern governments. Non-Western NGOs have added their voice, asking whether 'the High Commissioner will be able to focus upon human rights violations within Western societies themselves? Will the High Commissioner be given the opportunity to assess the rise of racism in both Europe and the United States and the fears it has generated among minorities living in the West or will he be ordered to keep the spotlight on Tiananmen and China? A number of governments and citizens' groups in the South are aware of this. It explains their cautious attitude towards the High Commissioner's post. Perhaps the only way of ensuring that the High Commissioner is relatively free of the powerful forces which control the global system is for Western human rights and other citizens' groups to monitor carefully the pronouncements and actions of the High Commissioner.'[23]

Because the main constituency for enhancing the human rights work of the United Nations is Western governments whose political constituencies are vocal – and often effective – in changing international policies of their

---

20 Strohal, C. – 'The United Nations responses to human rights violations', in: Mahoney, K.E. and Mahoney, P. (eds.) – *Human Rights in the Twenty-First Century: A Global Challenge*, Martinus Nijhoff Publishers, Dordrecht, 1993, p. 354.

21 United Nations – High Commissioner for the promotion and protection of all human rights, General Assembly resolution 48/141 of 20 December 1993, paras. 3(c) and (f).

22 Awanohara, S. – Asian compromise. UN gets human rights chief with trimmed powers, *Far Eastern Economic Review*, 30 December 1993 – 6 January 1994.

23 Muzaffar, C. – *Just Commentary*, No. 7, January 1994, Just World Trust, Penang.

own governments, pressure for change can make an impact on the United Nations. This, however, requires a profound change in the policies of Western governments themselves. The first necessary change looks simple, but will be difficult to put into practice: it necessitates acceptance of the fact that human rights are universal, geographically and conceptually, hence human rights violations in the North (racial discrimination, for example) and by the North (notably, those committed in the name of 'development') should be addressed as violations. Obstacles to introducing this change are many. They range from the rejection of economic and social rights, increasingly visible not only at the international level, but also within the North. Reducing human rights to individual freedom – in conditions of deep inequalities – is contrary to the core concept of human rights. This concept is jeopardising the very 'human' in human rights: instead of equal rights of all human beings, human rights are increasingly seen as yet another barrier between 'us' and 'them'. The human rights movement emerged much before human rights rhetoric, more than a hundred years ago, to combat slavery. In the 1960s it started spreading worldwide, with those whose rights were protected working on behalf of those whose rights were violated. In the 1990s it has come dangerously close to those whose rights are already protected denying the equal rights of others. This necessitates the recognition of a simple fact – that our rights are limited by the equal rights of all other members of the human family. It is easy to illustrate this point: no Northern government has ratified the Convention on the Protection of Human Rights of Migrant Workers despite the fact that the increasing rejection of migrants is visible throughout the North; the Northern human rights movement remains silent on this issue. Attempts to escape from desperate poverty are treated as economic rather than political issues, and borders fortified so that victims of unequal access of resources have nowhere to flee to. The myth that human rights require no more than the political will of a government is perpetuated rather than challenged. Decisions on resource allocations are by definition political, and the political will of Northern governments could be, but is not, challenged when it comes to abuses of economic power. As the human rights movement emerged in the 1960s with the focus on abuses of physical power by governments, to respond effectively to this challenge of the 1990s it would have to focus on abuses on economic power. As already emphasised, in the field of human rights governments respond to public pressure and where there is none, they are unlikely to move.

5. UN humanitarian machinery
The need for good and just practice

ANGELA PENROSE

According to the first Under-Secretary General for Humanitarian Affairs and Emergency Relief Coordinator, Jan Eliasson, the creation in 1992 of the United Nations Department of Humanitarian Affairs (DHA) coincided with 'an extraordinary demand on the United Nations to provide humanitarian assistance under unprecedented conditions of complexity and insecurity'.[1] The establishment of the DHA in 1992 was, however, not coincidental. It was an attempt to improve the institutional response to this demand. The new arrangements were based on the UN's 'central and unique role ... in providing leadership and coordinating the efforts of the international community to support the affected countries'.[2]

The nature of contemporary humanitarian challenges

Throughout the 1980s concern grew that the international response to humanitarian crises was inadequate. General Assembly Resolution 46/182 of December 1991, *Strengthening the Coordination of Humanitarian Emergency Assistance of the United Nations,* which led to the creation of DHA and the appointment of the Emergency Relief Coordinator, was the culmination of mounting pressure from donor governments and non-governmental organisations involved in the delivery of emergency relief.

Increasing complexities
Emergencies have never been simple, but operational effectiveness in response to natural disasters such as floods, cyclones and disasters has, over

---

1 Jan Eliasson, 1993.
2 UN GA Resolution 46/182.

time, improved. Increasingly, however, disasters are 'man-made', and those involved in the provision of humanitarian assistance are confronted with unprecedented dilemmas. These man-made disasters may be considered as 'complex emergencies', and they have been defined by the DHA as occurring when political and/or military conflicts, are one of the main causes of humanitarian disaster.[3]

The winding down of the Cold War has had global repercussions. Some of these have been positive, resulting in moves towards peace in Ethiopia and Cambodia, but the sudden end of support for regimes by one or another Cold War adversary has brought many long-impending weaknesses to the surface. Nation-state structures that were imposed during the age of empires, and then bolstered by Cold War contest, have begun to collapse, as in Somalia. States have tended to fragment as demands for self-determination and autonomy emerge from the long rigidities.

There has been considerable progress in the period since the second world war in developing mechanisms for preventing or mitigating interstate wars. However, internal conflicts have become a greater security issue. The root of much civil unrest is to be found in the desire for self-determination and for ethnic expression, exacerbated by political and religious ideology; competition for resources; and the lack of representative political structures through which frustrations might otherwise be expressed.

The roots of conflict and disaster did not all lie within Cold War rivalries, however. On analysis many of the current conflicts derive from an earlier period of liberation struggles from colonial empires. Angola has suffered almost continuous war since the struggle for independence began in the 1950s. Conflict has interfered with development agendas throughout the post-colonial era.

Increased unrest has led to the massive displacement of populations, and the increasing need for relief has led to a considerable rise in the flow of humanitarian assistance from OECD countries in recent years. Between 1989 and 1990 humanitarian aid increased by 30 per cent. In 1990-91 it jumped by nearly 130 per cent. Yet resources fall far short of demand and only in a few cases does the provision of humanitarian aid in itself resolve the problem.

Dissatisfaction with the slow, inadequate and often inappropriate international humanitarian response resulted from experience of a range of very different crises. Undoubtedly the main impetus for reform arose out of the Kurdish refugee crisis of April 1991. The plight of over one and a

---

3 'Complex Emergencies: A United Approach', DHA/UNDRO News, July/August 1992, pp. 4-6.

half million Iraqi Kurds fleeing towards the Turkish and Iranian borders after attacks from Saddam Hussein's forces convinced observers that important precedents had been set which represented a new era of international humanitarian response. Security Council Resolution 688 of April 1991 required 'that Iraq allow immediate access by international organisations to all those in need of assistance in all parts of Iraq'. United States, British, French and Dutch forces took action to re-establish safe havens within northern Iraq in order to enable the displaced Kurds to move to more sheltered and accessible sites where they were provided with emergency assistance.

The infringement of Iraqi sovereignty was significant, but the nature of the crisis and the response to it were not necessarily typical of the previous emergencies which had raised concerns. The high profile nature of the action which was carried out in the aftermath of the Gulf War distracted attention from the real nature of the problems of humanitarian response. The operation in Iraqi Kurdistan was only possible in the context of the end of the Cold War and the immediate aftermath of the Gulf War. Ironically, while the massive emergency operation in which military forces played a part raised awareness of the limitations of the international community's ability to respond, at the same time it sidetracked the movement to improve humanitarian response, and took it down dangerous, expensive and interventionist paths.

In the short period since the end of the Cold War appeared to augur a new international climate, there has been dangerous experimentation in dealing with internal strife, disintegration of states, internal displacement and rising national security concerns. The UN has pursued more actively the resolution of conflict and humanitarian crises, but it has gone through a troubled transitional phase as it seeks ways of meeting the increased demands made upon it.

The main challenge is to deliver humanitarian assistance in the midst of civil conflict, disputed sovereignty or government breakdown. In such a context the present UN faces a diverse and often contradictory task. The apparent new range of options which are open to the international community allows the UN and its most powerful member states in the Security Council to become directly involved in humanitarian response. This involvement has taken the form of increased intervention through military action, sanctions, and preventive and humanitarian diplomacy. The more complex the political and military role of the UN in an emergency, the more its humanitarian operation is compromised by association.

The humanitarian operation in Iraqi Kurdistan is an example of the

problems facing the United Nations:
- incompatibility of political, military and humanitarian roles;
- the need for consistency of response;
- the state-centric mandates of UN Agencies;
- the need for improved operational performance;
- the need for timely and appropriate response;
- the need to recognise the long-term nature of humanitarian emergencies.

Principles or politics

Events in Iraq, as well as other recent emergencies, reveal that equal levels of humanitarian assistance are not applied consistently in every emergency. The selective and discriminating nature of the international community's involvement suggests that equity and need are not necessarily the main criteria of international assistance. Considerable thought is being given by those involved in the provision of humanitarian assistance to establishing principles of conduct.

The first edition of a training manual *Humanitarian Principles and Operational Dilemmas in War Zones*[4], prepared by the DHA in collaboration with the UNDP, is based upon the Providence Principles of Humanitarian Action, the first two of which are 'relief of life-threatening suffering' and 'proportionality to need'. In reality, however, humanitarian action is still driven by political attitudes towards governments, strategic priorities, intercultural factors and media attention, and not even lip service is paid to these principles.

Failures in Somalia and Bosnia have dampened the enthusiasm for humanitarian intervention. At the opening session of the UN General Assembly in September 1993, US President Clinton and Britain's Foreign Secretary Douglas Hurd, both representing governments which had encouraged the development of the UN's peace-keeping activities, demanded restraints on peace-keeping operations. 'If the American people are to say yes to peacekeeping', said President Clinton, 'the United Nations must know when to say no'. Within days the United Nations said 'No' to Burundi.

The diversity of interests and the uneven allocation of power and resources which exist between the member states inevitably lead to the political and financial prioritisation of humanitarian assistance. Humanitarian

---

4 Larry Minear and Thomas Weiss, *Humanitarian Principles and Operational Dilemmas in War Zones*, UNDP and DHA Disaster Management Training Programme, 1993

response inevitably has resource implications, especially when it is support-ed by military intervention. It has become increasingly clear that resource constraints will mean that humanitarian response becomes discretionary. Whilst it may become the case that means have to be found to regulate the discretionary response, current steps towards devising criteria are worry-ing. The purport of President Clinton's speech to the General Assembly was formulated in May 1994 as Presidential Decision Directive 25 (PDD 25), laying down strict guidelines for US participation in or approval of a UN operation, with or without troops. It is reasonable to expect criteria such as that the crisis must represent a threat to international peace and security, but to assert that any intervention must have the consent of all parties and a realistic exit strategy represents considerable backtracking.

UN involvement in the sustained protection and assistance to those in need in Iraqi Kurdistan lessened as the international community's priori-ties shifted after the most acute emergency phase. In order to maintain re-lations with the government of Iraq, the DHA signed a new Memorandum of Understanding with it on 22 October 1992, which gives Baghdad a great deal of control over the type, volume and destination of aid to the north. Some NGOs felt unable to sign. Agencies like the United Nations Develop-ment Programme (UNDP), the Food and Agriculture Organisation of the UN (FAO) and the World Health Organisation (WHO) are accustomed to working through national governments and are obliged to operate through Baghdad, but ways must be found of working directly with the Kurdish administration in the north.

Wrong perceptions of crisis

Categorising emergencies as periods of sudden, unusual and short-term stress is a misrepresentation of many current areas of humanitarian need. They are seldom temporary crises after which society returns to 'normal'. In Iraqi Kurdistan the provision of emergency relief and protection through the temporary deployment of Western military forces did not ad-dress the broader political and economic issues which gave rise to the orig-inal crisis. The lack of attention paid to the Kurds since the establishment of the safe havens underlines the limitations of providing short-term solu-tions for complex, long-term problems.[5] In countries like Angola, Somalia, Southern Sudan, Liberia and Iraqi Kurdistan the provision of humanitari-an assistance should become a long-term process of supporting communi-

5   David Keen, *The Kurds in Iraq: How safe is their haven now?*, Save the Children, 1993.

ties while they cope with and adapt to the reality of continual crisis.

The response in Iraq suggests that the increased demands and increased expectations have not been fused with an increased understanding of the nature of humanitarian crises and the appropriate response.

The serious drought-related famines in the mid-1980s in the Sahel and Horn of Africa resulted in a better understanding of response mechanisms. (In these cases 'response' is defined as the provision of additional resources, over and above normal development aid, channelled to famine-prone people, which assists them to withstand the effects of declining access to food.)[6] There was also better understanding of why certain populations are vulnerable, and why appropriate response should be geared to the saving of livelihoods and not just lives. Although relief operations are often perceived as timely because they succeed in averting widespread famine deaths, they are often too late to avert a serious deterioration in livelihoods. Once livelihoods have been destroyed, a population remains vulnerable and dependent upon assistance until their livelihoods have been restored.

A man in a highland village in Tigray, Ethiopia, expressed his predicament in 1993, a year when there were better than average rains in northern Ethiopia.

'I would say that more than two-thirds of the people in this place went to Sudan in 1984-85, and I was one of them. Many of the rest went for resettlement. I sold every last one of my livestock some time before we finally went. We walked nearly all the way to Sudan: I remember we had only one journey in a truck. In Sudan we lived first at Kassala and then at a smaller town, and we were in tents the whole time – more than two and a half years. Most of the time we had nothing to do, but sometimes we could make money carrying water in the town or doing other bits of work...

What I want to tell you is that we manage to get just enough to live, but we have never been able to buy animals to make up for what we lost in 1984. We can't improve our lives since we came back, that is our problem. Now we survive, but we don't prosper.'[7]

---

6 Hussein, K., Buchanan-Smith, M., Davies S., Petty, C., *Predicting and Preventing Famine:An Agenda for the 1990s*, Report of the Conference at Wiston House, Sussex, 4-6 November 1992.

7 Holt, J., Lawrence, M., *Making Ends Meet: A survey of the food economy of the Ethiopian north-east highlands*, Save the Children UK, 1993.

Large parts of highland Ethiopia are in food deficit for most of the year. Since the beginning of the 1980s, billions of dollars have been spent on food aid in Ethiopia and the effectiveness of this relief operation should not be undervalued. The Save the Children survey quoted above established that food aid deliveries bore a reasonable relationship to food deficits, as identified by villagers. In the bad harvest year of 1990/91, food aid managed to meet a considerable level of need. One of the main successes of food aid was that it reached almost all the villages in Tigray and some 82 per cent of villages in north Wollo, the two major areas affected by drought.

Despite great resilience, however, there is little that the remote inhabitants of this area can do to lesson their own vulnerability and dependence on food aid without rehabilitation measures. These include access to seeds, fertilisers, pest control measures and veterinary services to increase productivity. Access to all of these is severely limited by the lack of infrastructure.

The experience of the last 20 years in Ethiopia and elsewhere teaches that food crises and conflicts are not exceptional events. The roots of conflict and disaster do not all lie in Cold War rivalries but in economic and social disparities that interact with struggles for power and rights. Long-term processes are at work, such as environmental degradation, human displacement, diminishing access to land under population increase and declining terms of trade. Those responsible for deliberately exacerbating the historical ethnic tensions between Hutu and Tutsi in Rwanda, with such appalling results in 1994, were only able to do so in the context of human insecurity engendered by these long-term forces. Any form of intervention in times of crisis demands an understanding of these processes, and will fail unless root causes are quickly addressed.

The main machinery of international response and actors in the 'international community'

How can there be an effective response to crises when causes are long-term and complex? Is it possible to develop a 'system' that can respond?

Humanitarian response is based upon the premise that individuals have rights, including claims to subsistence, that are basic to humanity rather than dependent on membership of a nation state. These rights are now firmly embedded in an international framework of humanitarian law including the UN Charter, the Geneva Conventions of 1949, and the Additional Protocols of 1977. The maintenance of this law is problematic, however, despite the existence of impartial humanitarian organisations whose purpose is to provide humanitarian assistance.

The international 'system'

It has become customary to speak of the international community as operating an international system for humanitarian response. The main members of this community are considered to be intergovernmental organisations, including the specialised agencies of the UN and other multilateral donors, in particular the European Union; bilateral donors such as the Overseas Development Administration (ODA); international agencies, in particular the International Committee of the Red Cross; and non-governmental organisations. Mandates and capacities may vary but each actor in the system is dependent upon donor governments and/or the general public for funding.

There are limitations to defining the 'international system' in this way. The most obvious limitation is the difficulty of extending the description of the system to those in need of assistance and describing how the international community engages with them. All too frequently, the analysis becomes reduced to an international community on one side which channels or delivers assistance to 'beneficiaries' on the other. The roles of the various types of recipient are often less clearly defined.

The political context is acknowledged to be an inescapable factor in determining how the 'system' will function. It is often the nature of the governing structures of the affected communities which determine which actors within the international community play a role. It has been said that current debates on improving the UN's response tend 'to conflate the institutional or technical difficulties with the political problems and thus to exacerbate the difficulties in dealing with either'.[8] There is no doubt that institutional and political factors are inextricably linked. It has been demonstrated in many circumstances that however expertly technical issues may have been refined, there are political or institutional constraints on their application.

Current and recent humanitarian crises demonstrate the variety and intractability of the political dimension. In Liberia, Angola, Somalia and Southern Sudan, agencies face the problem of maintaining the non-partisan delivery of aid in theatres of contested sovereignty. There are several

---

8 Reginald Herbold Green, 'Calamities and Catastrophes: Extending the UN Response', *Third World Quarterly* 14 (1993): 31-55

instances where, despite accurate early warning systems providing information on impending food crises, political factors such as the relationship between donors and governments impede timely response. In Ethiopia, during the Mengistu regime, Northern donors' dislike of the regime undoubtedly led to delays in response to famine in 1984. Early warning information became ensnared in controversy and political negotiation between donors and the Sudanese government in 1990/91.

The situation in the former Yugoslavia illustrates the definitive role of antagonists with complete disregard for international humanitarian law in restricting humanitarian action in contemporary emergencies. Within each of the countries, political leaders lacked authority over military commanders who targeted civilians, complicated the convoy approval processes and insisted upon reciprocity before granting humanitarian access or evacuating the most vulnerable.[9]

The question is not whether political, institutional and technical issues are conflated, but whether it is feasible that a state-centric, global organisation which is committed to finding a political solution can maintain neutral humanitarian operations at the same time. Is the type of response 'co-ordinated' by the United Nations likely to lead to solutions, or will it in fact exacerbate the problems?

Analysis of the international response to the crisis in Somalia from the fall of Mohamed Siad Barre in January 1991 (see chart, pages 122-123) suggests that there is a mismatch between the nature of the problem and the response, based on the inability of the 'system' to analyse the problem. The intense fighting of the civil war rendered the work of international agencies working in Somalia ineffective and dangerous. By early January 1991, most agencies, governments and non-governmental organisations had removed their remaining expatriate staff. By the end of February the International Committee of the Red Cross (ICRC), and a small number of non-governmental organisations (NGOs) including Médecins Sans Frontières and Save the Children, had resumed their activities and were attempting to draw attention to the deteriorating humanitarian situation.

At this stage the need for UN agencies with development-related mandates to re-engage with structures in Somalia was as great, if not greater, than the need for those with humanitarian components in their mandates.

---

9   Larry Minear et al, *Humanitarian Action in the Former Yugoslavia: the UN's Role 1991-1993*, Providence, The Thomas J. Watson Jr Institute for International Studies, 1994.

UN intervention in Somalia: A summary of UN action in Somalia 1991 to 1994

1991: 'The year of missed opportunities' [10]

Lack of urgency and inability of UN agencies to reengage with local structures because of disputed sovereignty, government breakdown and insecurity. The requirement of the UN agencies to relate operationally and politically to institutions of state limited their flexibility of response and the range of appropriate partners. The failure to engage earlier contributed to worsen a situation where more drastic intervention was made to appear necessary and inevitable.

Somalia was portrayed by the media as an intractable civil war. [11]

January to December 1992: UN ceasefire negotiations dominate proceedings and displace humanitarian action

Intense UN political activity to negotiate a ceasefire: 24 April, Security Council (SC) Resolution 751 established a UN Operation in Somalia (UNOSOM); 4 May, Ambassador Mohammed Sahnoun, the Security Council's Special Representative, arrived in Somalia. Despite the relief plan and the arrival of first UN relief food, by November 1992 NGOs were still undertaking almost 90 per cent of all relief and rehabilitation work in the country. The lack of legitimate partners appeared to limit both UN relief and rehabilitation activities. No overall UN strategy combining political and humanitarian initiatives was formulated. There was a lack of information and contacts.

December 1992 to April 1993: UNITAF, the first phase of UN military intervention

SC Resolution 794 authorised US forces to 'use all necessary means to establish as soon as possible a secure environment for humanitarian

---

10 Mark Bowden, 'The Year of missed opportunities', *Conflict and International Relief in Contemporary African Famines,* Report on Conference organised by save the Children and the London School of Hygiene and Tropical Medicine, March 1992.

11 Hugo Slim and Emma Visman, 'Evacuation, Intervention and Retaliation: United Nations Humanitarian Operations in Somalia 1991-1993', in *Sovereignty and Suffering,* ed. John Harris, Pinter/Save the Children, 1994.

relief operations in Somalia'. US-led 'Operation Restore Hope' was launched immediately. Initially the securing of main ports and airports appeared to enable major food deliverers to provide a better service. A general improvement in nutritional status and overall security was observed. But many agencies believe that the level of looting was exaggerated and the worst of the famine had already passed. The timing, justification, and conduct of UNITAF thus raise serious policy issues. Mohammed Sahnoun resigned.

April to June 1993: the handover to UNOSOM II

Under SC Resolution 814 UNOSOM II assumed an increased responsibility for peace enforcement under Admiral Howe, new Special Representative of the Secretary General (SRSG). UNOSOM commanders interpreted the mandate in a manner that led to military conflict with the most powerful faction;[12] 23 Pakistani UNOSOM II troops were killed on 5 June.

June to December 1993: escalation of conflict and the impact of UN military operations on humanitarian aid

SC Resolution 837 called for an investigation into those responsible for the killings and demanded the 'relocation' of expatriate staff in anticipation of reprisals. There was an escalation of violence and concern over not only the UN's neutrality but all international humanitarian assistance. All humanitarian programmes were severely disrupted. In August 1993 UNOSOM Humanitarian moved from UNOSOM II HQ to distance itself from political and military activities.[13]

December 1993 to September 1994: revised UN mandate; phasing out of extensive military operations

Withdrawal of French, Belgian and finally US forces.

---

12 Tom Farer, 'United States Military Participation in United Nations Operations in Somalia: Roots of the conflict with General Mohamed, Farah Aideed and a Basis for Accommodation and Renewed Progress', submission to the Committee on Armed Services of the House of Representatives, 14 October 1993.

13 Emma Visman, *Military Humanitarian Intervention in Somalia*, Report, Save the Children, London, December 1993.

Action at this stage would have been rehabilitative and arguably preemptive.[14]

At the time of Siad Barre's fall there was extensive need for reconstruction. There was total economic breakdown at all levels, including the collapse of local food markets. The banking system was also destroyed, resulting in a cessation of once substantial remittances from abroad. Operational NGOs, and Somalis themselves as represented by the putative government of the United Somali Congress (USC)[15], identified a major humanitarian crisis fusing with the political crisis, creating a 'complex emergency'.

As the situation deteriorated an increasing number of NGOs, many of them without previous experience in Somalia, began to undertake programmes to avoid or alleviate the impending disaster. Observing this familiar scenario, Save the Children's regional representative highlighted the 'need for (a) Somalia relief coordinator immediately'.[16] Many NGOs were based in Nairobi, and in February a meeting between the UNDP Somalia Resident Representative and NGO representatives was held at which the need for the UN to return to Mogadishu specifically to assume a coordinating role was expressed.

Security

Closely enmeshed with the political and humanitarian issues are issues of security. It is difficult to unravel the role played by security during 1991 and 1992 in Somalia. Guidelines on the security of UN personnel appear to have prevented the UN from dealing with a humanitarian emergency.

The UNDP Resident Representative stated that an early return to Somalia was not feasible on the grounds of the lack of a stable security situation.[17] A UN Reconnaissance Mission to Mogadishu in February also gave the absence of security and the lack of sovereignty as reasons for not re-establishing a UN presence. Neither the security nor the sovereignty factors prevented some NGOs and the ICRC from working between February and August 1991. Throughout 1991 and 1992, SCF pursued the objective of rehabilitating basic health services not damaged by fighting.

In its slowness to engage at that early period the UN missed the opportu-

---

14 House of Commons Foreign Affairs Committee, *The Role of the UN in Emergencies*, submission by Save the Children Fund UK.
15 USC Appeal to all Governments, Humanitarian Organisations and Agencies, 27 January 1991.
16 Telex, Ben Foot to SCF, London 6 February 1991.
17 Minutes of Meeting between UN and NGOs, 7 February 1991.

nity to conserve and strengthen government structures and to support the many committed and competent Somalis who demonstrated their willingness to keep systems operating. As the situation deteriorated, the humanitarian imperative became predominant, but from the end of the civil war there was also the imperative to halt the damage being done to the development process. It was vital to re-establish trade and resuscitate the local economy. It would have been easier to attempt this early in 1991 than very late in 1992.

Security has become a major issue in the former Yugoslavia where, in a 13-month period beginning in September 1992, United Nations High Commission for Refugees (UNHCR) and other humanitarian personnel were involved in 660 separate security incidents. Nine people involved in UNHCR operations and 58 United Nations Protection Force (UNPRO-FOR) soldiers were killed. However, the mandate of the United Nations Protection Force in the former Yugoslavia was limited, and eventually concern for the security of UN military and humanitarian personnel inhibited more forceful attempts to bring conflict to an end. The effectiveness of protection personnel travelling around in armoured vehicles was also limited.

Recent attempts to reform the international system

At a theoretical level, General Assembly Resolution 46/182, *Strengthening the Coordination of Humanitarian Assistance of the United Nations*, attempted to address many of the problems affecting humanitarian assistance. In particular, the Guiding Principles of the Resolution explicitly recognise the link between the underlying crisis in development faced by many less developed countries and emergencies. The need to build in a continuum from relief to rehabilitation during emergency response is firmly stated, and it is affirmed that 'emergency assistance should be provided in ways that will be supportive of recovery and long-term development'.

Many people with practical experience of attempting to provide humanitarian assistance in different contexts were encouraged to see such fundamental principles expressed, but many were pessimistic about a small new department's ability to bring about the necessary change in attitude and approach within the UN. There were particular concerns regarding the ability of the DHA to coordinate the activities of the funds and specialised agencies – UNHCR, UNICEF, WFP, WHO, UNDP, FAO (all of which have a key role to play in the first response to disasters) – that had a role in emergency response. There is good reason to believe that these fears have been fulfilled.

The UN Disaster Relief Organisation (UNDRO) was a forerunner of the DHA. It was beset with problems since it was set up in 1971. UNDRO was also intended to coordinate the relief activities of the components of the UN system and UN assistance with other sources. UNDRO did not control resources being channelled to emergencies, nor did it become directly involved in the delivery of relief. It therefore never succeeded in fulfilling its coordination role adequately.

Many aspects of its performance were criticised, in particular the calibre of its personnel. As the text of GA 46/182 was being transformed into institutional reality, the decision was made to absorb UNDRO complete with its existing staff into the new DHA. There is no doubt that Jan Eliasson espoused the humanitarian diplomacy aspect of his role assiduously, but this legacy of over 100 officials tuned to the existing mandate of UNDRO was a serious encumbrance for the new organisation.

In order to become a truly persuasive facilitator within the system, the DHA has still to demonstrate its expertise in the critical areas of information gathering, assessment, networking, fundraising and monitoring which complement the expertise of the operational agencies and NGOs in affected countries. This expertise should include the ability to combine an understanding of problems in the field with the capacity to formulate a strategic overview. As the DHA inherited a large number of its staff which were not selected for their competence in these areas of expertise or field experience, it found it difficult to convince those within the UN system and the wider international system of its competence at an early enough stage.

This was not the only factor which contributed to the DHA's failure to make an early impact on the system. The division of responsibilities between New York and Geneva led to inefficiency and delays which have not yet been resolved despite attempts at restructuring. Other factors that have contributed to the early difficulties of the DHA are the polycentric nature of the UN and coordination with funds and agencies; the reluctance of the main humanitarian assistance agencies to collaborate on substantiating what coordination would mean in practice; and the lack of resources arising from the failure of member states to provide the DHA with necessary backing.

---

18 Paul Taylor, *Options for Reform of the International System for Humanitarian Response*, London School of Economics, Centre for Global Governance/Save the Children, 1993, and in *Sovereignty and Suffering*, ed. John Harris, Pinter/Save the Children, 1994.

Coordination

The problems of the polycentric nature of the system and the lack of a central 'brain' have often been deplored.[18] The Specialised Agencies have constitutional independence from one another and no central authority has legal authority over them. The UN funds involved are all legally responsible to the Secretary-General, but the funds have never been brought under proper UN authority. Proper coordination would entail the managed transfer of responsibilities and staff between agencies as appropriate. There has been little tradition of such coordination within the UN system and the development of the DHA is perceived to involve a reduction in the area of competence of the funds and agencies.

The principle of coordination is at the centre of the new arrangements and was identified as a critical factor required in the strengthening of the UN's humanitarian system. Despite the public support given to DHA by the heads of the agencies, there is as yet little evidence of agreement within the system on the nature of the coordination function required of DHA. There appears to be agreement that DHA does not have a supra-agency or supra-national role, but agreement on a less threatening role is less easy to obtain.

At least three of DHA's specific functions were designed to aid coordination: the preparation of 'consolidated appeals' for funds and relief materials; to serve as 'a central focal point with governments and inter-governmental and non-governmental organisations concerning United Nations relief operations'; and 'to facilitate a rapid and coordinated response of the organisations of the system' by means of the Central Emergency Revolving Fund (CERF), initially of $50 million. It was also 'to be involved with the systematic pooling and analysis of early warning information'.

The consolidated appeal process (CAP) presented the potential for the UN to assess need, develop an operational plan, request funds and track expenditure. In most cases to date, however, the consolidated appeal has been a funding document based on a list of projects with little or no attempt to formulate them into an integrated plan. The potential for devising an overall strategy based on a better analysis of needs, and involving all parties, received theoretical recognition in a review of the consolidated appeal process conducted by DHA. General Assembly Resolution 46/182 envisaged two functions for the CAP: a means by which the UN agencies could mobilise resources in order to implement programmes that would meet the needs of people affected by complex emergencies; and a mechanism to coordinate the response of various actors involved in meeting the emergency needs throughout the course of an emergency. DHA's review attempted to widen the definition to incorporate a genuine process through which all the actors in the system would be mobilised. It defined the process in terms of a continuum from initial disaster planning through assessment, the development of a strategy which would 'provide the blue print on which all agencies and organisations agree to work together', the inter-agency appeal to the post-appeal activities.

The development of this process was in direct response to the demand from donors that the entire UN system should synthesise its resource needs into a single appeal. The criticism of the appeals in Somalia and the former Yugoslavia was that they have been a list of existing or planned projects rather than a statement of objectives and articulation of strategy. Nonetheless, donor government response to this new approach to appeals has averaged only 25 per cent of the sums requested.[19] A self-defeating result of this tendency is for the UN to attempt to make more 'realistic' appeals based on what they are likely to get rather than what needs have been assessed to be. The Consolidated Appeal for UN activities in the former Yugoslavia for the first half of 1994 stated that it did 'not attempt to assess and respond to the totality of needs throughout Yugoslavia, but rather focuses upon those which are within the capacity and competence of its agencies and their partners to deliver and implement'.

The original regulations governing use of CERF funds were too restrictive, encouraging caution rather than action. UN agencies had to secure undertakings from donors to replace money drawn down from CERF in advance of using the funds.

The Inter-Agency Standing Committee

The Inter-Agency Standing Committee (IASC), which brings together all UN agencies and other actors such as the ICRC and key NGOs, was designed to be an essential component of the process of strengthening the coordination of international humanitarian response. The main committee had met only six times by the end of 1993, hardly frequently enough for a body expected to be the nerve centre of systematic cooperation. Although various Working Groups of the IASC met regularly, important matters raised in these groups were seldom considered at the higher policy and decision making level.

---

19 UN Department of Humanitarian Affairs, Consolidated Inter-Agency Humanitarian Assistance Appeals: Summary of Requirements and Contributions, Summary #4, 20 April 1994.

The IASC represented the best opportunity to create a coordinating body which truly represented the wider international community. Such a body had the potential to make key strategic decisions about appropriate coordination mechanisms on a case by case basis. It may also have prevented the DHA from becoming subordinate, not just to the funds and agencies, but to the more knowledgeable departments of peacekeeping and political affairs.

Jan Eliasson noted in July 1993 that 'only US$1 was being spent on the humanitarian assistance for every US$10 spent on the military peace-enforcement operation', and that the $US166 million requested by the UN for humanitarian operations in Somalia remained underfunded. Member states have not followed through the creation of the DHA, which to a high degree was designed to their own specifications, so that it has the resources needed to reform and equip itself for the role of facilitation and leadership which they claimed was needed.

In Somalia the UN humanitarian operations were marginalised. In the former Yugoslavia the relationship between DHA and UNHCR, which received its mandate as lead agency two months before the GA Resolution called for the creation of DHA, was never clarified. The Under-Secretary-General was sometimes excluded from meetings involving the political affairs and peace-keeping departments even when humanitarian programmes were closely involved. Jan Eliasson made no public complaint, but there is no doubt that the combined effects of constant criticism of DHA performance, lack of genuine support from UN agencies, the non-consultative style of the Secretary-General and the lack of security in the post (the Secretary-General has a policy of granting Under-Secretary-General contracts of no more than one year at a time) contributed to his decision to resign.

As Peter Hansen succeeds Jan Eliasson as the new Emergency Relief Coordinator there are scaled down expectations of the DHA. Talk of a relief 'Supremo' was always unrealistic, but the more modest hopes engendered by Resolution 46/182 have yet to be realised. The task of the new head of DHA is to convince the different actors that there are benefits in participating in the coordination process. Peter Hansen began by undertaking a major reorganisation of DHA which attempts to address one cause of confusion, the split between Geneva and New York. All complex emergencies are now to be dealt with in New York under a special Complex Emergency Branch which is intended to strengthen contacts with policy making organs of the UN, the Secretary-General and the peace-keeping and political departments. There is also to be a Policy Analysis Branch and a Task Force on Quick Response.

The Security Council has recently emerged as the main forum for debating and planning international humanitarian action. Increasingly it is the Security Council that authorises and sets the parameters of the international community's response to complex emergencies. This action is determined on an ad hoc case by case basis. There is as yet no overall humanitarian policy that sets criteria for interventions and which is transparent to the whole international community.

The neutrality of humanitarian aid

Throughout the Cold War and since its 'end', international armed conflicts have become fewer while non-international armed conflicts have shown higher levels of violence. Different types of conflict are creating new types of challenges for humanitarian work. Even the ICRC is encountering operational conditions very different from its former experience. In some internal conflicts it has been prevented from carrying out its humanitarian mandate because it has been unable to obtain the agreement of all parties involved to respect its neutrality.[20] In May 1992 when an ICRC delegate was killed near Sarajevo, apparently quite deliberately, the ICRC temporarily suspended work. An increasing lack of respect for the provisions of international law is becoming an obstacle, even to the work of the ICRC with transparently humanitarian motives. It is inevitable that in the highly politicised environment of conflicts, the involvement of organisations with multiple objectives and agendas is easily perceived to have political implications.

One outcome of the first UN Security Council meeting to be held at Head of State level in January 1992, was a request to Dr Boutros Boutros-Ghali to suggest ways in which the UN could carry out its peacekeeping and peacemaking roles more effectively. His report, *An Agenda for Peace*, published in July 1992, dealt with the capacity of the UN to expand its preventive diplomacy and peacekeeping roles and introduced proposals for 'post-conflict peace building' and for the funding of peacekeeping operations.

Resolution 46/182 commits the international community to providing humanitarian assistance 'in accordance with the principles of humanity,

---

20 Caratsch, C, *Humanitarian Design and Political Interference: Red Cross Work in the Post-Cold War Period*, *International Relations* Vol XI, Number 4 April 1993.

neutrality and impartiality'. As the UN has felt freer to act in a more dramatic, interventionist style, however, there is concern that the international community's commitment to humanitarian assistance as outlined in Resolution 46/182 has been superseded by the more political and security orientated priorities of *An Agenda for Peace*. These priorities form the new *raison d'être* of the post-Cold War UN. There is growing concern that humanitarian assistance is being perceived as a means to these ends rather than an urgent and inalienable right in itself. There is even concern that the meaning of 'humanitarian' is becoming distorted.

In a variety of contexts – Somalia, the former Yugoslavia, Iraq, Angola – the challenge is to deliver humanitarian assistance in the midst of civil conflict. In such a context the UN is taking on multiple roles – political, military as well as humanitarian. The more complex the political and military role of the UN in an emergency, the more its humanitarian operation is compromised by association. An example of the marginalisation of humanitarian operations was evident in Somalia after the killing of UN Pakistani troops on 5 June 1993, when UN military action destabilised the environment for humanitarian aid.

In situations like Somalia and Iraqi Kurdistan, when NGOs have been looking to the UN humanitarian operation to provide a framework, they have been forced to employ distancing tactics to avoid association with compromised UN efforts. The ICRC normally seeks to distance itself from the UN's humanitarian, political and military activities. It negotiates its own agreement with local authorities and combatants and is unwilling to be associated with either economic or military force.

It was not just NGOs that felt compromised and took action to dissociate themselves from UN policy in Somalia. In August 1993 part of the UN's operation in Somalia, UNOSOM Humanitarian, established its headquarters separately from UNOSOM Force Headquarters in order to distance itself from the UNOSOM military. There have been a number of recent attempts to merge the management of political, security and humanitarian affairs but it is doubtful whether the defence of humanitarian neutrality and impartiality could survive under a closer administrative arrangement.

In Yugoslavia the compatibility of the UN's humanitarian role with its protection role has also been questioned. Far fewer resources and personnel were allocated to protection activities. UNHCR employed 25 officers with protection activities by the end of 1993, although human rights monitors from the UN Centre for Human Rights and UNPROFOR Civilian Police also undertook protection activities. Whilst complementary in theory, the two activities competed in practice when, for example, UNHCR field officers expressed the fear that 'an active human rights policy would complicate our assistance role'.[21]

A more controversial aspect of the protection policies adopted by UNHCR within the former Yugoslavia is that the four million displaced people have had to be 'protected' within the old borders of the country. Initially UNHCR attempted to protect and assist people where they were trying to resist ethnic cleansing. This was seen by some as a dilution of its traditional protection policy, which was based on the right to seek asylum, and as condoning the attitude of many European governments as they ignored their responsibilities to asylum seekers. In the absence of any political solutions, however, UNHCR was forced into the position of assisting people being forcibly ejected from their homes. The humanitarian imperative took over from discussions on complicity with ethnic cleansing.

More than in any other situation, however, can the humanitarian efforts of UN agencies and others be seen to have been undermined by the lack of effective international political efforts to deal with the underlying causes of the suffering. Here, in contrast to Somalia, shrinking from any application of force is considered by many to have lengthened the tragedy. Humanitarian organisations initially saw themselves as buying time for a political solution, but as time passed without a solution the humanitarian organisations were themselves partially blamed for the continuation of suffering. 'The failure of the international community to reverse the logic of war,' said the UNHCR Special Envoy Nicholas Morris in mid-1993, 'has meant the failure of humanitarian operations predicated on the logic of war being reversed'.[22]

These different experiences have led to increasingly disparate views on the compatibility of the varying UN roles. The DHA holds that political, military and humanitarian objectives 'can be carried out effectively in integrated and unified operations...'[23] but there is a growing opinion among non-UN actors that the roles are incompatible.

The relief to development continuum

Incorporating the concept of a phased response that works along the so-called 'relief and development continuum' into General Assembly Resol-

---

21 Larry Minear et al, *Humanitarian Action in the former Yugoslavia: The UN's Role 1991-3*, Providence, The Thomas J. Watson Jr Institute for International Studies, 1994, p25.

22 ibid p 8.

23 UN DHA, 'Humanitarian Mandates in Conflict Situations', Geneva. Consultative paper prepared in Geneva during 1994 and 1995.

ution 46/182 must be seen as a positive step forward. There is a danger, however, that as institutions try to operationalise such a concept they introduce a fixed menu of responses still based on the premise that emergencies are temporary crises after which societies return to 'normal'. It seems clear that in many of today's crises conflict, hunger, displacement and economic hardship are becoming normal features of life for whole generations. In these conditions, UN agencies need to be able to develop more pragmatic and less state-centric mandates that allow them to respond to the needs of victims. Such mandates could give UN humanitarian operations space to work with service-related governing structures (clinics, schools, agricultural services) in the absence of a recognised political government, or with alternative community structures in areas of disputed sovereignty.

The UN and donors appear unable to make, both conceptually and in practice, the distinction between the government – the political leadership – and the governing structures. There appears to be an unwillingness within the international community to engage in a systematic manner to try to restore governing structures. Donors have accepted the international community's responsibility not to suffer what has been termed the 'double jeopardy' of the problems of war and starvation and willingly channel relief assistance through voluntary agencies. They do not, however, explore the full consequences of this. This philosophy ignores the need to sustain the basic structures of society. Furthermore, it fails to explore ways of doing this that do not necessarily entail the legitimisation of a political grouping or recognition of a sovereign state. Whilst the state of Somalia preoccupied the UN, the secessionist north western sector, calling itself the Republic of Somaliland, struggled to maintain order, to rebuild its infrastructure and to organise elections. The former provincial ministries attempted to provide education and health services as national ministries. A serious attempt was made to disarm the population but, as in Somalia, the window of opportunity closed before external agencies responded.[24] Here the political objective of a 'greater Somalia' constrained the UN agencies and was a major obstacle to recovery.

Recommendations

Despite the importance attached to it in *Agenda for Peace*, preventive diplomacy remains a low priority in UN thinking and operations. An early-

---

24 Nicholas Hinton, 'A United Nations for the 21st Century', *RSA Journal*, Vol CXLII, No. 5449, May 1994, p. 22-34.

warning system for crises should be given greater priority. As it develops its information-sharing role the DHA should pay more attention to this, involving NGOs in the analysis.

UN humanitarian operations require independence from UN military and political operations. The Security Council should give more consideration to the humanitarian implications of its decisions and humanitarian organisations should be fully involved in the planning of peace-keeping operations. Military personnel should receive training on working in a way which is compatible with humanitarian principles.

People affected by humanitarian emergencies have a right to expect that the international community is making an equal effort to respond to each emergency on the basis of need. Greater effort should be made to formulate an international humanitarian policy and new mechanisms devised to ensure accountability.

A permanent and independent body should be established to act as a guardian of human rights in emergencies and to monitor the means undertaken to fulfil them. An independent commission on humanitarian assistance would be able to report on the needs of affected populations and on the conduct of all parties in responding to those needs. Over time this would make an important contribution to the consistent development of good and just practice in the field of humanitarian assistance.

6. Renewing the quest for disarmament
Arms control North and South

PAUL ROGERS

With the ending of the Cold War at the beginning of the 1990s, there were expectations of a more peaceful world order. This has not come to pass. Instead, a more disordered, insecure and unpeaceful world appears to be emerging. The United Nations was formed in an era of hope, which was quickly dashed by the emergence of the Cold War. Now, 50 years later, it has to come to terms with quite different forms of insecurity, often rooted in socio-economic conflict. The causes of, and responses to, this insecurity do not lie solely or even largely in the military dimension, though this is one of the central factors. In responding to new problems, the UN must work as much with political and economic instruments as in furthering de-militarisation.

The Second World War, fought mainly between 1939 and 1945, is considered to be the most devastating war in human history, with more than 20 million killed. Since then, there have been no global wars, yet the past half century has witnessed one of the most protracted periods of violence and conflict, albeit in the form of numerous wars, many of them in regions away from the greatest areas of military concentration.

Since 1945 there have been close to 150 wars fought in most regions of the world. Defined as conflicts causing deaths estimated at more than 1,000 per year, these wars are likely to have killed around 23 million people, most of them civilian. At least 50 million people have been injured, many of them maimed for life.[1]

Some regions of the world have been particularly prone to conflict, the most significant being parts of the Middle East and south east Asia, with

---

1 See Ruth Leger Sivard's survey: *World Military and Social Expenditure (WMSE)* 1991, World Priorities Inc, Washington DC.

five major conflicts involving Israel and its neighbours, and an almost continuing conflict in Indo-China from 1946 to the late 1980s. Two broad themes of war have been decolonisation processes, mainly from the early 1950s to the late 1960s, and wars which have indirectly involved the two major power blocs represented by NATO and the Warsaw Pact. The latter have included wars in Korea, Vietnam, Afghanistan, the Horn of Africa and Central America.

Overshadowing the many wars of the late 20th century was the super-power confrontation from the late 1940s, lasting more than 40 years and involving a series of arms races including an intense competition over nuclear weapons. By 1987, the East-West confrontation was responsible for more than 80 per cent of a world annual military expenditure in the region of US $1,000 billion. It involved successive waves of militarisation, including the development of nuclear and thermonuclear weapons, long-range strategic bombers, intercontinental ballistic missiles (ICBMs), submarine-launched ballistic missiles, cruise missiles, cluster bombs and a massive variety of advanced high-technology weaponry.

At the height of the Cold War in the early 1980s, the weapons reached appalling levels of destructiveness. A single giant Soviet ICBM such as the SS-18 could carry ten H-bomb warheads, each 40 times as powerful as the Hiroshima bomb, while an American B-52 strategic bomber could launch 20 powerful nuclear-armed cruise missiles at targets hundreds of miles apart.

From the 1960s onwards, persistent efforts were made to bring the process of militarisation under control, many of them under UN auspices. They included the 1963 Limited Test Ban Treaty, the Nuclear Non-Proliferation Treaty of 1968, the Biological Weapons Convention of 1972 and the Strategic Arms Limitation Treaties (SALT I and II) of the late 1960s and 1970s. Each had some small effect but none was successful in truly curbing military competition. It was only in the late 1980s that rapid progress became possible.

In the Soviet Union, when President Gorbachev came to power in 1985 he was faced with an economy being crippled by high military spending. His administration initiated a series of radical changes in defence policy, including unilateral actions such as short-term bans on nuclear testing. All were intended to try and break the arms deadlock of the Cold War.

This was parallelled in Europe by intense public campaigning against a new generation of intermediate-range nuclear missiles, such as the American ground-launched cruise missile and Pershing II ballistic missile and the Soviet SS-20 ballistic missile. Actions in Britain, especially at Greenham Common, and in Germany, the Netherlands and Italy, all demonstrated the considerable power of public pressure. They formed part of a more general anti-nuclear sentiment, including the influential Freeze Movement in the US which aimed to freeze all nuclear developments as a first step towards reversing the arms race.

Public pressure on western politicians, coupled with the changed policy of the Soviet Union, resulted in a much more favourable climate for nuclear arms control. An Intermediate Nuclear Force (INF) agreement was finally signed in 1987, with these and other missiles removed in the following three years.

As the Cold War finally came to an end, the pace of nuclear disarmament speeded up. The superpowers had originally planned to deploy around 30,000 strategic nuclear warheads and nearly as many tactical weapons by the mid-1990s. Changes in military policy resulted in massive cuts in the tactical arsenals, while the levels of strategic weapons were negotiated down in two rounds of the Strategic Arms Reduction Treaty (START I and II) at the beginning of the 1990s.

As a result of START II, in particular, the superpower strategic arsenals are likely to decline to under 7,000 nuclear warheads by the end of the 1990s. These are still massive deployments of devastating weapons, of course, yet barely a quarter of the numbers originally expected.

Conventional military spending, too, has declined from the peak year of 1987. There was a worldwide reduction of nearly 10 per cent between 1987 and 1991, with more cuts expected through much of the 1990s. But most of the cuts have fallen in the former Soviet bloc, where deep economic problems have led to far greater defence budget cuts than in the West. In developing countries, the cuts in military budgets have been minimal, and in some regions – the Middle East and south east Asia for example – military spending is increasing.

Even so, the overarching fear of East-West confrontation and nuclear war, so much a concern of the late Cold War years, diminished by the end of the 1980s. It was replaced by hopes for some kind of more peaceful new world order: hopes which were dashed while they were still fresh.

War and peace in the 1990s

By 1992, within three years of the ending of the Cold War, there were 29 major conflicts taking place in the world. This was the highest number ever recorded, while deaths due to war were the highest in 17 years. For the first time in several decades, these included major conflicts in the industrialised world, including the protracted war in former-Yugoslavia and bitter disputes in several former Soviet republics.[2]

To these must be added the continuing wars in Angola, Somalia and Afghanistan, the Gulf War of 1991, rebellions and uprisings in Latin America and many other conflicts in Africa and Asia. As a direct result of defence budget cuts in industrialised countries, major arms industries sought to develop their overseas markets, leading to intense sales efforts, especially in the Middle East and south east Asia. As the armed forces of the North were re-equipped with relatively smaller numbers of high-technology weapons, they tried to sell their second-hand equipment at low prices in overseas markets. This process is known as 'cascading' which serves to lock in the recipients to particular sources of supply.

Cascading now works at almost every level, from missiles to tanks and from warships to small arms. The massive surpluses of light weapons now flooding the world's unofficial arms markets have resulted in remarkably high levels of militarisation in many areas of conflict. This process can be seen especially clearly in southern Africa and south Asia, where the ready availability of small arms has added greatly to the human costs of local and regional conflicts.

The existence of numerous wars in the mid-1990s must be balanced by some areas of progress, however tentative. Some signs of reconciliation in the Middle East and southern Africa, and democratisation in Latin America, are indications of the possibility of progress. Furthermore, the very ending of the Cold War has made us more aware of many regional conflicts previously fought in its shadow. Conflicts in Afghanistan, the Horn of Africa and Central America were all too often seen as part of the East/West confrontation, and their human costs were largely ignored in the supposed battle between good and evil.

Even so, the overall trend is at least for the maintenance of high levels of regional conflict and the possibility of its increase. There is only some consolation in the fact that conflicts in former-Yugoslavia, Rwanda and elsewhere are now more clearly seen in terms of the intense human suffering that they cause. During the Cold War years, the media paid little attention to the cost of conflict. Now, though, the suffering in war zones, whether it be children maimed in Bosnia, land-mine victims in Cambodia, or the suffering in Sudan, Rwanda or Liberia, is more likely to be depicted.

In the immediate future, therefore, there is a great need for international action to curb the processes of militarisation, to facilitate conflict prevention, conflict resolution and peace-building. Yet there are indica-

---

2 *Ibid*, 1993

tions that this immediate need may be surpassed by longer-term trends towards international insecurity, trends which reach beyond conventional interpretations of peace and security.

A new world disorder

Three factors seem likely to influence trends in international peace and security around and beyond the turn of the century.

Polarisation between rich and poor

The first is the deep polarisation of the world's population into small areas of relative wealth and much larger areas of relative poverty. The distribution is by no means clear-cut but, essentially, one-fifth of the population uses around three-quarters of the wealth and physical resources. This alone is a source of potential instability, and is seen most graphically in the increasing incidence of mass migration and underclass rebellion, such as that becoming common in Europe and North America.

This wealth-poverty polarisation is steadily worsening because the regions of wealth have largely passed through the demographic transition to relative population stability, whereas the populations of the South are likely to increase for at least the next 60 years. In barely half that time, only one-seventh of the world's population will control three-quarters of the world's wealth, and pressures on those 'islands of wealth' will grow stronger.

A crisis of unsatisfied expectations might be avoided if prospects for international cooperation were greater. All the indications are, however, that it will be slow and tortuous, hindered not just by severe historic and continuing trading disadvantages but by a continuing debt crisis, economic exploitation and political instability. The numbers of people experiencing absolute poverty and malnutrition have increased substantially in the past two decades.

Some progress in development has been made, and much further progress is possible, as discussed elsewhere in this book. However, it has to be assumed that, at least on current trends, the massive disparities in global wealth and poverty will increase still further. The Northern states, which still exert control over the world economy, show little commitment to cooperative international development, which is hardly surprising since that very control is so advantageous to them.[3]

---

3 For a comprehensive study of UN activities on trade and development, see Nassau Adams, *Worlds Apart*, Zed Books, London, 1993.

Environmental constraints and resource conflict

Added to this is the second factor: the recognition that the entire global system appears to be approaching limits of human activity set by environmental constraints. At a regional level, these include immense problems of deforestation, water shortages, desertification, salinisation and atmospheric and marine pollution. At the global level, they already include ozone depletion and global warming. They also involve an intensifying competition for resources, especially strategic resources such as oil, which are now found predominantly in the South despite being consumed primarily in the North. On occasion, as in the Persian Gulf in 1991, this competition contributes to open warfare.

Resource conflict is both a regional and global phenomenon. Pressure on land is common throughout the world, water resources are particularly problematic in the Middle East and South Asia, and conflict over marine fisheries is particularly severe in the North Atlantic and West Pacific.

At the global level, the disparities are most severe for energy and mineral resources. About 65 per cent of all of the world's proved oil reserves are located in a handful of states around the Persian Gulf, all of which have larger reserves than traditional 'giants' such as the United States and Russia. Kuwait, Iran and Iraq, for example, each have three times the reserves of the whole of the United States including Alaska, and the Saudi reserves are far larger still. At present rates of use, the United States will have seriously depleted its remaining reserves within a decade, whereas Gulf states have up to a century of supplies.

Most of the world's trade in metals originates in the South, and some strategic minerals are almost exclusively located in very specific areas. Tungsten is a crucial metal in producing cutting and milling machinery throughout industry, yet two-thirds of the world's tungsten reserves are in China. Cobalt, another strategic metal used extensively in the arms industry, is produced mainly in Central Africa. Half of the world's cobalt production is located in a few mines in the Shaba Province of Zaire, a factor which undoubtedly contributed to western intervention in Shaba during the 1978 crisis. Similarly, one of the world's most lucrative deposits of rock phosphate, an essential component of compound fertilisers, is to be found at Bu Craa in Western Sahara, contributing to the intense desire of Morocco to control the territory.

Overall, with the energy and mineral reserves of the North far closer to exhaustion than those of the South, there is a real risk of increased competition and conflict. Even in such an environment though, Northern states still exert considerable power. They have economic and military strength, they produce most of the food surpluses and they are steadily consolidating their control of science and technology, especially through the maintenance of intellectual property rights.

In short, ecological constraints on development interact with the realities of economic inequality and political power. The overall development potential of the world is environmentally constrained, and, within the current global system, environmental limitations increase the risk of conflict.

Global militarisation

Thirdly, within this ecologically limited and economically polarised world system there is the primary legacy of the Cold War: world-wide militarisation. Although the excesses of East-West military confrontation are past, they leave behind a massive array of weapons, postures and attitudes. Many governments are searching for new 'threats' to provide further bogeyman roles at a time of declining defence budgets.

North/South confrontation and new 'threats'

Thus a combination of grossly unequal distribution of wealth, a crisis in development, environmental limits to human activity and continuing militarisation make it probable that the main risk to global peace and security in the coming decades will lie primarily on a North/South axis of confrontation.[4]

This may express itself in a number of ways, not least in competition for the control of resources and markets. With Western Europe, Japan and now, crucially, the United States dominantly dependent for continued industrial growth on access to resources and markets in the South, fears of a renewed hegemony are likely to grow. In particular, the region of greatest potential competition for physical resources is most likely to be the Middle East, especially the Persian Gulf with its remarkable concentration of energy resources. The resource wealth of southern Africa, Amazonia and eastern Asia will also, however, be significant. This is not to suggest that all forms of competition will be between Europe, North America and Japan on the one hand and the third world on the other. Some Southern economies, notably in south east Asia, are already competitive with the North, comfortably outpacing the sluggish economies of Europe and North America in particular. Their very success, however, will put even

---

4 These issues are explored in Paul Rogers and Malcolm Dando, *A Violent Peace, Global Security After the Cold War*, Brassey's, London, 1992.

more pressure on environment and resources.

Secondly, the transnational juxtaposition of wealth and poverty is likely to increase migratory pressures leading, in turn, to an anti-immigration reaction which is already a feature of European politics.

Finally, an increasingly vigorous political and military response is likely in a polarised world economy and will come largely from within the South. This is already in evidence in the evolving foreign policies of major states such as China and India, and in the pursuit of advanced weapons capabilities by a number of states. However, it is complicated by aspects of anti-elitism, militant nationalisms, regional separatism, radical and even messianic political movements and a variety of religious and ethnic fundamentalisms. It is almost impossible to predict the evolution of such responses and whether they come from groups within states or from states themselves. They may express themselves in guerrilla campaigns of remarkable fervour, such as the Sendero Luminoso phenomenon in Peru, militant nationalism in South Asia or religious fundamentalism in North Africa and the Middle East. Even before they involve whole states, they can be perceived as presenting threats to the established order and as requiring military responses.

In consequence, the military forces of the industrialised North redefine their international security roles as being to control regional threats to Northern interests. Far greater attention is given to the ability to project military force over long distances with great rapidity, while nuclear targeting is reconfigured to include the possibility of small-scale nuclear threats from the South. In addition research programmes are accelerated to adapt Star Wars technology to meet a perceived threat from the proliferation of missile technology in the Middle East and Asia.

It is not surprising that, at a time of defence budget cuts, military strategists look for new 'threats', but the pace of their change in attitudes, and the intensity of their changed perception, must be recognised. For one leading US naval magazine, the threat came from:

> '...that swirling pot of poison made up of zealots, crazies, drug runners and terrorists'. [5]

while an official US Air Force study spoke of the belief that:

> 'the growing wealth of petro-nations and newly hegemonic powers is

---

5 *Proceedings of the US Naval Institute*, Washington DC, January 1990, p 36.

available to bullies and crazies, if they gain control to wreak havoc on world tranquillity'.[6]

This rapid change in security attitudes was put clearly by the new Director of the CIA, James Woolsey, speaking early in 1993, when he characterised the ending of the Cold War and the developing new world disorder thus:

'...we have slain the dragon but now live in a jungle full of poisonous snakes.'[7]

Some years earlier, the economic geographer Edwin Brooks stood back from the narrow attitudes of the military and gave it a more global vision, warning of the risk of:

'...a crowded, glowering planet of massive inequalities of wealth, buttressed by stark force yet endlessly threatened by desperate people in the global ghettoes of the underprivileged.'[8]

The need for an integrated response

The early post-Cold War period has been characterised by a disorderly international system with numerous conflicts. Because these are taking place beyond the era of rigid East/West polarisation, the international community, primarily in the form of the United Nations, is able to be far more responsive in attempts to ameliorate the effects of conflict, through an increase in humanitarian relief, peacekeeping and, to a lesser extent, peacebuilding. It is also a period in which there is increased potential for the international control of militarisation. Neither process, however, addresses the core longer-term problems of insecurity, especially socio-economic polarisation and environmental constraints. These require, in addition, a multi-dimensional response encompassing many issues of economic and political cooperation for human progress, sustainable development and environmental management. Such responses are discussed elsewhere in this book, but relate directly to issues of peace and security. That they cannot be separated is increasingly recognised, not least in current thinking

---

6 Reported in *Navy News and Undersea Technology*, Washington DC, 13 January 1992.
7 Statement by James Woolsey at Senate Hearings, Washington DC, February 1993.
8 In *Human Ecology and World Development*, edited by Anthony Vann and Paul Rogers, Plenum Press, London, 1974.

on the role of the United Nations in promoting peace, through initiatives such as the *Agenda for Peace* in 1993.

If it is accepted that the major causes of insecurity, conflict and the consequent human suffering will increasingly arise from the deepening socio-economic differences among humankind, then the very institutions of the United Nations concerned with these issues need strengthening.

Within this wider context, the evolution of the United Nations System will have a particular and crucial relevance for the control of militarisation, peacekeeping, conflict resolution and peacebuilding, and for broad international cooperation towards common security. If it is possible slowly to move the world community towards a greater concern for socio-economic well-being and sustainable development, then the process of demilitarisation has some chance of becoming a reality. Starting with the core issues of arms control and disarmament, the role of the UN could substantially increase.

Arms control and disarmament

The most significant arms control agreements of the last ten years have been primarily bilateral, between the United States and Russia as the successor state to the Soviet Union. These have been the Intermediate Nuclear Forces Treaty and the Strategic Arms Reduction Treaties. While these, and the unilateral withdrawal of many tactical nuclear forces, represent remarkable progress, they do not in any sense involve substantial moves to abolish nuclear forces or to control proliferation.

Nuclear weapons

A number of treaties developed under UN auspices seek to control the development of nuclear weapons. These include early attempts to produce nuclear-free zones such as the 1967 Treaty of Tlatelolco covering Latin America, the 1967 Outer Space Treaty and the Seabed Treaty of 1970. The Limited Test Ban Treaty agreed in 1963 by the United States, the then Soviet Union and the United Kingdom and concerned primarily with banning atmospheric tests, now has over 100 signatories. The Threshold Test Ban Treaty of 1974 went on to limit the size of nuclear tests to 150 kilotons, but the most important potential agreement, the Comprehensive Test Ban Treaty (CTBT), remains under negotiation. Although at least in part symbolic, since nuclear tests can be partially simulated, its completion is widely regarded as the most likely indication of a willingness by nuclear powers to move, at least hesitantly, towards a post-nuclear world.

Parallel to the CTBT is the renegotiation of the Nuclear Non-Proliferation Treaty (NPT). The NPT dates from 1968, with review conferences held every five years from 1975 leading to an extension conference in 1995. Some significant states, including India, have regarded the NPT as little more than a device used by leading nuclear states to maintain the nuclear status quo. Against this, some would argue that the progress in nuclear arms control by states such as the US and Russia in the past five years improves the prospect of a successful extension of the NPT, especially if a Comprehensive Test Ban Treaty can also be negotiated.

Even so, the reality is that not one of the major nuclear states (the US, Russia, Britain, France and China) has any intention whatsoever of giving up its nuclear arsenals entirely. Indeed, the tendency is to develop weapons and strategies designed for small-scale nuclear confrontations in the post-Cold War world. This presents a continuing source of encouragement to would-be nuclear states, especially those in the Middle East and elsewhere that see themselves as 'threatened' by powerful states.

It follows that any attempt to control proliferation cannot expect more than limited success unless there is a radical change of political attitude by existing nuclear-armed states. This would need to involve an acceptance of the need for agreed general nuclear disarmament, for which the extension of the NPT and the negotiation of a comprehensive test ban would be no more than initial steps.

Chemical weapons

Concerning chemical weapons, the UN Committee on Disarmament in Geneva has provided the means for developing a Chemical Weapons Convention (CWC), tentatively agreed in 1989 and steadily receiving signatories since then. The CWC has made more progress than expected during the mid-1980s, and its negotiation was accompanied by mutual decisions by the United States and Russia to progressively dismantle their substantial chemical arsenals. At the same time, though, opposition to the treaty remains in some regions, especially in the Middle East, where some states are concerned at regional incidence of small nuclear arsenals.

Biological weapons

The Biological Weapons Convention (BWC), also under UN auspices, came into force in 1972 when it was widely believed that biological weapons had little military utility. Rapid developments in genetic engineering and other forms of biotechnology now indicate a much greater utility, with a consequent risk of a biological arms race. While the BWC is of historic importance, with over 100 signatories, its verification procedures are now widely regarded as fundamentally inadequate. It follows that some form of revision of the convention, with greatly improved verification procedures and transparency, is required.

Conventional arms

In contrast to the three main classes of weapons of mass destruction, nuclear, chemical and biological, the reality of current conflicts is that almost all deaths and injuries are caused by conventional weapons. Increasingly important are 'area-impact munitions' (AIMs), such as cluster bombs, fuel-air explosives, multiple rocket launchers and mass dispersal of anti-personnel mines. Some of these weapons are as devastating as small nuclear warheads: a single salvo from the US Multiple Rocket Launch System (MLRS) disperses nearly 8,000 anti-personnel 'bomblets' over an area of 30 hectares (66 acres). Over 1,000 salvoes were fired in the last few days of the Gulf War in 1991.

For these, and for other conventional weapons, multilateral arms control and disarmament processes are minimal. There exists a limited programme to control the proliferation of ballistic missiles, the Missile Technology Control Regime, but this is an agreement between a few industrial states. There are also agreements which have some effect on the control of inhumane weapons and potentially dangerous military incidents. There is, finally, the recent UN Arms Transfers Register. While this does not exercise any control over international arms sales, and only covers narrow categories of weapons, it does require signatory states to publish details of arms transfers and, as such, represents an initial step towards transparency.

The proliferation of advanced conventional military technology, especially ballistic missiles, anti-personnel mines and cluster bombs, is a process which is becoming increasingly global. It is aided by the need for the arms industries of industrial countries to establish new markets, often by co-production agreements, and by the desire of a number of Southern states to develop an indigenous capacity in the face of some unilateral government attempts to control technology transfer.

One main effect of the new generations of area-impact munitions such as cluster bombs is to make conflict inherently more destructive of life. A multiple rocket launcher can be far more damaging than conventional artillery, an aircraft dropping cluster bombs can kill and injure many more people than if equipped with conventional bombs. Because of this, we have to face the fact that conventional wars are likely to become steadily more devastating, with much higher casualties. It follows that there has to be a much greater commitment to this wider field of arms control, and most of this commitment has to come from the major producers of these weapons, the northern industrial states. Otherwise they will bear the greater responsibility for the increasing destructiveness of future wars, wherever they take place.

Priorities in arms control and disarmament

Priorities would appear to be multilateral negotiations, under the auspices of the UN Committee on Disarmament, to control the spread of long-range ballistic and cruise missiles and area-impact weapons including anti-personnel land mines. Given, though, that the main developers and deployers of such weapons are the industrialised states of the North, it is highly unlikely that negotiations would have any significant chance of success unless such states were willing to exercise considerable restraint themselves.

In this context, the work of the UN Committee on Disarmament (UNCD), based in Geneva, is revealing. The committee is maintained as a permanent body and works on disarmament issues through a number of committees. The most significant of these is the ad hoc committee on chemical weapons disarmament responsible for the Chemical Weapons Convention. Essentially, the UNCD exists as a body which, together with support from the UN Institute for Disarmament Research (UNIDIR), also in Geneva, provides a vehicle for negotiations on many disarmament issues. The problem, as ever, is the political will of the principal participants. If there is truly an increasing desire for successful negotiations by the leading states, then progress is possible, with the UNCD playing a potentially important role. Lacking such motivation, the work of the UNCD has limited value.

Beyond the control of the particularly devastating classes of weapons of mass destruction lies the even more substantial arena of the control of all conventional weapons. Progress here requires building on the Arms Transfers Register so that limits can be negotiated on the holding of categories of weapons such as heavy artillery and main battle tanks. This might best be approached on a regional basis, using the negotiating and verification procedures which resulted in agreed reductions in conventional force levels in Europe at the end of the 1980s. The Middle East and south and south east Asia are regions of primary concern.

Substantive negotiations on conventional weapons would, though, best be aided by extensive international cooperation on the practice of defence industry diversification and conversion. This is a core issue in demilitarisation. In most advanced industrial societies, the armaments industries have been lucrative enterprises with very powerful lobbying activities. They have been highly reluctant to engage in any kind of systematic arms conversion and diversification activities. Indeed, most of these activities have been promoted by trades unions and government agencies.

This is also an area in which the UN itself is very weak, even more so than in its arms control activities. Nonetheless, it is an area where there is a critical need for transnational studies to learn from the experience of successful arms conversion processes where they have occurred. Although under very different circumstances, there was a massive process of demobilisation and arms industry conversion in countries such as the United States and Britain after 1945. In recent years, some individual states within the USA have established arms conversion agencies which have aided companies diversifying out of arms production.

Against this, the predominant free market approaches of many western governments in the late 1980s and early 1990s meant that governments showed little or no interest in aiding defence diversification by industry. This resulted in millions of jobs and skills being lost that could have been applied to civil industries. In this context, the best role for the UN would be to ensure that relevant agencies such as UNIDIR and the International Labour Office (ILO) at least include a greater commitment to communicating the results of successful arms conversion and diversification experiences.

Conclusion

The end of the Cold War, and the partial success of some arms control agreements, gives some hope that a more peaceful and just world order might be established. This must involve an accelerating process of demilitarisation, but there is little chance that this can be achieved without parallel progress in countering the deep socio-economic polarisation of the world's peoples and in coming to terms with the environmental constraints on human activity.

If such progress can be made, then there is a very strong argument for making the major processes of arms control, arms industry conversion and demilitarisation part of a UN system of organisation. This has, to a limited extent, been the case for some decades, but much of the progress made in the late 1980s was on a bilateral basis between the United States and the Soviet Union. Now there is a much more urgent need to develop fully multilateral agencies for these tasks. The UN Security Council's Charter (Article 26) was required to establish a system for regulating arms. This was never fully undertaken, but the time is now right.

Article 26

In order to promote the establishment and maintenance of international peace and security with the least diversion for armaments of the world's human and economic resources, the Security Council shall be responsible for formulating, with the assistance of the Military Staff Committee referred to in Article 47, plans to be submitted to the Members of the United Nations for the establishment of a system for the regulation of armaments.

Where progress in demilitarisation and arms control has occurred, it has usually resulted from specific discussions that have arisen because of public pressure or the perceived risks of existing policies. This was true of the banning of atmospheric nuclear tests in the 1960s, and of the Intermediate Nuclear Forces (INF) treaty in the 1980s. Most significant treaties have emerged from bilateral processes, yet the demands of the future have to be met by a global approach.

As a general principle, any proposal for arms control and disarmament, whether originating with one or two countries, or in a larger region, should be expanded to a global process normally under UN auspices. Furthermore, it should be linked, wherever possible, to programmes of sustainable and cooperative development.

It will take much of the next 50 years to bring about a more just, more peaceful and less militarised world, and it will require fundamental reform of the global socio-economic system in the process. The alternative is a bitter, divided and deeply insecure world, heavily militarised and conflict-ridden. In many ways, the challenge facing the UN is even greater than in the post-war world of the 1940s. Then, the emphasis was on repairing the war-ravaged regions of the North. Now, the challenge is truly global.

Major Arms Control Agreements

Non-Proliferation Treaty (NPT)

Aims to control spread of nuclear weapons.

Agreed in 1968 and came into effect in 1970 – a multilateral treaty under UN auspices.

Reviewed every five years with final review and renegotiation in 1995. Seen by some states as a means of regularising nuclear possession by states such as US, UK and Russia while trying to prevent others acquiring them.

Limited Test Ban Treaty (LTBT)

Bans atmospheric nuclear testing and limits size of underground tests.

Negotiated rapidly between USA, USSR and UK in 1963 in wake of Cuba Missile crisis of 1962. Over 100 more states have since signed up.

Helped bring under control the environmental disaster of massive atmospheric testing in the 1950s, but it can be argued that it induced complacency and prevented agreement on a comprehensive test ban.

Comprehensive Test Ban Treaty

Would ban all nuclear testing.

Multilateral process under auspices of UN Committee on Disarmament in Geneva.

After sporadic negotiations for decades, became high profile issue from early 1990s as many non-nuclear states sought a CTBT from the nuclear states in return for their support for more effective control of proliferation.

Strategic Arms Limitation Treaty I (SALT 1)

Limited long-range nuclear delivery vehicles (missiles and bombers).

Agreed in 1972 between the US and the USSR.

Set high limits for numbers of bombers and missiles. Even this was largely irrelevant, as it allowed both sides to fit multiple warheads to missiles and thus continue the arms race in a new direction.

Strategic Arms Limitation Treaty II (SALT II)

Limited long-range warhead numbers

Agreed in 1979 between US and USSR after seven years' negotiations.

The participants doubled their warhead numbers during the seven years of negotiations. Classic example of arms control not keeping pace with arms race.

Intermediate Nuclear Forces Treaty (INF)

Eliminated US and Soviet immediate range nuclear missiles.
Bilateral Treaty Agreed in 1987.
First real nuclear arms control breakthrough, largely due to major concessions by Gorbachev. Cleared out Cruise, Pershing and SS20 missiles, among others, from Europe and signalled the start of serious, if partial, East/West nuclear arms control.

Strategic Arms Reduction Treaties I and II (START I/START II)

Reduces numbers of long-range nuclear weapons.
Agreed in 1991 and 1992 between US and USSR/Russia.
Rapid progress made end of Cold War after 10 years' procrastination. Will cut East/West strategic nuclear arsenals from around 24,000 to 8,000 by 2003, though still leaving more than enough for an apocalypse or two.

Chemical Weapons Convention (CWC)

Aims to eliminate chemical weapons.
Multilateral agreement under UN (Committee on Disarmament) auspices, available for signing from 1992.
Progress made in early 1990s after many years stagnation. Success will only come with large numbers of signatories, and verification will remain a problem. US and Russian commitment to eliminate their CW arsenals politically important and helped change climate of opinion.

Biological Weapons Convention (BWC)

Aims to eliminate biological weapons.
Multilateral treaty under UN auspices came into effect in 1972.
Agreed at a time when biological weapons considered ineffective. Pre-dates biotechnology developments which have transformed BW potential, and now widely recognised as hopelessly inadequate and unverifiable treaty. Tougher revised treaty is urgently needed but progress is very slow.

UN Arms Transfers Register

Makes public the sale and transfer of large weapons systems between states.
Commenced operations in 1993 – broad-based multilateral process under UN auspices.
Limited first step towards controlling the arms race. Modest aims are to make transfer of items such as warplanes, ships and tanks more transparent. Does not cover weapons such as small arms or land mines and does not exert any control over trade, though it may make the processes a little more open.

7. Blue Helmets
For what? Under whom?

PHYLLIS BENNIS

As the United Nations approached its 50th year, peacekeeping operations with new and broadened mandates remained the centrepiece of attention. By mid-1994, the UN was fielding almost 80,000 Blue Helmets around the world. Unlike traditional operations in which both sides had to authorise border observers or other monitors, most of the post-Cold War peacekeepers were stationed within, rather than between, countries racked by bloody divisions over ethnic or power-access conflict. Most were based in countries of the South. Most were deployed without the consent of one or more parties to the conflicts. And, despite well-meaning, often heroic efforts, most were failing even to staunch the bloodshed.

After the Cold War

The United Nations evolved parallel to, and indeed was shaped in the crucible of, the Cold War. Inside the UN, United States-Soviet rivalry was played out through threats and vetoes, UN back-room deals over membership and voting rights, and in the often paralysed Security Council. Even outside headquarters, the super-power conflict limited the arenas in which the UN would be allowed to intervene.

During the Cold War years, most local and regional conflicts either started as, or quickly became, proxy wars between governments and their opponents. Most were linked to and, crucially, armed by the US or the Soviet Union. The opposing sides were by no means symmetrical. From the 1950s through the 1970s, the US largely kept in power old-style colonial regimes and repressive governments following a pro-Western agenda overlaid with a gloss of official independence. The Soviet Union, in the main, backed anti-colonial guerrilla forces as well as non-aligned and socialist governments in power in the third world. During the 1970s, the US focused more on creating and arming guerrilla forces aimed at overthrowing popular but impoverished governments in countries such as Angola and Nicaragua, while continuing to back pro-Western governments like those in El Salvador and Guatemala against popular insurgencies.

In the short and dramatic period between 1989 and 1991, the world's conflicts were transformed. The end of super-power competition meant that proxy wars held little appeal for the rich nations; they were unnecessary to assert or maintain hegemony in the absence of a key super-power contender. But many of the hot wars fomented or inflamed by Cold War tensions did not disappear. There were new possibilities for solutions, to be sure, but the old sponsors of the warring factions simply wanted out. Furthermore, in areas of the world where bureaucratic socialism or armament-rich dictators had formerly kept control, such as the former Yugoslavia and Somalia, long-simmering conflicts (sometimes ethnically defined, but most with their roots in poverty and economic inequity) exploded into brutal cycles of rage and violence. In all those cases, the powerful nations on their way out of troublesome Cold War-era hot spots, or watching newly unleashed unrest from afar, began to turn to the United Nations to impose new notions of 'peacekeeping' – even in areas which had no peace to keep.

A new definition

UN peacekeeping is often defined in the context of the search for international peace and security. So far, in most theatres of deployment, the new UN operations have brought neither peace nor security to those caught up in the brutal wars of the 'new world order'. And beyond the failure of the UN's increasingly military efforts themselves, the organisation has paid a high price for the redirection of its resources. Colombia's Ambassador Luis Fernando Jaramillo, handing over his chair of the Non-Aligned Group of 77 to the Algerian Ambassador in January 1994, criticised the continuous demands on the UN 'to devote greater efforts to peacekeeping operations and security *in detriment of its functions and responsibilities in the area of economic and social development*'. (Emphasis added.) Within the UN Charter, peacekeeping themes emerge in three sections. Chapter VI, Pacific Settlement of Disputes, places responsibility on states themselves, regional organisations, the Security Council, the International Court of Justice and the General Assembly of the UN to help settle conflicts between states that threaten international peace and stability. A wide range of advisory possibilities and mediation methods are posed, all designed to settle inter-state disputes without resorting to military force. Chapter VIII further defines and encourages regional settlements. It is in Chapter VII that the UN response to 'threats to the peace, breaches of the peace and acts of aggression' escalates.

Chapter VII calls for severing diplomatic relations, disrupting economic ties, boycotts, and then, if those methods fail, describes how and in what circumstances the Security Council may authorise the use of military force. It is the only section of the Charter that deviates from the broad UN commitment to the peaceable settlement of conflicts. Chapter VII created a Military Staff Committee, composed of the Chiefs of Staff of the five permanent members, to advise the Council on military action. Peace enforcement was to be based on personnel provided to the UN on a voluntary basis by member states, operating under UN command and control. (The nucleus of permanent UN enforcement troops is hinted at in Article 45's call that 'to enable the United Nations to take urgent military measures, Members shall hold immediately available national air-force contingents for combined international enforcement action'.) Super-power tensions prevented the Military Staff Committee from functioning during most of the Cold War years, and the 'immediately available' forces were rarely seen. Financing of peacekeeping and peace enforcement operations is arranged on a case-by-case basis, with each member state assessed a pre-arranged percentage of the cost. The US is committed to pay close to 30 per cent of peacekeeping costs, but in 1994 it remained hundreds of millions of dollars in arrears.

Beginning with the US-driven militarisation of response to the 1990-91 Gulf crisis, the United Nations has concentrated far greater attention on military solutions to local and regional problems than ever before. Much of the Security Council's, and especially the five permanent members', debate over appropriate responses to post-Cold War crises exploding in Bosnia, Somalia, Haiti, Rwanda, and elsewhere begins and ends with the military provisions of Article 42 of Chapter VII: 'action by air, sea, or land forces as may be necessary to maintain or restore international peace and security'. The Security Council peacekeeping decisions have often relied on an extremely narrow, military interpretation. While Article 42 does speak of direct military action, it also discusses 'demonstrations, blockade, and other operations'. Further, the entire legitimacy of military action is rooted in the Charter's assumption that the Security Council has already determined that non-military measures such as 'complete or partial interruption of economic relations and of rail, sea, air, postal, telegraphic, radio and other means of communication, and the severance of diplomatic relations' (Article 41) 'would be inadequate or have proved to be inadequate' (Article 42). In far too many discussions of Council responses to regional crises, the potential power of these alternative sanctions is considered late, given inadequate time to take effect, or ignored altogether. During the Haiti crisis, for example, the initial weak and unenforced sanctions, imposed from 1991 until early 1994, allowed massive transit of embargoed goods, especially gasoline. These were carried both across the porous Dominican border and in sanctions-busting ships that 'escaped' the scrutiny of the US fleet (which was looking for refugees off the Haitian Coast). Once the sanctions resolution was hardened in mid-1994, with potentially serious consequences for the Haitian elite, talk immediately shifted to military options; the year or more estimated for the sanctions to bite was not allowed to elapse.

Peaceful settlement efforts first

Even more importantly, the mandates of Chapter VI – positioned before Chapter VII precisely to indicate its pre-military prerequisites – are routinely ignored. Chapter VI, Pacific Settlement of Disputes, provides a checklist of investigation, mediation and settlement-prodding for the Security Council and – also often ignored – a role for the General Assembly in solving local or regional disputes. From 1990, a key goal of the US and other permanent members of the Security Council was to bolster the Council as the sole locus of power within the United Nations. That goal was largely achieved, as the General Assembly, the International Court of Justice and other UN branches were relegated to strategic marginality. But while it is often assumed that the Charter grants the Security Council the sole UN mandate for issues of international peace and security, Chapter VI refers directly to an Assembly role in considering 'any dispute, or any situation which might lead to international friction or give rise to a dispute' (Articles 34 and 35). Further, the Charter's discussion of the Assembly's role itself calls on it to 'discuss any questions relating to the maintenance of international peace and security brought before it'. The role of the Assembly, by far the most democratic organ within the United Nations, stands in urgent need of reassertion and rehabilitation.

The mandates of Chapter VIII also remind the international organisation, especially the Security Council with its power to declare war and impose peace, of the primary importance of seeking out and respecting regionally-based solutions. While retaining the right of armed intervention, the Charter encourages the UN to rely on regional bodies for initial solutions to regional problems – the clear goal being the ability to solve emerging problems before they become international conflagrations. Under what circumstances, then, should the Council-only debate aimed at Chapter VII's military goals be invoked? Ultimately, reliance on the threat or use of military intervention to solve local or regional crises that are rooted in endemic poverty, legacies of colonial rule or left-over Cold War tensions, or exploding ethnic antagonisms, reflects a fundamental failure of the international community and the UN's own mandate to 'save succeeding generations from the scourge of war... and to promote social progress and better standards of life in larger freedom'. Sending the Blue Helmets to apply a tourniquet to a nation's bleeding jugular should not be heralded as a success for multilateral collaboration. Such a decision indicates rather the international community's failure towards one of its own.

Peacekeeping operations in the 1990s

A number of existing peacekeeping operations (PKOs) are of the traditional Cold War-era variety, in which both sides to a conflict agree to UN patrolling of still-tense borders or monitoring of fragile ceasefires. By 1994 these Chapter VI-authorised PKOs were functioning in the Middle East, Kashmir and Cyprus.

The Gulf Crisis operation

A more recent kind of UN military involvement emerged during the Gulf crisis. By offering a wide variety of political and economic carrots (including military, humanitarian and development aid) and by wielding sticks threatening dire consequences for failure to toe the pro-attack line (of which impoverished Yemen was a particularly tragic victim, losing its already-paltry $70 million in US aid), US diplomats were able to impose a Security Council decision. Falsely presented as a 'consensus', this provided a UN Chapter VII credential to Washington's Desert Storm. The UN was kept out of the decision-making loop, with even the Security Council and Secretary General ignorant of the planned assault on Baghdad. However, the organisation's sanction made possible the continuing US claim of international legitimacy, a global coalition, and its leadership of 'the world' against Saddam Hussein. (UNIKOM monitors the demilitarisation of the Iraq-Kuwait border, but it was imposed without Iraq's consent under Chapter VII as part of the punitive post-Desert Storm ceasefire terms.)

Several of the most highly visible, most contentious, and least successful of the newer peacekeeping operations are those that began by providing armed protection for relief agencies trying to provide humanitarian assistance. In Bosnia and Somalia especially, the Security Council looked on as the situations deteriorated. Eventually media-driven popular pressure, as well as calls from non-governmental organisations such as the International Committee of the Red Cross (ICRC) and the UN High Commission for Refugees (UNHCR), forced the Council to act. However, they sent Chapter VII peacekeepers only as guards for relief workers. To no one's surprise, conditions in both countries, though vastly different, continued to deteriorate. The root causes of unrest in both cases were ignored by UN – and, crucially, US – strategists.

The Somalia operation

The Somalia operation, especially, reflected a particularly cruel twist. The crisis was one for which the international community bore direct responsibility: Somalia had been a key playing field of Cold War rivalries, supported first by Moscow and later by Washington. The result was an extraordinary surfeit of powerful weapons 'left over' in the country. The empowerment of certain local leaders, and to some degree the exacerbation of clan-based competition, were also the legacy of that global conflict. But when the unstable government that replaced the Cold War-era dictator Mohamed Siad Barre fell into crisis and famine loomed, the international community, instead of attempting to help rehabilitate Somalia along Somali lines, largely ignored the Somali people and tried to impose solutions from outside. The UN mandate was limited and the small, slow successes of the early efforts of soon-deposed Special Envoy Mohammad Sahnoun were undermined. Finally, the small scale, lack of training and poor equipping of the initial contingent of UN troops ensured that the UN mission was bound to miscarry. Its failure guaranteed that the replacement US mission, heralded by the Marines' assault on Mogadishu's empty (except for reporters) beach, would capture international public attention as that of heroic American saviours – in harsh contrast to the UN's 'failed' Pakistani Blue Helmets.

A particular note about Ambassador Sahnoun is in order. Early warnings by the International Committee of the Red Cross, in December 1991 and March 1992, that mass starvation in Somalia was imminent, were largely ignored. International action came only at the end of the summer, when CNN-driven public demand forced the West into an emergency response. By the time that UN-protected food deliveries arrived, the hunger emergency was largely over, although serious danger from famine-driven

Summary of contributions to peacekeeping operations by country as of 31 August 1994

Glossary

UNTSO	United Nations Truce Supervision Organisation (June 1948 – to present)
UNMOGIP	United Nations Military Observer Group in India and Pakistan (January 1949 – to present)
UNFICYP	United Nations Peacekeeping Force in Cyprus (March 1964 – to present)
UNDOF	United Nations Disengagement Observer Force (June 1974 – to present)
UNIFIL	United Nations Interim Force in Lebanon (March 1978 – to present)
UNIKOM	United Nations Iraq-Kuwait Observation Mission (April 1991 – to present)
UNAVEM II	United Nations Angola Verification Mission II (June 1991 – to present)
ONUSAL	United Nations Observer Mission in El Salvador (July 1991 – to present)
MINURSO	United Nations Mission for the Referendum in Western Sahara (September 1991 – to present)
UNPROFOR	United Nations Protection Force (March 1992 – to present)
ONUMOZ	United Nations Operation in Mozambique (December 1992 – to present)
UNOSOM II	United Nations Operation in Somalia II (May 1993 – to present)
UNOMUR	United Nations Observer Mission Uganda-Rwanda (June 1993 – to present)
UNOMIG	United Nations Observer Mission in Georgia (August 1993 – to present)
UNOMIL	United Nations Observer Mission in Liberia (September 1993 – to present)
UNAMIR	United Nations Assistance Mission for Rwanda (October 1993 – to present)

P = civilian police   T = troops   O = military observers

#	COUNTRY		UNTSO	UNMOGIP	UNFICYP	UNDOF	UNIFIL	UNIKOM	UNAVEM	ONUSAL	MINURSO	UNPROFOR	ONUMOZ	UNOSOM	UNOMUR	UNOMIG	UNOMIL	UNAMIR	TOTALS	GRAND TOTAL
1	ARGENTINA	P							3			23							26	
		T			376			50		2		862	40						1330	1388
		O	6					6	2		5	5	8						32	
2	AUSTRALIA	P			20								16	1					37	
		T											4	67				314	385	435
		O	13																13	
3	AUSTRIA	P								2	10		19						31	
		T			346	459		12											817	907
		O	16		4			7			4						10	16	59	
4	BANGLADESH	P										34	99	1					134	
		T						790					1035	987			65	4	2881	3220
		O						9			7	39	35		20	8	35	52	205	
5	BELGIUM	P																		
		T										1019							1019	1034
		O									1	6	10						15	
6	BOLIVIA	P																		
		T																		
		O	6	2												2			10	10
7	BOTSWANA	P											15						15	
		T											752	423					1175	1201
		O											2		9				11	
8	BRAZIL	P							5	2		10	67						84	
		T							11				171						182	349
		O							7	3		33	27		13				83	
9	CANADA	P										46							46	
		T			10	223						2000						407	2640	2745
		O	14					5				15	4					21	59	
10	CAPE VERDE	O											18						18	18
11	CHAD	T																129	129	129

#	COUNTRY		UNTSO	UNMOGIP	UNFICYP	UNDOF	UNIFIL	UNIKOM	UNAVEM	ONUSAL	MINURSO	UNPROFOR	ONUMOZ	UNOSOM	UNOMUR	UNOMIG	UNOMIL	UNAMIR	TOTALS	GRAND TOTAL
12	CHILE	P								20									20	26
		O	3	3															6	
13	CHINA	O	5					15			20		10				15		65	65
14	COLOMBIA	P								27		12							39	41
		O								2									2	
15	CONGO	T																40	40	42
		O							2										2	
16	CZECH REPUBLIC	T										911							911	967
		O										23	19				14		56	
17	DENMARK	P										45							45	1383
		T						45				1237				1			1283	
		O	11	6				6				28				4			55	
18	EGYPT	P											50	6					56	2230
		T										425		1688					2113	
		O									9	13	20			4	15		61	
19	ETHIOPIA	T																800	800	800
20	FIJI	T					650												650	658
		O						7										1	8	
21	FINLAND	P										10	5						15	944
		T			1		552					334							887	
		O	17	7				6				12							42	
22	FRANCE	P								1		41							42	6304
		T					440					5751							6191	
		O	14					15			30	12							71	
23	GERMANY	P									5								5	13
		O														8			8	

COUNTRY		UNTSO	UNMOGIP	UNFICYP	UNDOF	UNIFIL	UNIKOM	UNAVEM	ONUSAL	MINURSO	UNPROFOR	ONUMOZ	UNOSOM	UNOMUR	UNOMIG	UNOMIL	UNAMIR	TOTALS	GRAND TOTAL
24 GHANA	P											40	6					46	1751
	T					783				8							820	1611	
	O						6			3	29						56	94	
25 GREECE	O						7			1					5			13	13
26 GUINEA	O									1							15	16	16
27 GUINEA BISSAU	P											65						65	159
	T																35	35	
	O							2				37				16	4	59	
28 GUYANA	O								5									5	5
29 HONDURAS	P									2								2	16
	O									14								14	
30 HUNGARY	P											20						20	61
	O						6	4				22		4	5			41	
31 INDIA	P											75						75	5173
	T											88	4963					5051	
	O						6	3				18				20		47	
32 INDONESIA	P											15						15	59
	T												7					7	
	O						7				30							37	
33 IRELAND	P			15							20	20						55	874
	T			25		657							91					773	
	O	17		4			7			9	9							46	
34 ITALY	P								8				5					13	321
	T					43						234	7					284	
	O	7	5				6			6								24	
35 JAPAN	T											53						53	53

COUNTRY	P/T/O	UNTSO	UNMOGIP	UNFICYP	UNDOF	UNIFIL	UNIKOM	UNAVEM	ONUSAL	MINURSO	UNPROFOR	ONUMOZ	UNOSOM	UNOMUR	UNOMIG	UNOMIL	UNAMIR	TOTALS	GRAND TOTAL
36 JORDAN	P										71	45						116	3571
	T										3360							3360	
	O							2			48				8	37		95	
37 KENYA	P										35							35	1092
	T										980							980	
	O						7			10	37					17	6	77	
38 KOREA, REPUBLIC of	P												2					2	31
	T									21			6					27	
	O									2								2	
39 MALAWI	T																133	133	143
	O																10	10	
40 MALAYSIA	P							3		15		70	5					93	2825
	T										1520		1128					2648	
	O						7	1		6	21	24				25		84	
41 MALI	P																5	5	16
	O																11	11	
42 MEXICO	P								37									37	37
43 MOROCCO	P							2										2	2
44 NEPAL	P										50	49						99	2041
	T					721					901		314					1936	
	O										6							6	
45 NETHERLANDS	P							2			10		6					18	2008
	T										1902	11						1913	
	O	15						2			50			10				77	

COUNTRY		UNTSO	UNMOGIP	UNFICYP	UNDOF	UNIFIL	UNIKOM	UNAVEM	ONUSAL	MINURSO	UNPROFOR	ONUMOZ	UNOSOM	UNOMUR	UNOMIG	UNOMIL	UNAMIR	TOTALS	GRAND TOTAL
46 NEW ZEALAND	T											3	7					10	29
	O	7						3			9							19	
47 NIGER	T																43	43	43
48 NIGERIA	P						5	5			38							48	886
	T												798					798	
	O										11	9	5				15	40	
49 NORWAY	P						5			4	30		5					44	1576
	T					833					637							1470	
	O	15	4					4			39							62	
50 PAKISTAN	P											66						66	10189
	T										3037		7004					10041	
	O						7			4	30					41		82	
51 PHILIPPINES	P												1					1	1
52 POLAND	P										29							29	2134
	T				361	561					1151							2073	
	O						5			2	20				2		3	32	
53 PORTUGAL	P										41	31						72	239
	T										1	153						154	
	O										12	1						13	
54 ROMANIA	T												237					237	244
	O						7											7	
55 RUSSIAN FEDERATION	P										39							39	1482
	T										1342							1342	
	O	11					15			27	17	16					15	101	

#	COUNTRY		UNTSO	UNMOGIP	UNFICYP	UNDOF	UNIFIL	UNIKOM	UNAVEM	ONUSAL	MINURSO	UNPROFOR	ONUMOZ	UNOSOM	UNOMUR	UNOMIG	UNOMIL	UNAMIR	TOTALS	GRAND TOTAL
56	SENEGAL	T																43	43	61
		O						6							10			2	18	
		P																		
57	SINGAPORE	O						7											7	7
58	SLOVAK REPUBLIC	T										587							587	605
		O							5								8	5	18	
		P																		
59	SPAIN	T								80			40						120	1604
		O										1440							1440	
		P								4		19	21						44	
60	SRI LANKA	P											11						11	11
61	SWEDEN	T	17	8				6	3	1		35	13						83	1416
		O										1264							1264	
		P								1		18	45	2		3			69	
62	SWITZERLAND	T										7				2			9	27
		O										2							2	
		P	7									6	3						16	
63	THAILAND	O						6											6	6
64	TOGO	P									5		5						10	10
65	TUNISIA	T										10							10	19
		O									9								9	
66	TURKEY	T										1468							1468	1474
		O						6											6	
67	UKRAINE	T										9							9	1187
		O										1168							1168	
		P										10							10	

COUNTRY		UNTSO	UNMOGIP	UNFICYP	UNDOF	UNIFIL	UNIKOM	UNAVEM	ONUSAL	MINURSO	UNPROFOR	ONUMOZ	UNOSOM	UNOMUR	UNOMIG	UNOMIL	UNAMIR	TOTALS	GRAND TOTAL
68 UNITED KINGDOM	T			420							3270						590	4280	4315
	O						15				18				2			35	
69 UNITED STATES	T										873	1						874	935
	O	17					14			30								61	
70 URUGUAY	P									4		15						19	955
	T											840						840	
	O		3				6			15		27			1	17	27	96	
71 VENEZUELA	O						2		3		3							8	8
72 ZAMBIA	P												6					6	938
	T											807					107	914	
	O											8					10	18	
73 ZIMBABWE	P							2	5									7	1035
	T												998					998	
	O												5				25	30	
SUB TOTAL	P			35				17	183	49	644	905	51				5	1889	
SUB TOTAL	T			1178	1043	5240	897	11	2	31	37442	4192	18725		1	65	3465	72292	
SUB TOTAL	O	218	38	8			242	50	13	219	629	330		66	54	270	294	2431	
GRAND TOTAL		218	38	1221	1043	5240	1139	78	198	299	38715	5427	18776	66	55	335	3764		76612

disease remained. This was exacerbated by the Western-imposed methods of concentrating people away from their home villages in large feeding centres without adequate sanitation. Sahnoun, a distinguished Algerian diplomat, shaped a plan uniquely suited to the particularities of Somalia's crisis. He began to build on the clan system that had reemerged with the collapse of the Cold War-bolstered Somali state. He worked with, rather than against, clan leaders and grassroots organisations to renew the devastated local economies. He also tried to legitimise and professionalise, rather than forcibly disarm, the local militias as part of the process of rebuilding the shattered nation. But Sahnoun's plan was never implemented. Flying in the face of standard peacekeeping methods, it was bitterly opposed in the Security Council, most vociferously by the United States. Before his results could be consolidated, Ambassador Sahnoun was forced to resign, and the Somali operation was taken over by American military officials operating in the name of the UN. Their disastrous failure, criminalising then rehabilitating the 'warlord' Mohammad Farah Aidid, led to the deaths of 18 Americans, 24 Pakistani peacekeepers and hundreds of Somalis.

Into the fray: civil war peacekeeping

Other UN operations focused on preparing for and monitoring elections aimed at consolidating fragile ceasefires ending Cold War-driven, often decades-old civil wars. These operations sometimes involved huge contingents of UN staff, military as well as civilian, with virtually unlimited mandates equivalent to governing the country.

Overseeing elections

The Chapter VI UN Transitional Authority in Cambodia (UNTAC) operation in Cambodia, the largest in UN history, was of this type, as was the election monitoring/restoring civil society prescript of the Namibia deployment. In both examples, the immediate goals of fostering relatively free and fair elections, and preventing a large-scale renewal of civil war, appeared at least partly met. But Pol Pot's Khmer Rouge boycotted the election, and its results did not stop Cambodia's civil war. During just one week in the spring of 1994, 55,000 Cambodians fled their homes in the western part of the country in response to escalating Khmer Rouge attacks.[1] By mid-July 1994, the coalition government elected in the UN-run election had passed new legislation to outlaw the Khmer Rouge.[2]

---

1 *New York Times*, 4 May 1994.

Other PKOs that reflected the collapse of Cold War-driven rivalries were those in Angola, Western Sahara, Mozambique and El Salvador. In each, the incentive for accepting UN-sponsored negotiations was rooted in the withdrawal of superpower support for one or both sides in the longstanding wars. In El Salvador, the election process resulted in institutionalising a role for the opposition FMLN forces. The country has yet to overcome the legacy of massive economic inequality, right-wing death squads and extrajudicial murder, but a process of national reconciliation does appear to be underway. The promise of a UN-sponsored national referendum in Western Sahara, however, remains unfulfilled, with election plans consistently delayed. In Angola, the UN moved precipitately to hold elections long before the US-backed UNITA rebels had shown any real willingness to abide by the results. The consequence was an astonishingly overt failure of UN intervention, as UNITA leader Jonas Savimbi led his forces back into the bush to resume the civil war the day after their sound defeat in the UN-backed elections. The UN remains unable to respond, and the brutal civil war continues. Meanwhile in Mozambique, perhaps having learned the lesson of Angola, elections were postponed for more than a year until such time as the Western-backed RENAMO guerrillas ceased their assaults and destabilisation campaigns.

Overseeing violence

In all of these cases, the willingness of the UN to intervene was inextricably bound up with the expired superpower conflict that had raged within these countries. The legacy of that conflict lies at the root of the violence that continues to ravage some of these Cold War left-overs. With some of these wars, of course, the UN essentially agreed to let the parties fight it out: the bombing of Kabul in Afghanistan by one of the Mujahedin factions, provided with advanced weapons by the United States, was considered unworthy of UN peacekeeping efforts beyond some minimal assistance to refugees fleeing the assault.

In other countries, the UN's agreement to send peacekeepers was a reflection of the end of strategic bipolarity. It also reflected the renewed interest of the US as sole superpower to maintain some level of stability in the increasingly volatile nations of the South (including the 'new South' in some republics of the former Soviet Union). The political instability that racked Liberia in early 1994 was one of the few arenas in which a rapid international deployment was able to make relatively concrete gains. It is not

---

2 *Christian Science Monitor*, 8 July 1994.

coincidence, in this context, that the force sent to Monrovia was the only peacekeeping contingent made up solely of troops from the South – while the UN financed much of the operation, it was organised by the Organisation of African Unity (OAU) and all troops were from Africa.

Haiti and Rwanda

In Haiti and Rwanda, UN teams briefly attempted but quickly failed to impose order on nations shattered by the vestiges of their colonial or neo-colonial past. In Haiti, where the military junta ousted democratically elected President Aristide, the deployment of UN human rights monitors proved of little value in stemming the violence. UN reports of the corpses appearing more and more frequently on the streets of Port-au-Prince did little to stop the proliferation of death. The UN and the United States refused to respond beyond a for-appearances-only porous embargo. The US ship *Harlan County* turned and sailed away from a few hundred protestors at Port-au-Prince harbour while President Aristide languished in Washington; and desperate Haitians were turned over to their torturers by US Coast Guard ships: the failure of US and UN policy was unmistakeable. On 12 July 1994, when the military junta ordered the UN and Organisation of American States (OAS) human rights monitors out of Haiti, the Security Council responded only with a presidential statement, which lacked the force of international law inherent in a resolution. The language, nonetheless, escalated the UN assessment of the crisis to one which 'affects the peace and security of the region', thus paving the way for Chapter VII military force. But it appeared to be intended primarily as UN legitimation of a US military invasion targeted less on restoring Haitian democracy than at stemming the flood of refugees to the Florida coast. And then, in July, the Council gave explicit authorisation to a US-controlled, non-UN military invasion.

In wartorn Rwanda, meanwhile, the limited monitoring mandate of the UN peacekeepers meant that when the April 1994 carnage in the streets of Kigali broke out, the Blue Helmets could do virtually nothing. Instead of responding quickly to the emergency by, for example, organising and financing an all-African response contingent, the Security Council, fearing that its own small contingent would be unable to stop the violence, moved instead to reduce the UN troops on the ground still further from 2,500 to only 270. The Rwanda conflict, simplistically dismissed at first as a 'tribal massacre' by the West, was rooted in the legacy of colonialism and uncontrolled, profit-driven arms sales after the Cold War. Access to education, privilege, and ultimately derivative power was granted by the Belgians largely to the Tutsi minority, leading to years of colonially-augmented tribal enmity. A Hutu revolution shot them to power in 1959, leading to independence in 1962. Hostilities broke out again intermittently, especially in 1990, and were answered by a near stampede of international arms traders eager to dump advanced weapons in Rwanda. In 1994 this led to the systematic elimination of all opponents of the Hutu extremists, and fuelled one of the worst humanitarian disasters in African history.

The former Yugoslavia torn apart

In the former Yugoslavia, a cruel and bloody war of dislocation, torture and 'ethnic cleansing' festered unabated. Regional solutions failed and the Security Council's reluctance to challenge the North's support for the various factions (Russia's for the Serbs; Germany's for Croatia; and no one, beyond hollow American slogans, for the cosmopolitan ideal that lay at the root of Sarajevan or Bosnian identity) allowed a cruel and bloody war of dislocation, torture and 'ethnic cleansing' to fester unabated. Only Western European 'regional' forces – the European Union and NATO, both Cold War instruments – were brought into efforts to resolve the emerging Yugoslav crisis. The Conference on Security and Cooperation in Europe (CSCE), the one potential agency with a European-wide mandate encompassing both West and East, as well as Russia, was kept out of the Yugo-loop, even during the historic CSCE summit in November 1990. Instead, the multilateral responsibility for the crisis shifted too soon to the military-oriented discourse of the Security Council. Its new peacekeeping strategy of establishing UN-designated 'safe havens' collapsed as the Bosnian Serbs continued sniper fire in Sarajevo, called what turned out to be the West's monumental bluff in Gorazde, and continued virtually unchallenged their domination of the other largely Muslim towns in Bosnia identified as 'safe areas'. The European powers, especially the United Kingdom, exploited the danger posed to their soldiers within the UN Protection Force (UN-PROFOR) contingents as the basis for opposing air strikes or sending additional troops. However, they also refused to lift the one-sided arms embargo to allow the Bosnian government to defend itself, and even to provide support (diplomatic, financial, or otherwise) to the organisations of civil society fighting to preserve a semblance of national life in Bosnia. By the summer of 1994, the Security Council had turned over responsibility to a joint US-European-Russian alliance, whose proposed 'settlement' for the Bosnian conflict awarded 49 per cent of the territory to the Bosnian Serb forces who were responsible for the 'ethnic cleansing' of Bosnia's multi-ethnic, Muslim and Croatian populations.

The North-South chasm

The paradigm of the industrialised and generally wealthy North fighting for control of the impoverished and, therefore, often unstable South is a useful one for understanding the motives and imperatives shaping UN peacekeeping. But within those broad strokes is a crucial particularity: within the North, it is Washington alone that has the power to call the strategic shots, even if not at all times and on all issues. But the controlling intersection between US and broader Northern strategic interests, as well as the increasingly overlapping identities of the United States and the UN, mean that the US role is often determinative in whether and how the UN will respond to 'security' crises around the world. (Or, similarly, if the UN will be denied a place at the table, as has been appallingly true in Middle East diplomacy, especially since the Gulf War. But that's another story.)

One immediate and potentially long-lived consequence of the Somalia debacle was the souring of the Clinton administration on the 'aggressive multilateralism' that characterised its early foreign policy rhetoric. A new White House report on 'Reforming Multilateral Peace Operations', released in May 1994, reflected a clear decision to downplay UN peacekeeping in favour of a return to using UN operations largely to maximise US policy goals. That tactical use of the UN ensures that 'the US benefits from having to bear only a share of the burden. We also benefit by being able to invoke the voice of the community of nations on behalf of a cause we support'. Strengthening the United Nations itself is addressed only in the context of improving financial and tactical efficiency, and democratising UN decision-making does not appear as a goal at all. The report goes to great lengths to assure Congress that any agreement to place US troops under UN command would be limited and tactical – and that 'the greater the US military role, the less likely it will be that the US will agree to have a UN commander exercise overall operational control over US forces. Any large scale participation of US forces in a major peace enforcement mission that is likely to involve combat should ordinarily be conducted under US command and operational control or through competent regional organisations such as NATO'. NATO troops, as confirmed by a secret document (MC 327) issued by the Military Committee of the Alliance, will not be placed under UN command, nor will NATO share intelligence information with UN peacekeepers.

Perhaps it is not surprising, then, that when the US Marines landed in Mogadishu, the top UN official in Somalia with whom the American command was to coordinate was Admiral Jonathan Howe. Howe was a former

US Navy commander, who exploited his US rank to ensure that the UN was on board with Washington's preferred strategy for bringing Somalia's General Mohammad Aidid to heel. When an Italian unit, whose own colonial past provided, however ironically, a far deeper understanding of Somalia than that of the newly-arrived Americans, refused to participate in what it deemed the ill-advised UN military action to capture Aidid, its soldiers were branded virtual outlaws. Claiming that any national contingent participating in a UN operation must follow UN orders regardless of their legitimacy, the UN Secretary-General Boutros-Ghali attempted, though unsuccessfully, to have the Italian general recalled. (It is interesting to note the UN's legal office's acknowledgment that the Secretary-General had no legal basis to demand the recall of a national contingent's commander. The Italians stayed in Somalia, although they moved out of Mogadishu to avoid future entanglements in military actions that they deemed inappropriate.)

Power and democracy

The UN Charter, designed to institutionalise rather than to challenge the global control exerted by the Second World War victors, provides for the power of waging war in the name of international peace to rest in the Security Council. But the Council, with its five permanent veto-wielding members, represents perhaps the most undemocratic component of the United Nations organisation as a whole. Zimbabwe's Ambassador Simbarashe Mumbengegwi, for example, expressed in 1992 serious unease about the imbalance of power:

'The Security Council only consists of 15 members. There are 160 members who are not part of the Security Council. Therefore it would be a serious mistake to want to create a situation where 15 members can want to argue that they are much stronger as a body than the 160 who are not in that body. That would really undermine the very basis of the United Nations, which is basically democratic, [and based on] equality of states.'

As long as the Security Council remains a bastion of Northern power, decisions that lead to the deployment of peacekeepers or other troops cannot be said to reflect a democratic UN. Despite Boutros Boutros-Ghali's claim that 'multilateralism is the democracy of international society',[3] its practice

---

3 *New York Times*, 20 August 1993.

in the arena of UN peacekeeping is anything but democratic. With the current debate on Security Council reform focusing almost solely on bringing Germany and Japan onto the Council – in the words of President Clinton's campaign, 'in recognition of their economic strength and the contributions they make to the United Nations budget'[4] – the continuation of the Security Council as a citadel of the richest and most powerful nations seems assured.

The popular belief that a UN-led multilateral effort is somehow inherently safer for the South than a unilateral or bilateral US or US-British intervention is true only to the degree that UN democracy can be preserved and defended. And so long as the vast majority of the world's countries remain excluded from Security Council decision-making, UN democracy remains unachieved.

Secretary General Boutros-Ghali, far more activist than all his recent predecessors, has stated his specific desire to reshape the UN into a global cop. Speaking at a February 1994 press conference, he reminded reporters that:

> 'the United States is not eager to play the role of the policeman of the world. So *the United Nations is there to do the job.* And there is a consensus that, in spite of all the difficulties, in spite of all the contradictions existing, the only forum existing today that can play this role is the United Nations' (emphasis added).

Perhaps his effort to bring that startling goal to fruition is part of his rationale for establishing in his 1992 *Agenda for Peace*, without General Assembly authorisation, the seven-member international team in charge of the 'stand-by arrangement concept'. This worked throughout 1993 and into 1994, travelling the world to cajole and pressure capitals into commitments of troops, logistical supplies, money, airlift capability, and more, for what would become the nucleus of a UN quick-response team. Colonel Gambiez, head of the stand-by arrangement team, confirmed in a 14 April 1994 press conference that the quick-response goal is different to the peace enforcement units also called for in *Agenda for Peace*, and arguably consistent with the provisions of Articles 43, 45 and 47 of the Charter. 'Stand-by forces are not to be used for peace enforcement actions', he said. They also would not be under the control of the Military Staff Com-

---

4 *New York Times*, 12 January 1994.

mittee, which holds the Charter's mandate for command of UN troops. By early 1994, 23 countries had pledged to make stand-by troops available for as yet undefined future UN missions. It is interesting to note, however, that when the call came to make those troops available for the real here-and-now UN peacekeeping commitment in wartorn Rwanda, every single one of the 23 countries refused.

Conclusion

Although a standing international UN army remains far from reality, its potential parameters are already clear. If it were to be made accountable to the General Assembly, the repository of democratic legitimacy of the United Nations, it would perhaps be an admirable goal. If access to this standing army, or even to its supplies and cargo planes and medical-evacuation units, was made available to the regional organisations functioning in Africa, in Asia, in the Middle East, in Latin America; or if representatives of the Non-Aligned Movement, the Group of 77, were somehow institutionalised within its leadership; or if the links and accountability to the humanitarian and economic development providers within the UN system and the NGOs outside it could somehow be assured – then, and only then, would such a plan bode well for dealing with the root causes, economic and social, of the world's unrest. But the anticipated lines of authority bounce back and forth only between the Secretary General and the Security Council. The protection of smaller and weaker states, especially the states of the global-South, as well as even the ability of such a standing army to overcome escalating local and regional crises, therefore remains an unresolved challenge.

UN planning, from its earliest days, has considered 'trip wire' arrangements or other methods of early warning to head off crises before they explode out of control. In recent years, most of those efforts have failed. Not because the information doesn't exist, quite the contrary – in these days of live-time CNN-driven familiarity with horror stories throughout the world, no one can claim that they didn't know. Too often, however, the warnings go unanswered, like the efforts of the International Committee of the Red Cross in Somalia, until it is too late, and the only option seems to be to send troops. New kinds of international tripwires are required, based in local and regional organisations and aimed at identifying the root causes – poverty, disempowerment, disenfranchisement – of the explosions that come to be called, wrongly in most cases, 'ethnic warfare' or 'tribal hostility.'

Military peacekeeping, the sending of UN troops to impose or enforce a reluctant peace, is a sign of failure. As authorised under Chapter VII, it may be required in rare situations of absolutely desperate circumstances – but as has been seen in the accumulating peacekeeping operations of just the last few years, military peacekeeping is always difficult, and rarely successful. Its use should be that of a last resort. It should only be called on when the solutions proposed in Chapter VI and Chapter VIII, mandating that peaceful and regional efforts be exhausted before military remedies are tried, have proved in action, not merely by political pontification, to be insufficient.

The goal of UN reform must not be to improve military peacekeeping operations, but to improve the organisation's ability to carry out better pro-active, peace-supporting and peace-building work that will prevent military intervention from being required. A military peacekeeping operation, even if it appears narrowly successful, should never be upheld as an heroic example of glorious international cooperation. Its very success should be viewed with sadness, as a lesson of the international community's failure, the regional and global institutions' failure, to have acted in time.

What is needed is a redefinition of peacekeeping, away from soldiers, whether Blue Helmets or red, white and blue, and towards an understanding of what makes true peace possible. Martin Luther King defined peace as 'not simply the absence of war, but the presence of justice'. When one examines the causes of the collapse of peace around the world, the absence of justice, whether economic or political, remains a constant factor. The United Nations would do well to base its peacekeeping on Dr King's definition.

Article 43

1. All Members of the United Nations, in order to contribute to the maintenance of international peace and security, undertake to make available to the Security Council, on its call and in accordance with a special agreement or agreements, armed forces, assistance, and facilities, including rights of passage, necessary for the purpose of maintaining international peace and security.
2. Such agreement or agreements shall govern the numbers and types of forces, their degree of readiness and general location, and the nature of the facilities and assistance to be provided.
3. The agreement or agreements shall be negotiated as soon as possible on the initiative of the Security Council. They shall be concluded between

the Security Council and Members or between the Security Council and groups of Members and shall be subject to ratification by the signatory states in accordance with their respective constitutional processes.

Article 45

In order to enable the United Nations to take urgent military measures, Members shall hold immediately available national air-force contingents for combined international enforcement action. The strength and degree of readiness of these contingents and plans for their combined action shall be determined within the limits laid down in the special agreement or agreements referred to in Article 43, by the Security Council with the assistance of the Military Staff Committee.

Article 47

1. There shall be established a Military Staff Committee to advise and assist the Security Council on all questions relating to the Security Council's military requirements for the maintenance of international peace and security, the employment and command of forces placed at its disposal, the regulation of armaments, and possible disarmament.
2. The Military Staff Committee shall consist of the Chiefs of Staff of the permanent members of the Security Council or their representatives. Any Member of the United Nations not permanently represented on the Committee shall be invited by the Committee to be associated with it when the efficient discharge of the Committee's responsibilities requires the participation of that Member in its work.
3. The Military Staff Committee shall be responsible under the Security Council for the strategic direction of any armed forces placed at the disposal of the Security Council. Questions relating to the command of such forces shall be worked out subsequently.
4. The Military Staff Committee, with the authorisation of the Security Council and after consultation with appropriate regional agencies, may establish regional sub-committees.

8. The people's organisations and the UN: NGOs in international civil society

Barbara Adams

The United Nations is, on the one hand, a place where ideals are articulated and standards of conduct set. On the other, it is a place that reflects the inequalities of power distribution within and among member states, and where decision making is not as independent of national government priorities as the UN's name and image would suggest. The UN is a centre of democracy in terms of one nation, one vote, and in terms of the issues, such as apartheid, that are set on its agenda. It is also a forum for elites. The UN is an arena where non-governmental organisations (NGOs) have raised concerns and influenced agendas, for example during the UN Decade on Women and, more recently, in connection with the UN Conference on Environment and Development. Yet the system is largely financed by northern governments, and this has influenced decision-making and concepts of participation. These influences are exacerbated by hierarchial attitudes towards international work; international institutions have yet to view themselves as so many diverse pieces within a global puzzle.

The UN conjures up many different images: the Secretary-General; peacekeeping forces; the Security Council; refugee work; UNICEF; the struggle for independence. Its agenda is comprehensive. It has many different agencies and programmes. It is a donor, an organisation for service, research statistics and information dissemination, and a place for advocacy.

NGO activities, approaches and attitudes to the UN have reflected all of these aspects. NGOs have been supporters and publicists for the UN, advocates for the UN, critics of the UN, implementors or participants in UN programmes; they provide funding, expertise, consultancy and advocacy for equity and justice.

This chapter looks at public participation in the UN within the NGO framework; it examines context and contributions, and addresses challenges to the UN and NGOs.

The context for UN/NGO interaction

NGOs have had an impact on the UN, its programmes and deliberations in a multitude of ways that are impossible to trace. Public mobilisation and campaigning by organised groupings such as the women's movement, environmentalists, the peace movement, and those fighting apartheid have influenced the UN's agenda. Formal education, curriculum development and development education have supported UN goals and objectives. NGOs have provided means of communication across national, religious and cultural boundaries, from the local and grassroots level to the national and international levels, and between organisations of civil society. At the national level, NGOs influence parliaments and governments in determining policies pursued in international fora.

Formal mechanisms for NGO presence and participation (and assessment of performance) at the UN, however, are very limited compared to the breadth and depth of NGO involvement in world affairs. The UN Charter, which opens with 'We the Peoples', focuses formal NGO contributions on arrangements with the Economic and Social Council (ECOSOC). NGOs are viewed primarily as providing public support for the UN system and participating in the implementation of some of its programmes. The UN's formal procedures have not made it easy for NGOs to contribute their insights, experience and expertise to UN decision-making and policy-setting directly, other than through governments at the national level.

Challenges for NGOs

Operational development activities and recent world conferences have shown that there are many NGOs, especially in developing countries, that are active at local, national, regional and international levels but which are not represented at the UN. The UN is now to undertake a general review of its current arrangements for consultation with NGOs (discussed in more detail later in this chapter). This review is to be completed by the end of 1995, with a view to updating and improving NGO/UN interaction if necessary. It is taking place at a time marked by changes in international priorities and the role of the nation state, and by transboundary movements, problems and solutions. There is a new emphasis on 'democratisation' and greater attention is paid to the practice of governance. These factors have contributed to an increased openness on the part of the UN and member states to outside perspectives and expertise, and have encouraged them to provide a greater political space for NGOs.

> 'The United Nations was considered to be a forum for sovereign States alone. Within the space of a few short years, this attitude has changed. NGOs are now considered full participants in international life.'
> *Boutros Boutros-Ghali, Secretary-General of the UN addressing NGOs at a DPI conference, 19 September 1994.*

Views are mixed among member states about the merits of increased NGO participation in the UN. Some see it as an essential component of democratisation and the participation of civil society; others regard it as part of the political conditionality imposed by the North on the South; some see non-state involvement as vital to tackling problems and implementing programmes; still others view it as an abdication or weakening of state responsibilities, particularly in the area of social services and development.

These developments pose challenges for NGOs. NGOs need to expand their capacity, skills and expertise to work effectively at the international level, in addition to continuing their wide-ranging activities at the local, national and regional levels. A bigger challenge is posed for NGOs if they present themselves as representatives of civil society, which would require them to address the central issues of their democracy, accountability, and representation.

As the dimensions of a global society broaden, there is increasing attention to the importance of civil society and the role of the organisations of civil society. Organisations of civil society are intimately involved in shaping and responding to new understandings concerning international priorities, the role of the nation-state, the balancing and interdependence of economic and social priorities, human security and the imperatives of sustainability.

NGOs' participation in the international system

NGOs have long been recognised as essential participants in the struggle for international peace and justice. The NGO contribution is multifaceted: whilst mobilising resources for refugees and development projects, for example, and contributing to humanitarian assistance in emergency situations, NGOs also play an influential role in undertaking education and advocacy work. They are constantly active in seeking more responsive action

---

New institutions of a global civil society

The shape our societies take does not depend exclusively on governments. Individuals, families, community groups, international foundations, transnational corporations, the communications media – these and many others help mould civil society.

There also are thousands of non-governmental organisations operating nationally and internationally – monitoring human rights, organising humanitarian aid and promoting the interests of such groups as women, the disabled or indigenous people. And new organisations emerge each year, often sprouting up spontaneously in response to felt needs and forming new alliances for change. They can powerfully influence government policy, as many women's organisations and environmental groups have demonstrated.

UNDP 1994 Human Development Report

---

by governments at the national and multilateral levels to set high standards of human rights, to establish and maintain peace, and to address their citizens' aspirations and basic needs.

NGOs are frequently the source of new insights or alternative policies and approaches on, for example, the status of women and the monitoring of transnational corporation practices. Through national, regional, international and multilateral processes, NGOs engage in advocacy work to promote policies that reflect these insights. This involves representation to government and parliamentary bodies, the churches, the media, trade unions, professional associations, the membership and constituencies of NGOs and the general public.

There has been growing recognition on the part of state actors that NGO experience can serve to inform and deepen the policy-making processes of governments and the UN agencies. For example, the growing international interest in the contribution of development NGOs is not just a reflection of the magnitude of financial flows from NGOs to the developing world (which one UN report estimated at US\$16.6 billion in 1992). It also reflects changing international priorities, with the emphasis shifting towards a more people-centred approach, which is more concerned with social and human development, sustainable development and popular mobilisation and participation – areas in which NGOs have considerable expertise.

'New development models should specifically recognise the role of organisations of civil society in giving a voice to the people. Grassroots people's movements should be strengthened and supported. They are the best chance to engage people fully in the betterment of their own lives.'

Boutros Boutros-Ghali, Secretary-General of the UN, addressing the Preparatory Committee for the World Summit for Social Development, 22 August 1994.

Formal mechanisms for NGO participation

(This section is excerpted and adapted from the NGLS handbook for NGOs)
NGOs have been active in the United Nations since its founding in San Francisco. NGOs interact with the UN Secretariat and agencies and consult with the member states of the UN. UN- NGO work takes many forms, including information dissemination, projects, collaboration with UN agencies, advocacy and lobbying of governments individually and collectively. This work is undertaken at the national level, at the UN, and in formal and informal ways. The formal interaction and consultation is governed by the UN Charter and related resolutions.

The UN Charter
The preamble of the United Nations Charter affirms the aims and purposes which 'we, the peoples of the United Nations' are committed to realise through the world organisation. Article 71 states that: 'The Economic and Social Council may make suitable arrangements for consultation with non-governmental organisations which are concerned with matters within its competence. Such arrangements may be made with international organisations and, where appropriate, with national organisations after consultation with the Member of the United Nations concerned.' This article and the arrangements established by ECOSOC form the basis for NGO consultation with governments at the UN and set guidelines for UN Secretariat dealings with NGOs. These procedures and arrangements also govern or guide other agencies and programmes of the UN system in their relations with NGOs.

The ECOSOC is a 54-member inter-governmental body of the UN which coordinates and oversees work in the economic and social fields. The fact that the arrangements for consultative status are made with the ECOSOC formally limits NGO involvement to issues on the ECOSOC agenda and to meetings of the Council and its subsidiary bodies. In practice NGOs are also given access to the General Assembly and its committees but they have no rights to make oral and written statements unless special arrangements are made. NGOs have no formal status with the Security Council, although humanitarian and some human rights groups work closely with many of the situations and activities addressed by the Security Council.

Under the UN Charter ECOSOC is the UN organ which is primarily responsible for consultation with NGOs. To assist it in this task, ECOSOC formed an intergovernmental Committee on Non-Governmental Organisations, currently composed of 19 members. This reviews NGO applications for consultative or roster status with ECOSOC, reviews the work of NGOs already in consultative status, and addresses general questions concerning such NGOs. This is the only intergovernmental committee in the UN system whose exclusive purpose is to manage relations with NGOs.

The rules and procedures for consultation with NGOs are contained in Economic and Social Council (ECOSOC) Resolution 1296, which was adopted in May 1968. Resolution 1296 specifies criteria which NGOs – 'any international organisation which is not established by intergovernmental agreement' – must meet in order to gain consultative status with ECOSOC. It also sets out the rules governing their involvement in the meetings of ECOSOC and its subsidiary bodies. The resolution also spells out the functions of the ECOSOC Committee on Non-Governmental Organisations and specifies terms of NGO consultation with the UN Secretariat. It establishes three categories for NGOs: Category I for international NGOs whose concerns cover most of the agenda of ECOSOC; Category II for NGOs that have special competence in a few fields of activity of ECOSOC; and Roster Status for NGOs whose competence enables them to make occasional contributions to the work of the UN. NGOs in consultative status with ECOSOC have to report every four years on the activities undertaken. These quadrennial reports are submitted to the ECOSOC Committee on NGOs, which can revoke consultative status of NGOs that fail to report or behave in ways contrary to the goals of the UN Charter.

In addition to consultative arrangements with NGOs, UN resolutions require that the UN Department of Public Information (DPI): 'actively assist and encourage national information services, education and institutional and other governmental and non-governmental organisations of all kinds interested in spreading information about the United Nations'. In this context NGOs can apply for Associative Status with DPI based on established criteria relating to organisations' standing, their support of the UN Charter, purpose, membership and the scope and resources available to carry out information programmes.

In 1994, there are 411 NGOs with consultative status, 1,096 on the roster, and 1,312 that have associative status with DPI (554 of these are also in consultative/roster status with ECOSOC).

Recent trends in UN-NGO interaction

In the last few years there has been a noticeable increase in NGOs' interest in the UN (and vice versa). NGOs have become much more actively involved in the multilateral policy-setting process. This was most noticeable in preparations for and participation in the UN Conference on Environment and Development (UNCED), which was held in June 1992 in Rio de Janeiro, Brazil, and the International Conference on Population and Development which was held in September 1994 in Cairo, Egypt. On a smaller scale, NGOs have continued to be active in connection with the elaboration of the International Convention to combat Desertification, the Global Conference on the Sustainable Development of Small Island Developing States, the Convention on Climate Change, the Convention on Biological Diversity, the Global Environment Facility and the UN Commission on Sustainable Development.

This increased interest by NGOs can be observed across the board. Thus, in humanitarian work there is greater interaction between UN, governments and NGOs in emergency and relief work. Similarly, NGOs have consistently applied themselves to the work of the UN on human rights and the status of women. The World Conference on Human Rights in Vienna in June 1993 and the Fourth World Conference on Women in Beijing in September 1995 are major events in the NGO calendar. Likewise in economic and social matters there has been a significant expansion of NGO interest and engagement. After years of concentrating on implementing development projects at the local level, there is now much greater interest in presenting civil society perspectives on economic and social policy issues at the UN decision-making venues. Several major conferences, including the International Conference on Population and Development (ICPD) in September 1994, the World Summit for Social Development (WSSD) in March 1995 and the Second UN Conference on Human Settlements (HABITAT II) in Turkey in 1996, are providing a venue for developing ideas, strategies and networking among NGOs.

NGO participation at major UN conferences has changed in recent years. Their increased attention has contributed to some changes in their practice in inter-governmental meetings, and in their monitoring of the ongoing work of the UN, particularly on issues relating to sustainable development. They have also been more active in lobbying national governments – as delegation members and in presenting policy recommendations on the conference issues – and in monitoring the development of the negotiations among governments. Women's organisations understood and siezed the opportunity, campaigning successfully to convey their positions in intergovernmental negotiations, for example through forming women's caucuses, which made particular advances at the World Conference on Human Rights and the International Conference on Population and Development. A report of the Secretary-General on the General Review of Arrangements for Consultations with Non-Governmental Organisations, of 26 May 1994, points out that 'NGOs have often been pioneers in national and international processes in drawing the attention of policy-makers and official development agencies to issues which have, in the last 20 years, become essential components of development strategies'.

Member states and the UN are showing increasing recognition of the importance of popular participation, including that of NGOs. This can be seen in the references to participation in Agenda 21, the comprehensive blueprint adopted at the UN Conference on Environment and Development and in the Programme of Action adopted at the International Conference on Population and Development. Agenda 21 devotes ten of its 40 chapters to elaborating ways to involve various 'major groups' in the follow-up, further development and implementation of sustainable development measures agreed by governments.

'NGOs are a basic form of popular representation in the present-day world. Their participation in international organisations is, in a way, a guarantee of the political legitimacy of those international organisations.' *Boutros Boutros-Ghali, Secretary-General of the UN, addressing NGOs at a DPI conference, 19 September 1994.*

UN-NGO Review

NGOs and the UN's new-found interest in each other has contributed to a recent ECOSOC decision to hold a general review of UN arrangements for consultations with NGOs. The review is to be conducted over two years with final recommendations going to the UN General Assembly in 1995. It provides a valuable opportunity for the UN, member states and NGOs to set a new standard for interaction. The UN could institute new rules and procedures to provide an environment that would enable organisations of civil society to participate in a more effective and serious manner and in a way which reflects their constituencies, insights and experiences.

There has been a general lack of recognition at the UN, which is reflected in its procedures, of the diversity of groups (in function as well as in outlook and stance). This has had the effect of homogenising the opportunities for NGO contributions – mainly in the form of oral and written statements – in a fashion that does not allow the breadth and depth of possible NGO contributions to develop. By and large, NGOs have increased their access to and influence on UN deliberations by influencing member states. National NGOs have become markedly more active in this area, and at recent world conferences there has been a increase in the number of NGO representatives on official delegations. However, the UN 'definition' of NGOs has not readily facilitated the participation of national or regional NGOs. This handicaps development NGOs, which are frequently either nationally-based or consortia of national NGOs. While many possess direct international experience, including active and effective North/South partnerships, they are not 'international' organisations per se, and have been viewed as being less relevant to the international community. In practice, the UN definition and opportunities for participation have favoured Northern-based international NGOs. Greater activity on the part of Southern NGOs, particularly with regard to world conference processes, has resulted in the 'discovery' of Southern NGO perspectives and networks. There is now growing pressure to distinguish between international and Northern NGOs. This is helping to open up international NGOs to more participation and representation by their Southern members.

Today, more attention is being paid to the differences between NGOs, recognising that separate groups have discrete priorities, constituencies and contributions – as shown by the recognition of major groups in Agenda 21 adopted at the Earth Summit. The NGO community is not homogenous, containing as it does substantial differences in positions between, for example, the industrial groupings and some not-for-profit NGOs.

Challenges for NGOs: Voice of civil society or a special interest group?

NGOs have been active throughout the life of the United Nations, notably in the areas of human rights and refugee work. Over the last decade, NGOs have played a greater role in domestic and international work. They themselves have proliferated, their resources have increased, and there has been a growing emphasis on professionalism, international networking, policy dialogue and advocacy.

Like the UN and member states, NGOs are being forced to rethink their roles. Recent demands are for them to increase their capacity for policy work and at the international level, whilst at the same time continuing to implement programmes at the local and household levels. If they are to be effective at the UN, many NGOs need to establish a more consistent presence and to present their experiences and recommendations in a more sustained and strategic manner.

NGOs face a dilemma. If they become more involved in international networking and lobbying, these activities may pull them away from their local or national work. This can lessen or undermine their accountability to their membership and to local communities. These factors, together with concerns about Northern and gender bias, present a challenge to NGOs on their own decision-making procedures and priorities. As they become more influential and gain more access to the decision-making, implementation and evaluation processes, the legitimacy of their voice and perspectives, and the transparency and accountability of their processes, will attract more scrutiny – and more criticism. NGO decision-making, their follow-up capacity, their resource and information sharing will become increasingly significant as NGOs present themselves as an important force in civil society. NGOs face a critical juncture.

Building bridges between the UN and civil society

Recent meetings and experiences of NGOs with the UN system and the intergovernmental process have given rise to a number of observations and suggestions concerning improved communication and collaboration between NGOs and the UN system. These include the following:

1 Broad public participation in decision-making is essential for equity and effectiveness.
2 Participation of people's organisations provides some essential elements of accountability and transparency regarding government and UN system policies and activities.
3 New forms of participation (within and between NGOs and the UN) are necessary. This includes the need of individuals, groups and organisations to know about and participate in decisions, particularly those which potentially affect the communities in which they live and work.
4 The diversity of experiences and insights that people's organisations and NGOs represent, as well as their autonomy and independence, need to be understood, welcomed and catered for by the UN and governments, and safeguarded by NGOs. Distinctions should be made, for example,

between the experiences and contributions of profit and non-profit organisations.

5 NGOs that represent 'people's organisations' should be viewed as voices of the civil society. Such NGOs should undertake the necessary procedures to ensure their democratic character.

'Non-governmental organisations are infinitely diverse by virtue of their size, statutes, fields of activity, methods, means and objectives. It is understandable that States are sometimes tempted to try to utilize or control non-governmental organisations in order to place them indirectly in the service of their own national policies. Non-governmental organisations must be beyond reproach in the political field... your independence is essential for you to be able to be full participants in the international peace process.' *Boutros Boutros-Ghali, Secretary-General of the UN addressing NGOs at a DPI conference, 19 September 1994.*

Primary activities and means include:
1 Enhanced NGO access to information.
2 Improved procedures for consultation with NGOs (including at regional, national and UN agency levels).
3 More opportunities to give testimony.
4 Assured representation of NGOs on UN advisory panels, committees, groups of experts, etc.
5 Broadening composition of delegations to UN to include representatives of civil society, for example, trade unions and indigenous peoples.
6 Improved procedures for NGO participation in inter-governmental meetings.
7 Securing resources for translation and interpretation for international and regional meetings of NGOs.
8 Earmarking of resources or establishment of a fund to ensure participation from developing country NGOs.

UN steps to support NGO participation:

1 Provision of regular, reliable and readable information on important policy processes. Also, information in a variety of forms (eg video, electronic communication), and to be made available in many languages.
2 Mandating and improving the capacity of UN offices around the world to work with NGOs on policy issues.
3 Developing mechanisms whereby the UN Secretariat, government representatives and NGOs can meet and debate on a regular and sometimes

informal basis.

4 Inviting NGOs to nominate participants on expert groups, high-level panels, etc.

5 Organising regular consultations with NGO representatives at the regional level, as well as annual consultations between the UN and, for example, development NGOs, with NGO participation based on criteria of regional and gender balance.

6 Facilitating NGO participation at inter-agency meetings.

7 Including the contributions of NGOs – experience, analysis, recommendations – in preparing UN substantive reports. To be practicable this requires advance notice, predictability, effective mechanisms and resources.

8 Making arrangements for NGO secondments to UN bodies.

Actions for consideration by NGOs:

1 Setting up a Southern NGO resource centre to ensure more equitable access to UN information.

2 Exploring the value of regional clearing houses for information.

3 Defining criteria to distinguish clearly between a briefing or information meeting and a decision-making meeting.

4 Supporting a process to develop criteria for accountability and representation at international meetings.

5 Further developing and using criteria for (rotating) membership of co-ordinating or steering committees, which takes into consideration region, gender, expertise, tasks to be fulfilled, reporting functions, follow-up capacity, etc.

6 Paying more attention to the differences between international, national and regional groups and elaborating a complementary division of labour which builds on respective strengths.

7 Advising some coalitions and networks of NGOs to apply for consultative status with the UN Economic and Social Council to enable representation at meetings.

8 Developing and making recommendations to the UN and to national governments on how UN procedures can be more accessible to NGO participation.

9 Making better use of electronic communications for information dissemination, communication and planning.

The views expressed in this chapter are those of the author. They do not necessarily represent those of the United Nations Non-Governmental Liaison Service (UN-NGLS) or any other part of the United Nations system.

9. Public Participation in the UN
And the Philippine experience

MAXIMO KALAW

'When the sense of the earth unites with the sense of one's body,
one becomes earth of the earth, a plant among plants,
an animal born from the soil and fertilising it.
In this union, the body is confirmed in its pantheism.

To exist in the fleet joy of becoming, to be a channel
for life as it flashes by in its gaiety and courage, cool water
glittering in the sunlight – in a world of sloth, anxiety and aggression.
To exist for the future of others without being suffocated by their
present.'

Dag Hammarksjold, Markings

The rise of national states – 'those cold monsters',[1] in the words of Charles de Gaulle, in whose backyard the French Revolution had started the process – was attended by an awareness of a new identity within the space carved out of the old regime. Historians like to stress that the transference of power takes time to play out and is never quite so clear-cut as the conceptual opposition of divine to natural rights, or of the old order to the new, summarily suggests. The devolution of power from the state system to civil society that we are witnessing today is a similarly complex process, which probably owes as much to advances in science and technology as to the decline of the idea of progress, as much to political alienation as to integration and globalisation processes. Be that as it may, what is beyond

---

1   Andre Malraux, *Anti-Memoirs*, tr. by Terence Kilmartin. Holt, Rinehart and Winston:1968.

doubt is that in our century the development of the nation state has been impassioned, accelerating with decolonisation, displaying a particular penchant for war – the ability to wage war being common to all states in their historical definition – amid a nearly universal popular impulse towards peace. Uneasy awareness of the dificulties inherent in steering between nation states' conflicting claims characterised the early efforts at international and intergovernmental, which is to say interstate, development of the League of Nations and the United Nations. Both had seemed at the time of their founding (after the First and Second World Wars respectively) to be necessary expressions of statehood with war-riven history their common medium. But their affirming of the value of peace, it has turned out, must involve the participation – beyond a dedicated bureaucracy – of organic constituencies, if such affirmation is to remain consistently meaningful. In this regard the UN has yet to meet the promise of its Charter Preamble.

Writing his autobiography in the shadow of the Hiroshima bombing, the English poet Stephen Spender said that after the First World War, 'people expected much of the League of Nations, but were not prepared to abandon national sovereignty. This time, a great many everywhere are prepared to sacrifice a great deal of nationhood and possessions which they formerly clung to, but they do not believe in the United Nations'. He added that, 'The most important condition of change – a widespread realism – has been achieved'.[2]

It can be argued that, starting out as an instrument of national identity – 'world within world' to appropriate the title of Spender's book – the UN System has now reached the stage where it is poised to accede to the pacifist, utopian will in its Charter declaration 'to save succeeding generations from the scourge of war'. It has the opportunity to promote sustainability as an alternative to the destructive ideology of growth that has dogged its development initiatives for well over a generation.

The Philippines in the UN

This chapter provides a shift to a microscopic focus. It posits one country's experience as a template for organised substantive response to the world body of the UN. The Philippines provides a good example of such organised response for a number of reasons.

---

2 Stephen Spender, *World Within World*. Hamish Hamilton, 1951.

Historical ties

The first is historical. The Philippines was in a shambles, and the devastation of its capital was second only to that of Warsaw in 1945, when it signed the UN Charter along with 50 other countries. China and India were the only other signatories from the Far East. The Philippines' career as an independent state, the depth of its aspiration towards peace and its facility in the idioms of Pax Americana coincide therefore with the evolution of the UN.

The Philippines was the first experiment of the United States in colonial government. The Americans had supplanted the Spaniards in the Philippines at the turn of the century, when they realised that, in the words of Senator Albert J. Beveridge in 1900, 'the Pacific is the ocean of the commerce of the future. Most future wars will be conflicts for commerce. The power that rules the Pacific, therefore, is the power that rules the world. And, with the Philippines, that power is and will forever be the American Republic.'[3]

Philippines independence, granted on 4 July 1946, might seem in retrospect an early signal of decolonisation. In fact, as early as 1898 the republic established by Filipinos after a successful revolution against Spanish rule had sent similarly hopeful signals. These had been doomed to disappointment by the sentiments of such as Senator Beveridge, who, in the same peroration cited above, observed chillingly: 'The wood of the Philippines can supply the furniture of the world for a century to come'.

Cultural links

The second reason is cultural. As a consequence of Spanish and US influences on its indigenous base, the Philippines is the only predominantly Christian and, for a long time, the most westernised country in Asia. This has made for a certain flexibility of policy which enables its people to uphold Asiatic traditions while keeping an eye on Western innovations. As a firm ally of the United States within and outside the UN, the English-speaking Filipinos early became acquainted with UN rhetoric and protocol.

The Philippines' perennial delegate to the UN, Carlos P. Romulo, was the first Asian to be elected president of the (Fourth) General Assembly. Twice head of the Security Council, Romulo had actively participated in the writing of the UN Charter itself. In the 1947 proceedings of the UN

---

3 Congressional Record, January 9, 1900.

Commission on Human Rights, he had been particularly eloquent in maintaining that the principle that man had certain inalienable rights was ancient and what was new was that 'these natural human rights need to be safeguarded by some authority more potent than the sovereignty of the State, by an instrument of common consent more stable and efficacious than the law of nations as we know it today.' It is said that Romulo did not miss a single session of the General Assembly in its formative years. In 1969, Secretary-General U Thant called him 'Mr United Nations'. Much later, when Romulo turned 80, he was asked what UN encounters he remembered best. He mentioned a run-in with the Russian delegate about a world map that did not reflect Philippine territory. On the scale used, the Russian had fulminated, the Philippines would be a mere dot, to which Romulo had replied: 'Well, then, put the dot in'.

The participation of small sovereign states in the UN process has been largely confined to making similar symbolic gestures. The ability of Filipinos to adjust to both Eastern and Western symbolic frameworks, which today might be considered paradigmatic, assured their perfect fit into the East-West axis on which the UN had turned throughout the Cold War. It may prove to be even more relevant today.

Authoritarian alliance

A third reason involves the way in which the UN has sometimes been used by repressive and authoritarian leaders. Thus the latter part of Ferdinand Marcos' martial law regime which started in 1972 saw the Philippines First Lady, Imelda Marcos, in her capacity as her husband's special envoy and as governor of a commission to direct development in the capital region, leading successive special missions to the UN. This occasionally had the effect of robbing her government's foreign minister, Mr United Nations himself, of the attention to which he was accustomed in New York.

In the late 1970s Mrs Marcos gave currency to human settlements and environmental planning concepts that she had appropriated from UN expertise. Although her numerous diplomatic missions had had concrete results, such as formalising ties with China, the Soviet Union and Cuba, she also generated political capital to justify and extend her tenure. Blunt criticism of her government's record of human rights violations, particularly against the proponents and sympathisers of the longest-playing communist insurgency in Asia, frequently attended Philippine negotiations with the IMF and World Bank, which eventually decided to turn their backs on the dictatorship they had helped prop up.

The four-day peaceful revolution of 1986 exiled President Marcos to the

United States, where a court of justice gave due course to charges of corruption against him and his wife, eventually upholding the latter's 'innocence' after a trial speeded up by his death. She was to use the acquittal by a New York court to make a strategic comeback to the Philippines through the 1992 presidential elections, where she bested two of her severest critics in the past, shedding light on the dynamics of political acceptance in developing countries.

State and civil society partnership

A fourth reason has to do with the historical response of member states to the challenge of the UN Conference on Environment and Development (UNCED) process, held in June 1992 in Rio de Janeiro, Brazil, and its agenda for sustainable development. The fact is that the present Philippine president, Fidel Ramos – a ranking general of Marcos' martial law regime but also its most powerful opponent in the 1986 revolution that ousted the regime – was the first head of state to create, in September 1992, within three months of what was known as the 'Earth Summit' in Rio de Janeiro, a Philippine Council for Sustainable Development that integrates non-government organisations (NGOs) and their grassroots constituencies in the implementation of the Summit's comprehensive statement of intent, Agenda 21. This effort to institutionalise state and civil society partnership in concretising the UNCED's blueprint for global sustainability in the 21st century has caught the attention of the global NGO community. It holds out promises of new ways of global cooperation and an alternative ecological basis for the peace that has eluded the global state system.

The involvement of non-governmental organisations in the UNCED process culminated in the International NGO Forum (INGOF) at Rio, working parallel to the intergovernmental conference (UNCED, or the Earth Summit). This development has posed a challenge to the established mode of NGO participation in the UN.

NGO involvement in international integration

The engagement of non-government agencies in the dream of 'international integration' had started with the League of Nations. Their participation falls under the rubric of 'consultations' undertaken by the Economic and Social Council (ECOSOC). ECOSOC worked initially on matters related to 'humanitarian' services such as war relief, with independent and international organisations like the Red Cross supplying an early model. This 'first generation' of NGOs made way in the period from the 1950s to the

1970s to a 'second generation' of largely professional, special-interest groups exemplified by the human rights organisation Amnesty International and women's groups. A third generation was born in the 1980s as a response of popular, representative, nationalist forces in developing countries to multilateral development aid and the Cold War in a loosely balanced bipolar system.

The Second UN Conference on the Least Developed Countries (Paris, 1990) prefigured UNCED. The two years that it took to negotiate the distance to the Earth Summit gave NGOs more leeway than any they had previously known in ECOSOC. The crafting at the International NGO Forum in Rio de Janeiro of 41 treaties by representatives of 4,000 NGOs from 70 countries described a quantum leap that contrasted starkly to the reluctance displayed by heads of state vis-à-vis Agenda 21. It also demonstrated in the wake of the Cold War a rational strength of which states may not have dreamed.

INGOF: blossoming of NGOs

The analytical framework of the INGOF, as heterogeneous a grouping as any forum could possibly hope to be, had focused a number of unmistakable global trends, the subject of ceaseless study by UN experts. These included: increasing poverty in the South alongside ecosystems destruction; urbanisation and migration to the cities; the globalisation of markets and economies, including international fund flows and the commodification of culture; intrusion into the natural order through biotechnology and genetic interference, on the one hand, and sustainable agriculture and natural pest control, on the other; the rise of information technologies with application to issues in biodiversity and medicine; the renewed importance of spirituality to human life; and the widening gap between the state and civil society.

The adumbration of these trends by NGOs in early preparatory committee meetings had already clarified their character as laboratories for the formation of new levels of meaning and identity. The INGOF realised the need to develop the capacity of these trends to help formulate new and global approaches to development. These approaches were to be anchored on the NGOs' practical experience of those values that engender and are engendered by sustainability (such as self-defined limits, real needs as opoosed to consumer wants, diversity and gender-balance, and popular participation).

The 41 NGO treaties in Rio de Janeiro outlined action plans in areas such as debt, biodiversity, technology transfer, consumption patterns and lifestyle, and alternative economic strategies. These plans had the immediate effect of eliciting the sympathetic interest of representatives of the media and academia, and expanding networks of advocacy. More significantly, they helped to configure what amounts to a grassroots-based alternative constituency to the General Assembly itself. At the INGOF the public realm expanded beyond the confines set by statist thinking and it is true to say that supranational actors became sharply aware of a new identity of non-governmental action emerging at the Earth Summit.

Taking much of the credit for the blossoming of NGOs in Rio, the UN System has since given the international steering committee responsible a seven-point mandate to continue the process they had started. This includes the organisation of regional and sub-regional meetings to determine parameters as well as mechanisms for future cooperation; and the identification of caretakers in each sub-region. In 1994 the members of the steering committee fanned out to disseminate the content of the treaties and to lay the groundwork for meetings expected to lead on to a new global cooperation treaty and thence to their participation in the UN Council for Sustainable Development (UNCSD) itself, whose purposely-kept-skeletal mandate to monitor the implementation by governments of Agenda 21 remains the major product of the Rio Conference.

If, however, no official consultative relations are established between NGOs and the General Assembly, where the mandate of the UNCSD is to be fleshed out, NGO participation in the UNCSD negotiations will be severely limited. Denying NGOs active participation in the discussions would amount to shutting the door on an historic opportunity to fill up a major lacuna in public participation in the UN System; it would effectively stunt the UN's ability to predict or correct the course of its own development.

Were it not for the restrictiveness of existing regulations in ECOSOC (itself subject to demands for reform due to its ineffectiveness as an economic and social affairs counterpart of the Security Council) the NGOs mobilised by the UNCED process would otherwise have the status of 'microobservers' in UN deliberations on the UNCSD, even under the wings of the Non-Government Liaison Service (NGLS) which had effectively interconnected them with the UNCED process and may be called upon in future to do so with the UNCSD process. This ancillary role of third generation NGOs in the UN system may be the result of the predominance enjoyed by Northern second generation NGOs. Equally, it may be due to distrust of NGOs by their governments, particularly in countries which claim to have been forced to build authoritarian structures of governance to speed up development, and which have guarded against the perceived destabilising effects of NGO advocacy and mobilisation activities. This apprehension, however, is not borne out by the history of NGOs. In the Philippines, where they helped topple an authoritarian regime, NGOs are the mechanism of civil society

Philippine NGOs: vital actors

The Philippine response to the challenges firmed up in Rio is embedded in the Philippine Council for Sustainable Development (PCSD), which was so structured as to respond directly to the major concerns of Agenda 21. The PCSD institutionalises NGO participation in sustainable development through a governmental/non-governmental counterpart system. It therefore provides a model whose evolution can be scrutinised by the rest of the global NGO community.

NGO participation in the PCSD is entirely self-determined down to the sub-committee level. In addition, a parallel grouping of NGOs and private organisations operates to support the seven NGO members of the 21-person PCSD. The Philippine government has recently formulated a medium-term development plan to propel the country's economy to Newly Industrialised Country (NIC) level. Philippine NGOs' principal concern is therefore to ensure that the development programmes on executive drawing boards, whether they be local private sector initiatives or a mix of multilateral and transnational persuasions, are truly sustainable.

Evolution of Philippine NGOs

Filipinos are not strangers to such an exercise. The Philippines has produced a vast if somewhat anarchic array of NGOs since colonial days. Their credibility is traditionally in direct proportion to their pro-active postures. This is the result in large measure of the alienation of local communities from colonial centres, whose number is necessarily limited by the country's archipelagic character. This, along with ethnic diversity, is the bane of the Northern ideal of political unity. Filipinos mounted the first successful revolution against a European colonial power in Asia, but succumbed to the superior military might of US intervention to become the subject of the first US experiment in 'imperialism'.

The organisation and networking of NGOs in the Philippines quickened upon President Marcos' declaration in 1972 of martial law. This, to all appearances succeeded in polarising Filipino society, but the dramatic non-violent overthrow of its author in 1986 by 'people power', a virtual coalition of NGOs, uncovered a moral consensus which showed that civil society had not been deceived by the martial law administration.

Since the painless four-day revolution Philippine NGOs have gained recognition as vital actors in development undertakings. Their roles have evolved through fundamentally different functions which now define the span of their activities. These activities range from the distribution of relief to livelihood project-management and resource-restoration; they include community organising as a necessary process for affecting social change; policy research; and advocacy on alternative models of development. The evolution of NGOs' role was determined to a large extent by the crisis in the Philippine environment, particularly the destruction of forest ecosystems as the habitat of endangered species possessing pronounced cultural and traditional significance. The Philippines' largest environmental NGO, for example, the Haribon Foundation, started fittingly as a bird-watching society, moved on to the conservation of indigenous culture and then administered the nation's first debt-for-nature swap, even as it engaged in scientific research on the global environmental impact of Mount Pinatubo's eruption. The astonishing span of their concerns measured against the scarcity of funds has understandably obliged Philippine NGOs to be largely self-steering, while rigorously focusing on the root causes of underdevelopment that structures have continued to foster.

Philippine NGOs have also launched an effort to transform the multilateral banks and the International Monetary Fund which they criticise for clinging to the post-Bretton Woods institutional archetype of economic expansion, and for their non-transparent, non-democratic and non-participatory process. The NGOs lobbied to set up a Global Environmental Facility (GEF) governance and secretariat functions independent of the World Bank, and have pressed for a review of the quality of aid and its allocation to basic human needs. They have also pushed to free aid from conditionalities, to regard it as payment for ecological debt incurred by developed countries in their exploitation of the natural resources of developing countries like the Philippines.

Philippine NGOs have called on the North to change consumption patterns, stressing that the biospheric system cannot carry more aggregate economic growth and its waste products. Maintaining that development is something that only the people can do for themselves, they view sustainable development as rooted in a personal choice of options about how to live, arguing that what is personal is of public interest and therefore political. They hold out NGOs and civil society with women taking a lead role, as instruments for correcting the imbalance and healing the rifts, imposed by the centralising tendencies of economic society and the state.

While the Filipino delegation at the INGOF was admittedly among the most energetic, their performance was by no means unique. The unanimous eschewal of bureaucracy and the uniform sense of urgency of 4,000 other NGOs at the INGOF painted a picture of a truly general assembly. The operative principle was, beyond one-member-one vote, that of democratic participation, and enough warmth was generated to thaw a legion of 'cold monsters'. It may very well prove to be the case that NGOs have prepared the state system for transition to the post-Cold War era, by functioning as a positive catalyst in the development process and by innovating where the state's cut-and-dried formulae have begun to fail.

Increasing responsibilities for NGOs globally

The available evidence suggests that everywhere in the world today, NGOs have been unavoidably drawn into the development process. In Zimbabwe, a savings development movement initiated by an NGO now yokes together local savings clubs, government agencies and fertiliser corporations to improve agricultural practices. In Kenya, an environmental NGO network is articulating what promises to be the core of a national biomass energy policy. In Brazil, NGOs defending the Amazonian Indians have come under attack by mining companies whose deep-seated interests they have disturbed. In Mexico City, NGOs helped to define and implement policies needed by the poor to cope with the traumas of earthquakes. In Sarawak, Borneo, indigenous people have set up successful blockades of logging operations. In Tokyo, they do not shrink from delineating Japanese responsibility for the plunder of the world's forests. In Sri Lanka and Indonesia, the critical attitudes of NGOs have moved the state to inquire into external sources of NGO funding as a security measure against 'the lackeys of imperialism'. Channels for the free flow of information in partnership with the Association for Progressive Communication have been set up in Nicaragua, Russia, the United Kingdom, Sweden, Germany, Bolivia and Costa Rica, and account for the first information links between Cuba and the United States since 1959. NGOs organise housing cooperatives in Uruguay, provide transport to market for local producers in Africa, address drug-related problems in Colombia and Ecuador, and prevent hardwood imports in Europe.

NGOs' work has been cut out for them by their environment. In the face of the continuing decline of global resources, it was probably inevitable that they should converge in an INGOF, and that the vision of sustainable development laid out before them through the UN System should now engage NGOs on a global scale. With Rio behind them, their main tasks are to ensure state compliance with the agreements on Agenda 21 as well as with the People's Agenda contained in the alternative treaties at INGOF. They must also constitute the Council for Sustainable Development (CSD) as a forum to which 'We the People' may have recourse in prosecuting violators of our environmental and developmental rights, much as Amnesty International represents in the public eye a forum to protest against state violence and abuse of our civil and political human rights.

With NGOs as members, the CSD offers more latitude than ordinary state machinery, more nearly resembling a compassionate council of tribal elders in a traditional society than a corporatist state in an industrial society. As a model of institutional response, it is bound to be more flexible than a review panel such as that initiated by the World Bank to respond to appeals in the interest of sustainable development.

The CSD represents, furthermore, an opportunity for NGOs to build a global constituency for earth issues. This they are doing through the newly created (1992) Earth Council, which publishes monthly 'alerts' from the perspective of the environment, human rights, development and peace movements. The Earth Council seeks popular participation in decision-making by, for example, urging people to write to the decision-makers in multilateral firms, in order to influence action.

Involving NGOs in the CSD negotiations is a good step towards the creation of more councils for sustainable development and effecting their efficient networking. It amounts to building the foundations of a bridge between government and civil society to facilitate the free flow of information between them, thus assuring the UN of the broadest basis for public participation such as its Charter had envisioned.

National NGOs have continued to attend follow-up conferences to the Earth Summit, such as the Down to Earth meeting in Copenhagen in December 1993. They have continued to participate in preparatory meetings for upcoming conferences on women, population, small island states, desertification and the summit on social development. These activities represent an emerging national and global process with the potential to address grey areas of governance such as the globalisation of capital and technology, the traffic in drugs and arms, and the increase in ethnic and religious conflicts. It will also help to provide a normative value system whereby people can regulate their behaviour, lifestyle and consumption as the bottomline of sustainable development.

As NGOs gain access to international decision-making fora like the UN, their mode of participation is likely to change more and more substantially, advancing beyond advocacy and resistance to the articulation of real alternatives. Being intimately familiar with poverty, they may be expected to function reliably in the next two decades, which are forecast to be particularly impecunious for the majority of humankind. Philippine NGOs' participation in the national development process offers a microcosm of the larger UN system in which NGOs must operate. The UN bureaucracy could do no worse than to ignore their rapping on the door.

10. A UN for all our children
A giant undertaking

ERSKINE CHILDERS

This book was not intended to be an encyclopaedia of the UN System. Rather, it has examined the most pervasive causes of the world's increasing restiveness, mass misery, and violence; how the UN System responds to them; and what needs to be done to improve its effectiveness.

It has been a severe analysis. The System manifestly does need improvement; but which institution within nation-state societies does not? Our first need is to stop seeing 'the UN' as impenetrably remote and intangible except to a handful of experts in each country, and to realise that it is simply the universal extension of our selves, our national behaviour. This realisation should lead to a second. It is that 'we', citizens of our countries, are also citizens of the United Nations, and have far more responsibility for it than either governments have appeared to understand or than most of us have shown interest in shouldering.

Along the way, many need to discard perceptual baggage about 'foreigners', and how difficult 'they' must be to work with. In over two decades of UN service and even more in close observation, I never found anything that 'they' were doing or not doing that could not find a reflection in societies closer to home. Indeed, the marvel is how well so many different nationalities, perceiving the world's problems from different cultural prisms and even thinking in different languages, can work together on a daily basis in the UN System for common goals.

The real problem is that although we have a world-community organisation, our governments too often allow it to function only in uncoordinated fits and power-distorted starts, and nothing like enough against root causes. Neglected causes are now producing upheavals and human degradation on an unprecedented scale, placing massive burdens on the also-neglected capabilities of the UN to respond to such consequences.

We therefore have no choice but to tackle both dimensions – causes and consequences – and very urgently.

We must see to it that governments equip the UN with an efficient Rapid Response force, instantly available to the Secretary-General, such as Sir Brian Urquhart has urged, to prevent such horrors as occurred in Rwanda *before* they expand into genocide.[1] We must insist that governments now learn the lessons of delayed response to drought and civil collapse in a Somalia on the one hand, or to ethnic demagoguery in a disintegrating Yugoslavia on the other. Ideally, regional organisations of governments, like the Organisation of African Unity (OAU) or the European Union (EU), should take first responsibility. Their capacities should be strengthened; but it is not presently safe to count on them, so the UN must have worldwide response capability.

Here again, there is cultural baggage to be offloaded. This is strikingly evident in the ease with which Northern commentators have criticised the OAU for its undoubted failure to respond quickly in Rwanda. Europeans are in no position to criticise the OAU in Rwanda or any other African crisis after the richly endowed EU's indecisiveness and uncoordinated initiatives in Yugoslavia.

Governments South and North have, however, moved extraordinary distances in only the last few years, forward from the traditional stance of sacrosanct national sovereignty. To lay solid foundations of trust we still need the General Assembly (not the Security Council) to adopt clear standing criteria and rules of engagement for interventions by the United Nations without the request of a government. The efficiency of UN command systems must be improved to the point where no major power will have excuse left for refusing to place its forces under UN direction, while expecting all other countries to do so. The powers' current practice of seeking UN approval for their own interventions is manifestly undesirable.

At the same time it is unconscionable for governments that were responsible for, or complicit in, the total destabilisation of countries like Angola and Mozambique now to leave the UN to try to cope, with little or no special assistance. It is also hypocritical for governments that are still promoting their own countries' arms sales to criticise levels of military expenditure in other countries. Perhaps the ultimate form of hypocrisy in arms issues is the holier-than-thou attitude of nuclear powers towards nuclear

---

1 See Brian Urquhart article, 'For a UN Volunteer Military Force', *The New York Review of Books*, New York, 10 June 1994.

'proliferation', while refusing to forgo the very weapons they themselves introduced to the world.

We are in serious danger of leaving to our children a world in which cynicism prevails over ethics in international decision-making. International relationships have been deeply poisoned by double standards: it is no more possible to achieve peaceful relations between nations than within them if the powerful can demand that their own aggressiveness (or that of their satrapies) be accepted, while others' is punished. Yet again, every member-state pledges to honour the UN Charter principle of 'the equal rights of nations large and small'. But in the Gulf Crisis and over many other UN issues, major powers have used outright economic intimidation of impoverished countries to secure their votes or their silence.

The Charter invokes the best in all of us when it asks that we 'practice tolerance and live together in peace with one another as good neighbours'. We must be far more vigilant and resolute in demanding that our decision-makers behave according to its noble principles.

Still in the dimension of response to consequences, there really is no sound excuse for the tangles of separately operating humanitarian relief funds that governments have created in fits and starts down the years in the UN System. Its scattered humanitarian emergency machinery must be urgently consolidated in an efficient Operations Branch of the UN Department of Humanitarian Affairs, organised in such a way that it can best help the front-line volunteer women and men of all the world's non-governmental organisations, those who mobilise the funds and supplies and those who do the work on the ground.

Turning now to causes, this book has made abundantly clear that 'aid' could never have been the means to enable three-quarters of humankind to struggle out of the poverty with which they had to begin their post-colonial independence. Genuine development co-operation has, of course, its valuable place. But the arithmetic alone exposes something between hallucination and hoax in the refusal of major industrial countries to formulate genuine, all-gain macro-economic policies at the United Nations.

All official 'aid' from the North to the South currently amounts to about US$56 billion a year. The trade, monetary and finance policies of the same 'donor' governments are currently depriving developing countries of over US$500 billion in *income* that they could be *earning* each year.[2]

As noted earlier in these pages, although the founders of the UN System

---

2 *Human Development Report 1992*, UN Development Programme, New York.

were not anticipating decolonisation in this century, the mandates and machinery that they gave the UN System are largely adequate to address the commanding heights of the universal world economy. The problem has been that major industrial powers have refused to implement those mandates.

They refused to complete the machinery with an equitable International Trade Organisation. They have allowed the IMF's role to be warped and distorted from its original role as a central bank of the world, equitably intervening in surplus as in deficit countries, to one that focuses only on the already-poorest countries in the world, imposing conditionalities that have caused one upheaval after another. They have persistently sought to weaken the UN Secretariat's capacities to formulate real-world macro-economic policies, while pretending to be caring for a 'global economy' which turns out to be only that of less than a quarter of humankind in Japan, North America, and Europe.

Here, we have more baggage to discard. Not least of the hoaxes involved in this reprehensible story has been the canard that proposals long made for reshaping the international economic system are only 'the third world poor trying to soak the rich'. We must urgently persuade the fumbling economic managers of key Northern countries to make better sense of what is in plain sight before them.

First, the costs of evading the causes of mass abject poverty in the South are already staggering when their consequences arrive in bills for peace-keeping and emergency relief. In a world where already one in every four of us only exists on the margins of daily survival, and soon it will be one in every three, these costs will increase exponentially unless their causes are at last addressed. Yesterday's apocryphal novel about masses of desperately poor people moving towards Northern affluence will be tomorrow's non-fiction reality unless Northern policies are changed. Secondly, the North is going to need the vast markets of the South, and it is the most elementary law of commerce that the would-be buyer has to have purchasing-power. Most of the South will not have it so long as it is kept in abject poverty.

In all of the issues discussed in this book, the role of European countries leaves a great deal to be desired. Far too often in recent years it has been impossible to discern any distinctive European view of the world at the UN, only a recurring joining of votes with those of the major Northern powers. Yet three points must be made about this phenomenon. There is, first, the irony that at the birth of the UN at San Francisco, when Europe lay in ruins, its governments showed far more courage vis-à-vis the powers than they do today. Secondly, again and again there is a marked divergence between policies expressed at UN fora by European governments and the known strong views of large groups of citizens and their parliamentarians in the same countries. Thirdly, the effect of this European acquiescence on North-South relations and on Southern confidence in the UN itself cannot be over-emphasised. Europe has enormous stakes in and bears a unique and vital responsibility for the future of global relationships and of the United Nations. European citizens are entitled to hold their governments to account in this.

We must, then, make the UN System's 50th anniversary the springboard for determined pressure on the citadels of economic power to join the rest of humankind in the UN System, to equip the Secretary-General with top-quality resources for macro-economic policy formulation, and to overhaul the machinery so that it does at last work for the real world. There is no time left, and there are no options about this: if it is not done, no amount of resourcing of UN peacekeeping will be sufficient to cope with the convulsions that lie ahead.

All of the improvements so far summarised will also involve improving the UN's leadership capabilities. Its Secretary-General must be the confidence-commanding and inspiring leader of an emergent world community that works as one. She or he should be chosen (for a single term of seven years) through a proper process of search, not merely within the diplomatic old-boy network but throughout the world. The membership as a whole must assert its Charter-given responsibility, informing the 'Permanent Five' that, even if they retain a veto over a candidate, the General Assembly is prepared to reject anyone not meeting optimal criteria. And to complete improved leadership, an independent commission of civil-service specialists should recommend how to restore the UN service to top quality, with a common UN System Staff College of existing teaching and training institutions.

Finally, there is the issue of the 'we' of whom I have been writing. Who are 'we' who must see to these initiatives and improvements? The UN has been kept so remote from its citizens that it is very seldom suggested they can do anything about it. The fallacy in this has been glimpsed in this book's discussions of the UN and environmental concerns, and if governments have recently been far more active in the field of human rights at the UN, it is also without question because they have been pressured to be by their citizens.

It is time, indeed it is overtime, to empower those whom the Charter proclaims to be the first authors of the United Nations – 'We, the Peoples'. In addition to the needed strengthening of NGO roles and access, we must press our governments now to do what even in 1945 Foreign Secretary Ernest Bevin (no 'dreamer') called a necessary 'completion' of the architecture of San Francisco.

We need a United Nations Parliamentary Assembly, where our directly elected representatives can monitor and contribute to the performance of executive governments. They do need help. Those who have been practising double standards need the realisation that the representatives of the citizens of this planet are close by, watching, and alert to expose all unethical international behaviour. Executive governments that wish to follow the Charter and to advance all of its democratic goals need the additional courage that they would derive from such an assembly in session next door to theirs. Creating such an assembly will, of course, be an enormous task, but so have been many of the advances we have managed to make in international relations in the last 50 years.

Despite all the UN System's constraints to date, its research and deliberations have brought us to the point where we know the whole of our world for the first time in human history. We have deprived ourselves of the last excuse, of ignorance of how most of our sisters and brothers have to live out their days. Now, we have to go forward in the giant undertaking of building a democratic United Nations to make the real world safe, just and sustainable, for all its children.

Note on contributors

Barbara Adams works for the United Nations Non-Governmental Liaison Service (UN-NGLS) at UN headquarters in New York. Before joining UN-NGLS Ms Adams was the Associate Director of the Quaker United Nations Office, working on issues of economic and social justice, women, peace and human rights. She has also served as a consultant to UNICEF. Ms Adams has authored and co-authored many articles, reports and booklets on the United Nations.

Dr Nassau Adams has had a distinguished career with the United Nations, being closely associated with the work of UNCTAD since its inception. During the 1970s he served as a member of ILO Employment Advisory Missions to Colombia and Kenya. Dr Adams' publications include *World's Apart: The North-South Divide and the International System* (Zed Books, 1993). He is currently an independent consultant based in Geneva and Kingston.

Phyllis Bennis is a journalist and writer based in New York. Her publications include numerous articles and books on the United Nations and Middle East issues. Ms Bennis is a research fellow at the Institute of Policy Studies, Washington DC. She was formerly senior investigator at the Office of the Public Defender, Contra Costa County, California.

Erskine Childers (Ireland) retired in 1989 as Senior Adviser to the UN Director-General for Development and International Economic Co-operation after 22 years as a UN civil servant. Before 1967, as an independent writer and broadcaster on international political and development affairs, he specialised in UN issues, serving as a periodic consultant, including a special mission in the Congo for Secretary-General U Thant. He has worked with most UN organisations at all levels and in all regions, and has especially studied UN problems of coordination, development and humanitarian operations, and public communication and constituency-building.

Dr Amir Habib Jamal has had a long and distinguished career in the Tanzanian government and international politics. Some of his many appointments include membership of the Brandt Commission (1977), head of the Tanzanian Permanent Mission to the United Nations Agencies (1985), Chairman of the GATT Council, Geneva (1987) and Honorary Executive Director of the South Centre (1990). Dr Jamal retired from public office in 1993.

Maximo Kalaw is president of the Green Forum-Philippines, a Manila based forum of non-governmental organisations (NGOs), people's organisations and church groups for sustainable development. Mr Kalaw is a member of the advisory boards of the South-North Development Initiative in New York, and Earth Action International in Brussels.

Angela Penrose is senior overseas information officer at Save the Children UK, with responsibility for disseminating the lessons of the organisation's operational experience, particularly in the field of humanitarian assistance. She has previously worked throughout Africa as a writer, teacher and journalist. Ms Penrose is co-author of *The Ethiopian Famine* (Zed Books, 1987).

Paul Rogers is professor of peace studies and head of department at the University of Bradford. He specialises in international security issues and North-South relations. Formerly Professor Rogers worked in rural development in Uganda. He has written and edited many books and articles including *A World Divided: Militarism and Development After the Cold War* (Earthscan/St. Martin's Press, 1994).

Dr Katarina Tomaševski works as a senior research associate at the Danish Centre for Human Rights in Copenhagen. She holds graduate degrees in international law from Harvard Law School and the University of Zagreb. Dr Tomaševski's main research area is human rights in international development cooperation. Her publications include *Development Aid and Human Rights Revisited* (Pinter Publishers, 1993).

Myriam Vander Stichele is trade programme coordinator at the International Coalition for Development Action (ICDA) in Brussels where she also manages the Coordination of European Non-governmental organisations Networking on Trade (CENNT). Ms Vander Stichele is a fellow of the Transnational Institute (TNI), Amsterdam.

Further reading

General

Kevin M. Cahill (ed), *A Framework for Survival: Health, Human Rights, and Humanitarian Assistance in Conflicts and Disasters*, Council on Foreign Relations & Basic Books (Harper/Collins, 1993.

Erskine Childers with Brian Urquhart, *Renewing the United Nations System*, Dag Hammarskjöld Foundation, Uppsala, 1994.

Peter Donaldson, *Worlds Apart: The Development Gap and What it Means*, Pelican Books, 1986.

Gareth Evans (Foreign Minister of Australia), *Cooperating for Peace*, Allen & Unwin, 1993.

R. Falk, S. Kim, S. Mendlovitz (eds), *The United Nations and a Just World Order*, Westview Press, 1991.

Julius K. Nyerere & South Centre, *Facing the Challenge*, Zed Books, 1993.

South Commission, *The Challenge to the South*, Oxford University Press, 1990.

Ford Foundation, *Financing an effective United Nations*, New York, 1993.

Brian Urquhart and Erskine Childers, *A World in Need of Leadership: Tomorrow's United Nations*, Development Dialogue 1990, 1-2, Dag Hammarskjöld Foundation, 1990.

Brian Urquhart, 'For a UN Volunteer Military Force', *The New York Review of Books*, New York, 10 June 1994.

United Nations, *Everyone's United Nations*, UN (recurringly up-dated handbook of the UN System, available at UN Sales Agents).

Barbara Walker (ed), *Uniting the Peoples and Nations*, World Federalist Association, 1993.

Important annual or periodic UN papers

Report of the Secretary-General on the Work of the Organisation

Equivalent reports of each specialised agency

State of the World's Children (UNICEF)

State of the World's Environment (UNEP)

State of the World's Population (UNFPA)

Human Development Report (UNDP)

The World's Women (UN)

Human Rights: A Compilation of International Instruments (UN)

Chapter 1

Nassau Adams, Worlds Apart: *The North-South Divide and the International System*, Zed Books, London 1993.

Francis Fukuyama, *The End of History and the Last Man*, Avon Books, New York, 1992.

Richard N.Gardner and Max F.Millikan, *The Global Partnership*, Praeger Publishers, New York, 1968.

Simon Kuznets, *Modern Economic Growth: Rate Structure and Spread*, Yale University Press, New Haven and London, 1966.

Chapter 2

Angelos Angelopoulos & Melvin Fagen, *The Rich and the Poor: the widening gap*, University Press of America, Lanham, New York and London, 1993.

Ross Hammond & Lisa McGowan, *The other side of the story: the real impact of World Bank and IMF structural adjustment programmes*, Development Group for Alternative Policies, Washington.

Ed. Thomas Callaghy and John Ravenhill, *Hemmed in – responses to Africa's economic decline*, Columbia University Press, 1993.

Chapter 3

Michael Barratt Brown and Pauline Tiffen, *Raw Deals: Africa and World Trade*, Transnational Institute, Netherlands, 1992.

Belinda Coote, *The Trade Trap*, Oxfam, 1992.

Peter Madden, *A Raw Deal* and *Winners and Losers – the impact of the GATT Uruguay Round on developing countries*, Christian Aid, 1993.

Chakravarthi Raghavan, R*ecolonisation – GATT, the Uruguay Round and the Third World*, Third World Network, 1990.

UN Conference on Trade and Development (UNCTAD), *Trade and Development Report* published annually.

Myriam Vander Stichele, *The democratic deficit of the Uruguay Round*, EECOD, Brussels, 1992.

Chapter 4

Alston, P. (ed), *The United Nations and Human Rights: A Critical Appraisal*, Clarendon Press, Oxford, 1992

An-Na'im, A.A. (ed), *Human Rights in Cross-Cultural Perspectives. A Quest for Consensus*, University of Pennsylvania Press, Philadelphia, 1991.

Claude, R.P. and Weston, B.H. (eds), *Human Rights in the World Community. Issues and Action*, University of Pennsylvania Press, Philadelphia, 1989.

Mahoney, K.E. and Mahoney, P. (eds), *Human Rights in the Twenty-first Century: A Global Challenge*, Martinus Nijhoff Publishers, Dordrecht, 1993.

Mbaye, K., *Les droits de l'homme en Afrique*, Commission internationale de juristes, Editions A. Pedone, Paris, 1992.

Ramcharan, B.G., *The Concept and Present Status of the International Protection of Human Rights Forty Years after the Universal Declaration*, Martinus Nijhoff Publishers, Drodrecht, 1989.

Tejedor Salguero, M. (ed), *The Reform of Internation Institutions for the Protection of Human Rights*, First International Colloquium on Human Rights, La Laguna, Tenerife, 1-4 November 1992, Bruylant, Bruxelles, 1993.

Katarina Tomaševski, *Development Aid and Human Rights Revisited*, Pinter Publishers, London 1993.

Chapter 5

David Keen, *The Kurds in Iraq: How safe is their haven now?*, Save the Children, 1993.

Larry Minear et al, *Humanitarian action in the former Yugoslavia: the UN's role 1991-3*, Providence, the Thomas J. Watson Jr Institute for International Studies, 1994.

Larry Minear and Thomas Weiss, *Humanitarian principles and Operational Dilemmas in War Zones*, UNDP and DHA Disaster Management Programme, 1993.

Hugo Slim and Emma Visman, 'Evacuation, Intervention and Retaliation: United Nations Humanitarian Operations in Somalia 1991-1993' in *Sovereignty and Suffering*, ed John Harris, Pinter/Save the Children, 1994.

Chapter 6

CND, *Blueprint for a Nuclear Weapon-Free World*, London, 1994.

Malcolm Dando, *Biological warfare in the 21st century*, Brassey's, 1994.

Ruth Leger Sivard, *World Military and Social Expenditure (WMSE)*, 1992-93, World Priorities Inc, Washington.

Geoff Tansey, Kath Tansey, Paul Rogers, *A World Divided: Militarism and Development after the Cold War*, Earthscan, 1994.

Chapter 7

Phyllis Bennis and Michel Moushabeck, *Beyond the Storm: A Gulf Crisis Reader*, Interlink Publishing Group, 1991.

Phyllis Bennis and Michel Moushabeck, *Altered States: A Reader in the New World Order*, Interlink Publishing Group, 1993.

Chapters 8 and 9

Economic and Social Council 1968. ECOSOC Resolution 1926 (XLIV). *Arrangements for Consultation with NGOs.*

Economic and Social Council 26 May 1994. ECOSOC document E/AC.70/1994/5. *General Review of Arrangements for Consultations with NGOs, Report of the Secretary-General.*

Economic and Social Council 5 July 1994. ECOSOC document E/1994/99. *Report of the open-ended working group on the review of arrangements for consultations with NGOs.*

Dag Hammarksjöld, *Markings*, Faber and Faber, 1964.

Joint Inspection Unit of the United Nations (JIU), 1993. *Working with NGOs: Operational Activities for Development of the UN System with NGOs and Governments at the Grassroots and National Levels.* Geneva: United Nations.

United Nations Non-Governmental Liaison Service (UN-NGLS), 1994. T*he NGLS Handbook.* Geneva: United Nations.

Index